The Writings

of

Sir Thomas Browne.

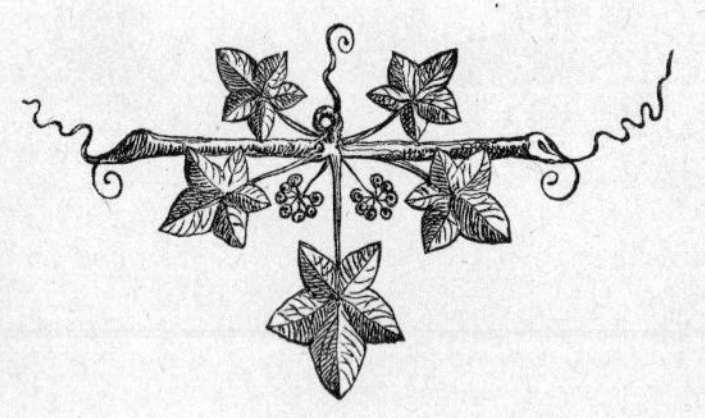

RELIGIO MEDICI

A LETTER TO A FRIEND
CHRISTIAN MORALS
URN-BURIAL
AND OTHER
PAPERS

BY

SIR THOMAS BROWNE, Kt. M. D.

BOSTON

TICKNOR AND FIELDS

1862

CAMBRIDGE, MASS.:
WELCH, BIGELOW, AND COMPANY,
PRINTERS TO THE UNIVERSITY.

TO

OLIVER WENDELL HOLMES, M. D.

AUTHOR OF "THE AUTOCRAT OF THE BREAKFAST-TABLE,"

AND

JOHN BROWN, M. D.

AUTHOR OF "RAB AND HIS FRIENDS,"

This Volume

OF THE ELOQUENT WRITINGS

OF AN OLD ENGLISH PHYSICIAN

IS INSCRIBED BY THE EDITOR.

CONTENTS.

Biographical Sketch of

The Author.

FOR a more detailed account of the life of SIR THOMAS BROWNE, the reader is referred to his Biography by Dr. Johnson, and the Supplementary Memoir by Simon Wilkin, Esq., both included in the London edition of the Complete Works, in four volumes. Coleridge, Lamb, Hazlitt, Hallam, Bulwer, and other distinguished writers, have put on record their estimate of his genius, and Cowper was so imbued with the spirit and beauty of the thought in the Religio Medici and other writings of Browne, that numerous resemblant passages in the Task have been frequently pointed out. The present Editor will content himself with giving a few dates of the principal occurrences in the author's life, and adding to these some interesting passages written by one who was for thirty years

Sir Thomas Browne's intimate friend. It is to be regretted that Mr. Whitefoot did not carry out his intention of writing an extended memoir of his well-beloved companion, for what he has left to us is conceived in so attractive a manner, we cannot but lament his original design was not fully completed. How much he valued Sir Thomas's friendship may be gathered from his remark, that he "ever esteemed it a special favour of Divine Providence to have had a more particular acquaintance with this excellent person, for two thirds of his life, than any other man that is now (1682) left alive."

Sir Thomas Browne was born in London on the 19th of October, 1605, and died on his birthday, at Norwich, in 1682. His father came of an ancient Upton family, in Cheshire, and enjoyed a good name as an honest merchant. A daughter of Sir Thomas has recorded of this worthy man an act very touching in its pious significance. She says, in a memorandum in her own hand, appended to a brief account of her distingushed parent, "his father used to open his breast when he was asleep, and kiss it in prayers over him, as 't is said of Origen's father, that the Holy Ghost would take possession there." This excellent person dying when his son Thomas was yet a lad, the boy was defrauded by one of his guardians, but found his way to the school of Winchester for his education. In 1623 he went to Oxford, entering as a gentleman-commoner, and graduated from the newly named Pembroke College in 1626–7. Turning his attention to physic after taking his degree of Master of Arts, he practised in his profession some time in Oxfordshire. He afterwards travelled into France and Italy, visiting Montpellier and Padua, then celebrated schools of physic, and, returning home through Holland, was created Doctor of Medicine at Leyden. In 1634 he is supposed to have returned to London, and to have written his "Religio Medici"* during the next year. This celebrated treatise was not printed till 1642, when, without his consent, the book was published. It at once attracted great attention, and was criticised in a volume by Sir Kenelm Digby, "who," says Lord Clarendon, "was a person very eminent and notorious throughout the whole course of his life, from his cradle to the grave." The "Religio Medici" was very soon translated into Latin, Italian, German, Dutch, and French.

Dr. Browne settled in Norwich, where his practice became very extensive, many patients

* "This book paints certain parts of my moral and intellectual being (the best parts, no doubt) better than any other book I have ever met with; — and the style is throughout delicious." — S. T. Coleridge.

coming from a distance to consult so eminent a physician, now made more famous by the publication of so admirable a book. In 1641, he married Mrs. Mileham, a most excellent lady, whose graces both of mind and body well fitted her to become the partner of her distinguished husband. They lived together forty-one years, and with their ten children formed a household singularly happy in all its relations. In 1646 Dr. Browne printed his "Enquiries into Vulgar and Common Errors"; in 1658, his "Hydriotaphia, or Urn Burial," adding to the treatise his "Garden of Cyrus." His other writings were published after his death, many of them being left corrected for the press by his own hand. Charles the Second conferred on him the honor of knighthood in 1671, while on a tour to Norwich; and Evelyn, who went down at that time to join the royal party, having, as he says, "a desire to see that famous scholar and physitian, Dr. T. Browne," paid him a visit. He makes eulogistic mention of Sir Thomas's home, and tells us that "his whole house and garden was a paradise and cabinet of rarities, and that of the best collections, especially medails, books, plants, and natural things." So the good physician's days passed onward, filled with high reputation, and devoted to constant usefulness in his profession, till in his seventy-sixth year he fell ill and died. Submission to the will of God and fearlessness of death were among the expressions last on his lips. His burial-place is in the Church of St. Peter, Mancroft, in Norwich, where a mural monument on the south pillar of the altar records his learning and his virtues.

The Rev. John Whitefoot, who lived so many years the constant friend and neighbour of Sir Thomas, was requested to draw up some "minutes" after the death of his old companion. He complied in these fitting and worthy-to-be-remembered words.

"For a character of his person, his complexion and hair were answerable to his name; his stature was moderate, and habit of body neither fat nor lean, but εὔσαρκος.

"In his habit of clothing, he had an aversion to all finery, and affected plainness both in the fashion and ornaments. He ever wore a cloak, or boots, when few others did. He kept himself always very warm, and thought it most safe so to do, though he never loaded himself with such a multitude of garments as Suetonius reports of Augustus, enough to clothe a good family.

"The horizon of his understanding was much larger than the hemisphere of the world. All that was visible in the heavens he comprehended so well, that few that are under them knew so much. He could tell the number of the visible stars in his horizon, and call them all by their names that had any; and of the earth he had such a minute and exact geographical knowledge, as if he had been by Divine Providence ordained surveyor-general of the whole terrestrial orb, and its products, minerals, plants, and animals. He was so curious a botanist, that, besides the specifical distinctions, he made nice and elaborate observations, equally useful as entertaining.

"His memory, though not so eminent as that of Seneca or Scaliger, was capacious and tenacious, insomuch that he remembered all that was remarkable in any book that he had read, and not only knew all persons again that he had ever seen at any distance of time, but remembered the circumstances of their bodies, and their particular discourses and speeches.

"In the Latin poets he remembered everything that was acute and pungent. He had read most of the historians, ancient and modern, wherein his observations were singular, nor taken notice of by common readers. He was excellent company when he was at leisure, and expressed more light than heat in the temper of his brain.

"He had no despotical power over his affections and passions, (that was a privilege of original perfection, forfeited by the neglect of the use of it,) but as large a political power over them as any Stoic or man of his time; whereof he gave so great experiment, that he hath very rarely been known to have been overcome with any of them. The strongest that were found in him, both of the irascible and concupiscible, were under the control of his reason. Of admiration, which is one of them, being the only product either of ignorance or uncommon knowledge, he had more and less than other men, upon the same account of his knowing more than others; so that, though he met with many rarities, he admired them not so much as others do.

"He was never seen to be transported with mirth, or dejected with sadness; always cheerful, but rarely merry, at any sensible rate; seldom heard to break a jest; and when he did, he would be apt to blush at the levity of it. His gravity was natural, without affectation.

"His modesty was visible in a natural, habitual blush, which was increased upon the least occasion, and oft discovered without any observable cause.

"They that knew no more of him than by the briskness of his writings, found themselves deceived in their expectation when they came in his company, noting the gravity and sobriety of his aspect and conversation, — so free from loquacity or much talkativeness, that he was something difficult to be engaged in any discourse, though when he was so, it was always singular, and never trite or vulgar. Parsimonious in nothing but his time, whereof he made as much improvement with as little loss as any man in it; when he had any to spare from his drudging practice, he was scarce patient of any diversion from his studies; so impatient of sloth and idleness, that he would say he could not do nothing.

"Sir Thomas understood most of the European languages; viz. all that are in Hutter's Bible, which he made use of. The Latin and Greek he understood critically. The Oriental languages, which never were vernacular in this part of the world, he thought the use of them would not answer the time and pains of learning them; yet had so great a veneration for the matrix of them, viz. the Hebrew, consecrated to the oracles of God, that he was not content to be totally ignorant of it, though very little of his science is to be found in any books of that primitive language. And though much is said to be written in the derivative idioms of that tongue, especially the Arabic, yet he was satisfied with the translations, wherein he found nothing admirable.

"In his religion, he continued in the same mind which he had declared in his first book, written when he was but thirty years old, his 'Religio Medici,' wherein he fully assented to that of the Church of England, preferring it before any in the world, as did the learned Grotius. He attended the public service very constantly when he was not withheld by his practice, never missed the sacrament in his parish if he were in town, read the best English sermons he could hear of with liberal applause, and delighted not in controversies. In his last sickness, wherein he continued about a week's time, enduring great pain of the colic, besides a continual fever, with as much patience as hath been seen in any man, without any pretence of stoical apathy, animosity, or vanity of not being concerned thereat, or suffering no impeachment of happiness, — 'Nihil agis, dolor.'

"His patience was founded upon the Christian philosophy and a sound faith of God's providence, and a meek and holy submission thereunto, which he expressed in few words. I visited him near his end, when he had not strength to hear or speak much; the last words which I heard from him were, besides some expressions of dearness, that he did freely submit to the will of God, being without fear. He had often triumphed over the king of terrors in others, and given many repulses in the defence of patients; but when his own turn came, he submitted with a meek, rational, and religious courage.

"He might have made good the old saying of 'Dat Galenus opes,' had he lived in a place that could have afforded it. But his indulgence and liberality to his children, especially in their travels, two of his sons in divers countries, and two of his daughters in France, spent him more than a little. He was liberal in his house-entertainments and in his charity. He left a comfortable but no great estate, both to his lady and children, gained by his own industry.

"Such was his sagacity and knowledge of all history, ancient and modern, and his observations thereupon so singular, that it hath been said by them that knew him best, that if his profession and place of abode would have suited his ability, he would have made an extraordinary man for the Privy Council, not much inferior to the famous Padre Paolo, the late oracle of the Venetian state.

"Though he were no prophet, nor son of a prophet, yet in that faculty which comes nearest it he excelled, i. e. the stochastic, wherein he was seldom mistaken as to future events, as well public as private, but not apt to discover any presages or superstition."

Dr. Johnson affirms that "it is not on the praises of others, but on his own writings, that Sir Thomas Browne is to depend for the esteem of posterity; of which he will not easily be deprived while learning shall have any reverence among men; for there is no science in which he does not discover some skill, and scarce any kind of knowledge, profane or sacred, abstruse or elegant, which he does not appear to have cultivated with success": and he also declares that "there is scarcely a writer to be found, whose profession was not divinity, that has so frequently testified his belief of the sacred writings, has appealed to them with such unlimited submission, or mentioned them with such unvaried reverence."

In arranging this edition, the notes and readings adopted by several other editors of Sir Thomas Browne's writings have been largely consulted. Especial use has been made of the labors of Henrv Gardiner, M. A. of Exeter College, Oxford, and of the late Rev. Alexander Young, D. D., of Boston. It is hoped that the endeavor to supply a more perfect text than has hitherto appeared has been a successful effort on the part of the Editor. and of those friends who have kindly aided him with their corrections and annotations.

The portrait which accompanies this volume is newly engraved from the head in the folio of 1686, the original painting of which is at Oxford.

J. T. F.

Boston, *December*, 1861.

Religio Medici.

To the Reader.

CERTAINLY that man were greedy of life, who should desire to live when all the world were at an end; and he must needs be very impatient, who would repine at death in the society of all things that suffer under it. Had not almost every man suffered by the press, or were not the tyranny thereof become universal, I had not wanted reason for complaint: but in times wherein I have lived to behold the highest perversion of that excellent invention, the name of his Majesty defamed, the honour of Parliament depraved, the writings of both depravedly, anticipatively, counterfeitly imprinted; complaints may seem ridiculous in private persons; and men of my condition may be as incapable of affronts, as hopeless of their reparations. And truly had not the duty I owe unto the importunity of friends, and the allegiance I must ever acknowledge unto truth, prevailed with me ; the inactivity of my disposition might have made these sufferings continual, and time, that brings other things to light, should have satisfied me in the remedy of its oblivion. But because things evidently false are not only printed, but many things of truth most falsely set forth ; in this latter I could not but think myself engaged : for though we have no power to redress the former, yet in the other the reparation being within ourselves, I have at present re-presented unto the world a full and intended copy of that piece, which was most imperfectly and surreptitiously published before.

This I confess, about seven years past, with some others of affinity thereto, for my private exercise and satisfaction, I had at leisurable hours composed ; which being communicated unto one, it became common unto many, and was by transcription successively corrupted, until it arrived in a most depraved copy at the press. He that shall peruse that work, and shall take notice of sundry particularities and personal expressions therein, will easily discern the intention was not publick : and being a private exercise directed to myself, what is delivered therein was rather a memorial unto me than an example or rule unto any other: and therefore, if there be any singularity therein correspondent unto the private conceptions of any man, it doth not advantage them; or if dissentaneous thereunto, it no way overthrows them. It was penned in such a place, and with such disadvantage, that (I protest) from the first setting of pen unto paper, I had not the assistance of any good book, whereby to promote my invention, or relieve my memory; and therefore there might be many real lapses therein, which others might take notice of, and more that I suspected myself. It was set down many years past, and was the sense of my conceptions at that time, not an immutable law unto my advancing judgment at all times; and therefore there might be many things therein plausible unto my passed apprehension, which are not agreeable unto my present self. Therefore are many things delivered rhetorically, many expressions therein merely tropical, and as they best illustrate my intention; and therefore also there are many things to be taken in a soft and flexible sense, and not to be called unto the rigid test of reason. Lastly, all that is contained therein is in submission unto maturer discernments; and as I have declared, shall no further father them than the best and learned judgments shall authorize them: under favour of which considerations, I have made its secrecy publick, and committed the truth thereof to every ingenuous Reader.

THOMAS BROWNE.

Religio Medici.

Our Physician a Christian.

FOR my religion, though there be several circumstances that might persuade the world I have none at all, as the general scandal of my profession, the natural course of my studies, the indifferency of my behaviour and discourse in matters of religion, neither violently defending one, nor with that common ardour and contention opposing another; yet in despite hereof I dare, without usurpation, assume the honourable style of a Christian. Not that I merely owe this title to the font, my education, or clime wherein I was born, as being bred up either to confirm those principles my parents instilled into my unwary understanding, or by a general consent to proceed in the religion of my country; but having, in my riper years and confirmed judgment, seen and examined all,* I find myself obliged by the principles of grace, and the law of mine own reason, to embrace no other name but this: neither doth herein my zeal so far make me forget the general charity I owe unto humanity, as rather to hate than pity Turks, infidels, and (what is worse) Jews; rather contenting myself to enjoy that happy style, than maligning those who refuse so glorious a title.

Quousque patiere, bone Jesu!
Judæi te semel, ego sæpius crucifixi;
Illi in Asia, ego in Britannia,
Gallia, Germania;
Bone Jesu, miserere mei, et Judæorum!

His belief defined.

II. But because the name of a Christian is become too general to express our faith, there being a geography of religion as well as lands, and every clime being distinguished not only by their laws and limits, but circumscribed by their doctrines and rules of faith; to be particular, I am of that reformed new-cast religion, wherein I dislike nothing but the name; of the same belief our Saviour taught, the apostles disseminated, the fathers authorized, and the martyrs confirmed; but by the sinister ends of princes, the ambition and avarice of prelates, and the fatal corruption of times, so decayed,

* According to the Apostolical precept, "Prove all things: hold fast that which is good." 1 Thess. v. 21.

impaired, and fallen from its native beauty, that it required the careful and charitable hands of these times to restore it to its primitive integrity. Now the accidental occasion whereon, the slender means whereby, the low and abject condition of the person by whom so good a work was set on foot, which in our adversaries begets contempt and scorn, fills me with wonder, and is the very same objection the insolent Pagans first cast at Christ and his disciples.

Differences of opinion need not separate Christians.

III. Yet have I not so shaken hands with those desperate resolutions, (who had rather venture at large their decayed bottom, than bring her in to be new trimmed in the dock; who had rather promiscuously retain all, than abridge any, and obstinately be what they are, than what they have been,) as to stand in diameter and sword's point with them: we have reformed from them, not against them; for omitting those improperations, and terms of scurrility betwixt us, which only difference our affections, and not our cause, there is between us one common name and appellation, one faith and necessary body of principles common to us both; and therefore I am not scrupulous to converse and live with them, to enter their churches in defect of ours, and either pray with them, or for them. I could never perceive any rational consequence from those many texts which prohibit the children of Israel to pollute themselves with the temples of the heathens; we being all Christians, and not divided by such detested impieties as might profane our prayers, or the place wherein we make them; or that a resolved conscience may not adore her Creator anywhere, especially in places devoted to his service; where, if their devotions offend him, mine may please him; if theirs profane it, mine may hallow it. Holy-water and crucifix (dangerous to the common people) deceive not my judgment, nor abuse my devotion at all: I am, I confess, naturally inclined to that which misguided zeal terms superstition. My common conversation I do acknowledge austere, my behaviour full of rigour, sometimes not without morosity; yet at my devotion I love to use the civility of my knee, my hat, and hand, with all those outward and sensible motions which may express or promote my invisible devotion. I should violate my own arm rather than a church; nor willingly deface the memory of saint or martyr. At the sight of a cross or crucifix I can dispense with my hat, but scarce with the thought or memory of my Saviour. I cannot laugh at, but rather pity, the fruitless journeys of pilgrims, nor contemn the miserable condition of friars; for though misplaced in circumstances, there is something in it of devotion. I could never hear the Ave Mary bell * without an elevation; or think it a sufficient warrant, because they erred in one circumstance, for me to err in all, that is, in silence and dumb contempt: whilst therefore they directed their devotions to her, I offered mine to God, and rectified the errors of their prayers, by rightly ordering mine own. At a solemn procession I have wept abundantly, while my consorts, blind with opposition and prejudice, have fallen into an access of scorn and laughter. There are, questionless, both in Greek, Roman, and African churches, solemnities and ceremonies, whereof the wiser zeals do make a Christian use, and stand condemned by us, not as evil in themselves, but as allurements and baits of superstition to those vulgar heads that look asquint on the face of truth, and those unstable judgments that cannot consist in the narrow point and centre of virtue without a reel or stagger to the circumference.†

Of Reformations.

IV. As there were many reformers, so likewise there were many reformations; every coun-

* A church bell that tolls every day at six and twelve of the clock; at the hearing whereof, every one in what place soever, either of house or street, betakes himself to his prayer, which is commonly directed to the Virgin.

† This figure is probably borrowed from Aristotle. Eth. Nic. ii. 9. "Wherefore it is hard to be good: for in each action to find the mean is difficult, as it is not every one that can find the centre of a circle, but he that is skilled to do so."

try proceeding in a particular way and method, according as their national interest, together with their constitution and clime, inclined them; some angrily, and with extremity; others calmly, and with mediocrity; not rending, but easily dividing the community, and leaving an honest possibility of a reconciliation; which though peaceable spirits do desire, and may conceive that revolution of time and the mercies of God may effect, yet that judgment that shall consider the present antipathies between the two extremes, their contrarieties in condition, affection, and opinion, may with the same hopes expect an union in the poles of heaven.

Of the Church of England.

V. But to difference myself nearer, and draw into a lesser circle: there is no church, whose every part so squares unto my conscience; whose articles, constitutions, and customs seem so consonant unto reason, and as it were framed to my particular devotion, as this whereof I hold my belief, the Church of England, to whose faith I am a sworn subject; and therefore in a double obligation subscribe unto her Articles, and endeavour to observe her constitutions: whatsoever is beyond, as points indifferent, I observe according to the rules of my private reason, or the humour and fashion of my devotion; neither believing this, because Luther affirmed it, nor disapproving that, because Calvin hath disavouched it. I condemn not all things in the council of Trent, nor approve all in the synod of Dort. In brief, where the Scripture is silent, the Church is my text; where that speaks, 't is but my comment: where there is a joint silence of both, I borrow not the rules of my religion from Rome or Geneva, but the dictates of my own reason. It is an unjust scandal of our adversaries, and a gross error in ourselves, to compute the nativity of our religion from Henry the Eighth, who, though he rejected the Pope, refused not the faith of Rome, and effected no more than what his own predecessors desired and assayed in ages past, and was conceived the state of Venice would have attempted in our days. It is as uncharitable a point in us to fall upon those popular scurrilities and opprobrious scoffs of the bishop of Rome, to whom, as a temporal prince, we owe the duty of good language. I confess there is cause of passion between us: by his sentence I stand excommunicated, heretic is the best language he affords me; yet can no ear witness I ever returned him the name Antichrist, man of sin, or whore of Babylon. It is the method of charity to suffer without reaction: those usual satires and invectives of the pulpit may perchance produce a good effect on the vulgar, whose ears are opener to rhetoric than logic;

yet do they in no wise confirm the faith of wiser believers, who know that a good cause needs not to be patron'd by passion, but can sustain itself upon a temperate dispute.

Disputes in religion wisely avoided.

VI. I could never divide myself from any man upon the difference of an opinion, or be angry with his judgment for not agreeing with me in that, from which within a few days I should dissent myself. I have no genius to disputes in religion, and have often thought it wisdom to decline them, especially upon a disadvantage, or when the cause of truth might suffer in the weakness of my patronage. Where we desire to be informed, 't is good to contest with men above ourselves; but to confirm and establish our opinions, 't is best to argue with judgments below our own, that the frequent spoils and victories over their reasons may settle in ourselves an esteem and confirmed opinion of our own. Every man is not a proper champion for truth, nor fit to take up the gauntlet in the cause of verity: many from the ignorance of these maxims, and an inconsiderate zeal for truth, have too rashly charged the troops of error, and remain as trophies unto the enemies of truth. A man may be in as just possession of truth as of a city, and yet be forced to surrender; 't is therefore far better to enjoy her with peace, than to hazard her on a battle: if therefore there rise any doubts in my way, I do forget them, or at least defer them, till my better settled judgment and more manly reason be able to resolve them; for I perceive every man's own reason is his best Œdipus, and will, upon a reasonable truce, find a way to loose those bonds wherewith the subtleties of error have enchained our more flexible and tender judgments. In philosophy, where truth seems double-faced, there is no man more paradoxical than myself: but in divinity I love to keep the road; and, though not in an implicit, yet an humble faith, follow the great wheel of the Church, by which I move, not reserving any proper poles or motion from the epicycle of my own brain; by these means I leave no gap for heresy, schisms, or errors, of which at present I hope I shall not injure truth to say I have no taint or tincture. I must confess my greener studies have been polluted with two or three, not any begotten in the latter centuries, but old and obsolete, such as could never have been revived, but by such extravagant and irregular heads as mine; for indeed heresies perish not with their authors, but like the river Arethusa,*

Fantasies in divinity dangerous as giving entrance to errors.

Whereof our Physician confesseth to have had two or three.

* Arethusa, a nymph of Achaia, while bathing, on her return from hunting in the Stymphalian wood, was surprised by the river god Alpheus, in whose waters she was disporting herself. She fled from him, and after a long chase was concealed in a cloud by Diana, just as her strength was failing. She thus re-

though they lose their currents in one place, they rise up again in another. One general council is not able to extirpate one single heresy: it may be cancelled for the present; but revolution of time and the like aspects from heaven, will restore it, when it will flourish till it be condemned again. For as though there was metempsychosis, and the soul of one man passed into another, opinions do find, after certain revolutions, men and minds like those that first begat them. To see ourselves again, we need not look for Plato's year: * every man is not only himself; there hath been many Diogenes, and as many Timons, though but few of that name: men are lived over again, the world is now as it was in ages past; there was none then, but there hath been some one since that parallels him, and as it were his revived self.

1st, That the soul might, in

VII. Now the first of mine was that of the Arabians,† that the souls of men perished with

lates (Ovid. Metam. v. 574) her transformation into the stream which bears her name, and with which the waters of Alpheus vainly sought to unite, Diana opening a way for her under ground and bringing her out again in Ortygia, near Syracuse in Sicily.

* A revolution of certain thousand years, when all things should return unto their former estate, and he be teaching again in his school as when he delivered this opinion.

† "It was not only in the point now mentioned, that the doctrine of the Gospel suffered, at this time, from the erroneous fancies of wrong-headed doctors. For there sprung up now, in Arabia, a certain sort of minute philosophers, the disciples of a

their bodies, but should yet be raised again at the last day. Not that I did absolutely conceive a mortality of the soul; but if that were, which faith, not philosophy, hath yet thoroughly disproved, and that both entered the grave together, yet I held the same conceit thereof, that we all do for the body, that it should rise again. Surely it is but the merits of our unworthy natures, if we sleep in darkness until the last alarum. A serious reflex upon my own unworthiness did make me backward from challenging this prerogative of my soul: so I might enjoy my Saviour at the last, I could with patience be nothing almost unto eternity. The second was that of Origen, that God would not persist in his vengeance forever, but after a definite time of his wrath, he would release the damned souls from torture: which error I fell into upon a serious contemplation of the great attribute of God, his Mercy; and did a

some sort, perish, and rise again with the body.

2d, That all men should finally be saved.

master whose obscurity has concealed him from the knowledge of after ages, who denied the immortality of the soul, and believed that it perished with the body: but maintained, at the same time, that it was to be recalled to life with the body, by the power of God. The philosophers who held this opinion were called Arabians, from their country. Origen was called from Egypt, to make head against this rising sect; and disputed against them in full council, with such remarkable success, that they abandoned their erroneous sentiments, and returned to the received doctrine of the Church." Mosheim, Eccl. Hist. vol. i. ch. 5, § 16, p. 307.

2

little cherish it in myself, because I found therein no malice, and a ready weight to sway me from the other extreme of despair, whereunto melancholy and contemplative natures are too easily disposed. A third there is which I did never positively maintain or practise, but have often wished it had been consonant to truth, and not offensive to my religion, and that is the prayer for the dead; whereunto I was inclined from some charitable inducements, whereby I could scarce contain my prayers for a friend at the ringing of a bell, or behold his corpse without an orison for his soul: 't was a good way, methought, to be remembered by posterity, and far more noble than a history. These opinions I never maintained with pertinacy, or endeavoured to inveigle any man's belief unto mine, nor so much as ever revealed or disputed them with my dearest friends; by which means I neither propagated them in others, nor confirmed them in myself; but suffering them to flame upon their own substance, without addition of new fuel, they went out insensibly of themselves: therefore these opinions, though condemned by lawful councils, were not heresies in me, but bare errors, and single lapses of my understanding without a joint depravity of my will. Those have not only depraved understandings, but diseased affections, who can-

3d, That we might pray for the dead.

But these he suffered not to grow into heresies.

not enjoy a singularity without an heresy, or be the author of an opinion without they be of a sect also: this was the villany of the first schism of Lucifer, who was not content to err alone, but drew into his faction many legions of spirits; and upon this experience he tempted only Eve, as well understanding the communicable nature of sin, and that to deceive but one, was tacitly and upon consequence to delude them both.

Of the manifold nature of schism, ever multiplying itself.

VIII. That heresies should arise, we have the prophecy of Christ; but that old ones should be abolished, we hold no prediction. That there must be heresies, is true, not only in our church, but also in any other: even in doctrines heretical, there will be super-heresies; and Arians not only divided from their church, but also among themselves: for heads that are disposed unto schism and complexionably propense to innovation, are naturally indisposed for a community; nor will be ever confined unto the order or economy of one body; and therefore when they separate from others, they knit but loosely among themselves; nor contented with a general breach or dichotomy with their church, do subdivide and mince themselves almost into atoms. 'T is true, that men of singular parts and humours have not been free from singular opinions and conceits in all ages; retaining something not only beside the opinion of their own church or any other, but also of any particular author; which notwithstanding a sober judgment may do without offence or heresy; for there is yet, after all the decrees of councils, and the niceties of schools, many things untouched, unimagined, wherein the liberty of an honest reason may play and expatiate with security, and far without the circle of an heresy.

Mysteries in divinity only to be approached in faith.

IX.* As for those wingy mysteries in divinity, and airy subtleties in religion, which have unhinged the brains of better heads, they never stretched the *pia mater* of mine: methinks there be not impossibilities enough in religion for an active faith; the deepest mysteries ours contains, have not only been illustrated, but maintained by syllogism, and the rule of reason. I love to lose myself in a mystery, to pursue my reason to an *O altitudo!* 'T is my solitary recreation to pose my apprehension with those involved enigmas and riddles of the Trinity, with Incarnation and Resurrection. I can answer all the objections of Satan and my rebellious reason, with that odd resolution I learned of Tertullian, *Certum est quia impossibile est.* I desire to exercise my faith in the difficultest point; for to credit ordinary and visible objects,

* See Aids to Reflection, p. 151.

is not faith, but persuasion. Some believe the better for seeing Christ's sepulchre; and when they have seen the Red Sea, doubt not of the miracle. Now contrarily, I bless myself, and am thankful that I live not in the days of miracles, that I never saw Christ nor his disciples: I would not have been one of those Israelites that passed the Red Sea, nor one of Christ's patients on whom he wrought his wonders; then had my faith been thrust upon me; nor should I enjoy that greater blessing pronounced to all that believe and saw not. 'T is an easy and necessary belief, to credit what our eye and sense hath examined:* I believe he was dead and buried, and rose again; and desire to see him in his glory, rather than to contemplate him in his cenotaph or sepulchre. Nor is this much to believe; as we have reason, we owe this faith unto history: they only had the advantage of a bold and noble faith, who lived before his coming, who upon obscure prophecies and mystical types could raise a belief, and expect apparent impossibilities.

Blessed are they that have not seen and yet have believed.

X. 'T is true, there is an edge in all firm belief, and with an easy metaphor we may say the sword of faith;† but in these obscurities I

The armour of a Christian.

* "God forbede but that men should believ
Well more thing than thei han seen with eye."
CHAUCER.

† Eph. vi. 16.

rather use it in the adjunct the apostle gives it, a buckler; under which I conceive a wary combatant may lie invulnerable. Since I was of understanding to know we knew nothing, my reason hath been more pliable to the will of faith; I am now content to understand a mystery without a rigid definition, in an easy and Platonic description. That allegorical description * of Hermes pleaseth me beyond all the metaphysical definitions of divines; where I cannot satisfy my reason, I love to humour my fancy: I had as lieve you tell me that *anima est angelus hominis, est corpus Dei*, as ἐντελέχεια; *Lux est umbra Dei*, as *actus perspicui*.† Where there is an obscurity too deep for our reason, 't is good to sit down with a description, peri-

* *Sphæra cujus centrum ubique, circumferentia nullibi.*

† Great variety of opinion there hath been amongst the ancient philosophers touching the definition of the soul. Thales's was, that it is a *nature without repose*. Asclepiades, that it is *an exercitation of sense:* Hesiod, that it is *a thing composed of earth and water:* Parmenides holds, *of earth and fire;* Galen, that it is *heat;* Hippocrates, that it is *a spirit diffused through the body:* some others have held it to be *light;* Plato saith, 't is *a substance moving itself;* after cometh Aristotle (whom the author here reproveth) and goeth a degree farther, and saith it is ἐντελέχεια, that is, that which naturally makes the body to move. But this definition is as rigid as any of the other; for this tells us not what the essence, origin, or nature of the soul is, but only marks an effect of it, and therefore signifieth no more than if he had said, that it is *angelus hominis*, or an intelligence that moveth man, as he supposed those other to do the heavens. K. Cf. Cic. Tusc. Disp. I. x.

phrasis, or adumbration; for by acquainting our reason how unable it is to display the visible and obvious effects of nature, it becomes more humble and submissive unto the subtleties of faith; and thus I teach my haggard and unreclaimed reason to stoop unto the lure of faith. I believe there was already a tree whose fruit our unhappy parents tasted; though in the same chapter, when God forbids it, 'tis positively said the plants of the fields were not yet grown, for God had not caused it to rain upon the earth. I believe that the serpent, (if we shall literally understand it,) from his proper form and figure, made his motion on his belly before the curse. I find the trial of the pucellage and virginity of women, which God ordained the Jews, is very fallible. Experience and history inform me, that not only many particular women, but likewise whole nations, have escaped the curse of childbirth, which God seems to pronounce upon the whole sex; yet do I believe that all this is true, which indeed my reason would persuade me to be false; and this I think is no vulgar part of faith, to believe a thing not only above, but contrary to reason, and against the arguments of our proper senses.

The Eternity of God.

XI. In my solitary and retired imagination,

——— Neque enim cum lectulus aut me
Porticus excepit, desum mihi —

I remember I am not alone, and therefore forget not to contemplate him and his attributes who is ever with me, especially those two mighty ones, his wisdom and eternity: with the one I recreate, with the other I confound my understanding; for who can speak of eternity without a solecism, or think thereof without an ecstasy? Time we may comprehend, it is but five days older than ourselves, and hath the same horoscope with the world; but to retire so far back as to apprehend a beginning, to give such an infinite start forward as to conceive an end in an essence that we affirm hath neither the one nor the other, it puts my reason to St. Paul's sanctuary: my philosophy dares not say the angels can do it; God hath not made a creature that can comprehend him; it is a privilege of his own nature: *I am that I am*, was his own definition unto Moses; and it was a short one, to confound mortality, that durst question God, or ask him what he was. Indeed he only is; all others have and shall be; but in eternity there is no distinction of tenses; and therefore that terrible term *predestination*, which hath troubled so many weak heads to conceive, and the wisest to explain, is in respect to God no prescious determination of our states to come, but a definitive blast of his will already fulfilled, and at the instant that he first decreed it; for to his eternity, which is indivisible, and all together, the last trump is already sounded, the reprobates in the flame, and the blessed in Abraham's bosom. St. Peter speaks modestly, when he saith,* a thousand years to God are but as one day; for to speak like a philosopher, those continued instances of time which flow into a thousand years, make not to him one moment: what to us is to come, to his eternity is present, his whole duration being but one permanent point, without succession, parts, flux, or division.

Of the Trinity.

XII. There is no attribute that adds more difficulty to the mystery of the Trinity, where, though in a relative way of Father and Son, we must deny a priority. I wonder how Aristotle could conceive the world eternal, or how he could make good two eternities: his similitude of a triangle, comprehended in a square, doth somewhat illustrate the trinity of our souls, and that the triple unity of God; for there is in us not three, but a trinity of souls, because there is in us, if not three distinct souls, yet differing faculties, that can and do subsist apart in different subjects, and yet in us are so united as to make but one soul and substance: if one soul were so perfect as to inform three distinct bodies, that were a petty trinity: conceive the distinct number of three, not divided nor separated

* 2 Pet. iii. 8.

by the intellect, but actually comprehended in its unity, and that is a perfect trinity. I have often admired the mystical way of Pythagoras, and the secret magic of numbers. "Beware of philosophy," is a precept not to be received in too large a sense: for in this mass of nature there is a set of things that carry in their front, though not in capital letters, yet in stenography and short characters, something of divinity, which to wiser reasons serve as luminaries in the abyss of knowledge, and to judicious beliefs as scales and roundles to mount the pinnacles and highest pieces of divinity. The severe schools shall never laugh me out of the philosophy of Hermes, that this visible world is but a picture of the invisible, wherein as in a portrait things are not truly, but in equivocal shapes, and as they counterfeit some more real substance in that invisible fabric.

The visible world a picture of the invisible.

The Wisdom of God.

XIII. That other attribute wherewith I recreate my devotion, is his Wisdom, in which I am happy; and for the contemplation of this only, do not repent me that I was bred in the way of study: the advantage I have of the vulgar, with the content and happiness I conceive therein, is an ample recompense for all my endeavours, in what part of knowledge soever. Wisdom is his most beauteous attribute; no man can attain unto it, yet Solomon pleased

God when he desired it. He is wise, because he knows all things; and he knoweth all things, because he made them all: but his greatest knowledge is in comprehending that he made not, that is, himself. And this is also the greatest knowledge in man: for this I do honour my own profession, and embrace the counsel even of the devil himself: had he read such a lecture in Paradise as he did at Delphos,* we had better known ourselves, nor had we stood in fear to know him. I know He is wise in all, wonderful in what we conceive, but far more in what we comprehend not; for we behold him but asquint, upon reflex or shadow; our understanding is dimmer than Moses' eye; we are ignorant of the back parts or lower side of his divinity; therefore to pry into the maze of his counsels, is not only folly in man, but presumption even in angels: like us, they are his servants, not his senators; he holds no council, but that mystical one of the Trinity, wherein though there be three persons, there is but one mind that decrees without contradiction: nor needs he any; his actions are not begot with deliberation, his wisdom naturally knows what is best; his intellect stands ready fraught with the superlative and purest ideas of goodness; consultation and election, which are two motions in us, make

* Γνῶθι σεαυτόν, *Nosce te ipsum.*

but one in him; his actions springing from his power, at the first touch of his will. These are contemplations metaphysical: my humble speculations have another method, and are content to trace and discover those expressions he hath left in his creatures, and the obvious effects of nature: there is no danger to profound these mysteries, no *sanctum sanctorum* in philosophy. The world was made to be inhabited by beasts, but studied and contemplated by man:* 't is the debt of our reason we owe unto God, and the homage we pay for not being beasts: without this, the world is still as though it had not been, or as it was before the sixth day, when as yet there was not a creature that could conceive or say there was a world. The wisdom of God receives small honour from those vulgar heads that rudely stare about, and with a gross rusticity admire his works: those highly magnify him, whose judicious inquiry into his acts, and deliberate research into his creatures, return the duty of a devout and learned admiration. Therefore,

No danger in attempting to trace the hand of God in his Works.

Search while thou wilt, and let thy reason go
To ransom truth, even to th' abyss below;
Rally the scattered causes; and that line
Which nature twists, be able to untwine.

* In the MS. (in the British Museum) this clause stands thus: "The world was made not so much to be inhabited by men, as to be contemplated, studied, and known, by man."

It is thy Maker's will, for unto none
But unto reason can he e'er be known.
The devils do know thee, but those damn'd meteors
Build not thy glory, but confound thy creatures.
Teach my endeavours so thy works to read,
That learning them in thee I may proceed.
Give thou my reason that instructive flight,
Whose weary wings may on thy hands still light.
Teach me to soar aloft, yet ever so,
When near the sun, to stoop again below.
Thus shall my humble feathers safely hover,
And though near earth, more than the heavens discover.
And then at last, when homeward I shall drive
Rich with the spoils of nature to my hive,
There will I sit like that industrious fly,
Buzzing thy praises, which shall never die,
Till death abrupts them, and succeeding glory
Bid me go on in a more lasting story.

And this is almost all wherein an humble creature may endeavour to requite, and some way to retribute unto his Creator: for if not he that saith, "Lord, Lord, but he that doth the will of his Father," shall be saved; certainly our wills must be our performances, and our intents make out our actions; otherwise our pious labours shall find anxiety in our graves, and our best endeavours not hope, but fear a resurrection.

St. Matt. vii. 21.

XIV. There is but one first cause, and four second causes of all things: some are without efficient, as God; others without matter, as angels; some without form, as the first matter: but every essence created or uncreated hath its

Every created essence hath its proper end.

final cause, and some positive end both of its essence and operation:* this is the cause I grope after in the works of nature; on this hangs the providence of God: to raise so beauteous a structure, as the world and the creatures thereof, was but his art; but their sundry and divided operations, with their predestinated ends, are from the treasury of his wisdom. In the causes, nature, and affections of the eclipses of the sun and moon, there is most excellent speculation; but to profound farther, and to contemplate a reason why his providence hath so disposed and ordered their motions in that vast circle, as to conjoin and obscure each other, is a sweeter piece of reason, and a diviner point of philosophy; therefore sometimes, and in some things, there appears to me as much divinity in Galen his books *De usu partium*, as in Suarez his Metaphysics: had Aristotle been as curious in the enquiry of this cause as he was of the other, he had not left behind him an imperfect piece of philosophy, but an absolute tract of divinity.

Nature doeth nothing in vain.

XV. *Natura nihil agit frustra*, is the only indisputable axiom in philosophy; there are no grotesques in nature; not any thing framed to

* "Eterne God, that thurgh thy purveance
Ledest this world by certain governance,
In idel, as men sain, ye nothing make."
CHAUCER, Frankeleine's Tale, 11176.

fill up empty cantons, and unnecessary spaces: in the most imperfect creatures, and such as were not preserved in the ark, but, having their seeds and principles in the womb of nature, are everywhere, where the power of the sun is; * in these is the wisdom of his hand discovered: out of this rank Solomon chose the object of his admiration; indeed, what reason may not go to school to the wisdom of bees, ants, and spiders? what wise hand teacheth them to do what reason cannot teach us? Ruder heads stand amazed at those prodigious pieces of nature, whales, elephants, dromedaries, and camels; these, I confess, are the colossi and majestic pieces of her hand: but in these narrow engines there is more curious mathematics; and the civility of these little citizens more neatly sets forth the wisdom of their Maker. Who admires not Regio-Montanus his fly beyond his eagle, or wonders not more at the operation of two souls in those little bodies, than but one in the trunk of a cedar? † I could never content my con-

Prov. vi. 6-8. xxx. 24-28.

* "Miraculous may seem to him that reades
So strange ensample of conception;
But reason teacheth that the fruitful seedes
Of all things living, thro' impression
Of the sun-beames in moyst complexion
Doe life conceive, and quick'ned are by kynd."
Faerie Queene.

† See Wordsworth's exquisite little poem entitled "Nutting," and Landor's Fæsulan Idyl: —

templation with those general pieces of wonder, the flux and reflux of the sea, the increase of the Nile, the conversion of the needle to the north; and have studied to match and parallel those in the more obvious and neglected pieces of nature, which without further travel I can do in the cosmography of myself: we carry with us the wonders we seek without us: there is all Africa and her prodigies in us; we are that bold and adventurous piece of nature, which he that studies wisely learns in a compendium, what others labour at in a divided piece and endless volume.

Nature a Bible open to all.

XVI. Thus there are two books from whence I collect my divinity; besides that written one of God, another of his servant nature, that universal and public manuscript, that lies expansed unto the eyes of all: those that never saw him in the one, have discovered him in the other. This was the Scripture and Theology of the heathens: the natural motion of the sun made them more admire him than its supernatural

"And 't is and ever was my wish and way
To let all flowers live freely, and all die,
Whene'er their Genius bids their souls depart,
Among their kindred in their native place.
I never pluck the rose; the violet's head
Hath shaken with my breath upon its bank,
And not reproached me; the ever sacred cup
Of the pure lily hath between my hands
Felt safe, unsoiled, nor lost one grain of gold."

station did the children of Israel; the ordinary effect of nature wrought more admiration in them, than in the other all his miracles: surely the heathens knew better how to join and read these mystical letters than we Christians, who cast a more careless eye on these common hieroglyphics, and disdain to suck divinity from the flowers of nature. Nor do I so forget God as to adore the name of nature; which I define not, with the schools, to be the principle of motion and rest, but that straight and regular line, that settled and constant course the wisdom of God hath ordained the actions of his creatures, according to their several kinds. To make a revolution every day, is the nature of the sun, because of that necessary course which God hath ordained it, from which it cannot swerve but by a faculty from that voice which first did give it motion.* Now this course of nature God seldom alters or perverts, but, like an excellent artist, hath so contrived his work, that with the selfsame instrument, without a new

Josh. x. 12, 13.

* See Wordsworth's Ode to Duty:—

"Thou dost preserve the stars from wrong;
And the most ancient heavens thro' thee are fresh and strong."

Cf. Cowper's Task, bk. vi:—

"Some say that in the origin of things,
When all creation started into birth,
The infant elements received a law

creation, he may effect his obscurest designs.
Ex. xv. 25. Thus he sweeteneth the water with a wood,
Ecclus. xxxviii. 5. preserveth the creatures in the ark, which the blast of his mouth might have as easily created; for God is like a skilful geometrician, who when more easily, and with one stroke of his compass, he might describe or divide a right line, had yet rather do this in a circle or longer way, according to the constituted and forelaid principles of his art: yet this rule of his he doth sometimes pervert, to acquaint the world with his prerogative, lest the arrogancy of our reason should question his power, and conclude he could not. And thus I call the effects of nature the works of God, whose hand and instrument she only is; and therefore to ascribe his actions unto her, is to devolve the honour of the principal agent upon the instrument; which if with reason we may do, then let our hammers rise up and boast they have built our houses, and our pens receive the honour of our writing. I hold there is a general beauty in the works of God, and there-

From which they swerve not since. That under force
Of that controlling ordinance they move,
And need not his immediate hand who first
Prescribed their course, to regulate it now.

. . . . .

The Lord of all, himself through all diffused,
Sustains and is the life of all that lives.
Nature is but a name for an effect,
Whose cause is God."

fore no deformity in any kind of species whatsoever: I cannot tell by what logic we call a toad, a bear, or an elephant ugly, they being created in those outward shapes and figures which best express those actions of their inward forms. And having passed that general visitation of God, who saw that all that he had made was good, that is, conformable to his will, which abhors deformity, and is the rule of order and beauty; there is no deformity but in monstrosity, wherein notwithstanding there is a kind of beauty, nature so ingeniously contriving the irregular parts, that they become sometimes more remarkable than the principal fabric. To speak yet more narrowly, there was never any thing ugly or misshapen, but the chaos; wherein, notwithstanding, to speak strictly, there was no deformity, because no form, nor was it yet impregnate by the voice of God; now nature is not at variance with art, nor art with nature, they being both servants of his providence: art is the perfection of nature: were the world now as it was the sixth day, there were yet a chaos; nature hath made one world, and art another. In brief, all things are artificial; for nature is the art of God.

Ecclus. xxxix. 33, 34. Wisd. xv. 18.

Gen. i. 31.

"Nature the art whereby God doth govern the world."

XVII. This is the ordinary and open way of his providence, which art and industry have in a good part discovered, whose effects we may

Providence often falsely called Fortune.

foretell without an oracle: to foreshow these, is not prophecy, but prognostication. There is another way, full of meanders and labyrinths, whereof the devil and spirits have no exact Ephemerides, and that is a more particular and obscure method of his providence, directing the operations of individuals and single essences: this we call fortune, that serpentine and crooked line, whereby he draws those actions his wisdom intends, in a more unknown and secret way. This cryptic and involved method of his providence have I ever admired; nor can I relate the history of my life, the occurrences of my days, the escapes of dangers, and hits of chance, with a *Bezo las Manos* to fortune, or
Gen. xxii. a bare gramercy to my good stars. Abraham
13. might have thought the ram in the thicket came
thither by accident; human reason would have
Ex. ii. said, that mere chance conveyed Moses in the
ark to the sight of Pharaoh's daughter: what a
Gen. labyrinth is there in the story of Joseph, able to
xxxvii. convert a stoic! Surely there are in every
man's life certain rubs, doublings, and wrenches, which pass awhile under the effects of chance, but at the last, well examined, prove the mere hand of God. It was not dumb chance that, to discover the fougade or powder-plot, contrived a miscarriage in the letter. I like the victory of '88 the better for that one occurrence, which

our enemies imputed to our dishonour, and the partiality of fortune, to wit, the tempests and contrariety of winds. King Philip did not detract from the nation, when he said he sent his armado to fight with men, and not to combat with the winds. Where there is a manifest disproportion between the powers and forces of two several agents, upon a maxim of reason we may promise the victory to the superior; but when unexpected accidents slip in, and unthought of occurrences intervene, these must proceed from a power that owes no obedience to those axioms; where, as in the writing upon the Dan. v. 5.
wall, we may behold the hand, but see not the spring that moves it. The success of that petty province of Holland (of which the Grand Seignior proudly said, if they should trouble him as they did the Spaniard, he would send his men with shovels and pickaxes, and throw it into the sea) I cannot altogether ascribe to the ingenuity and industry of the people, but the mercy of God, that hath disposed them to such a thriving genius; and to the will of his providence, that disposeth her favour to each country in their preordinate season. All cannot be happy at once; for, because the glory of one state depends upon the ruin of another, there is a revolution and vicissitude of their greatness; and they must obey the swing of that wheel, not

moved by intelligences, but by the hand of God, whereby all estates arise to their zenith and vertical points, according to their predestinated periods. For the lives, not only of men, but of commonwealths, and the whole world, run not upon an *helix* that still enlargeth, but on a circle, where arriving to their meridian, they decline in obscurity, and fall under the horizon again.*

The term Fortune used in a relative sense.

XVIII. These must not therefore be named the effects of fortune but in a relative way, and as we term the works of nature: it was the ignorance of man's reason that begat this very name, and by a careless term miscalled the providence of God; for there is no liberty for causes to operate in a loose and straggling way; nor any effect whatsoever, but hath its warrant from some universal or superior cause. It is not a ridiculous devotion to say a prayer before a game at tables; for even in *sortilegies* and matters of greatest uncertainty, there is a settled and preordered course of effects.† It is we that are blind, not fortune: because our eye is too dim to discover the mystery of her effects,

* This subject is discussed in an Essay by the Rev. A. P. Stanley, to which one of the Chancellor's Prizes was awarded. Oxford, 1840.

Cf. Herod. i. 207.

† "The lot is cast into the lap: but the whole disposing thereof is of the Lord." Prov. xvi. 33.

we foolishly paint her blind, and hoodwink the providence of the Almighty.* I cannot justify that contemptible provorb, *That fools only are fortunate*, or that insolent paradox, *That a wise man is out of the reach of fortune*, much less those opprobrious epithets of poets, *Whore*, *baud*, and *strumpet*.† It is, I confess, the common fate of men of singular gifts of mind, to be destitute of those of fortune, which doth not any way deject the spirit of wiser judgments, who thoroughly understand the justice of this proceeding; and being enriched with higher donatives, cast a more careless eye on these vulgar parts of felicity. It is a most unjust ambition to desire to engross the mercies of the Almighty, not to be content with the goods of mind, without a possession of those of body or fortune; and it is an error worse than heresy, to adore these complemental and circumstantial pieces of felicity, and undervalue those perfections and essential points of happiness wherein we resemble our Maker. To wiser desires it is satisfaction enough to deserve, though not to enjoy the favours of fortune: let providence provide for fools; it is not partiality, but equity in God,

* Cf. Bp. Butler's xvth Sermon.

† So Dryden:—

> "But when she dances on the wind,
> And shakes her wings, and will not stay,
> I puff the prostitute away."

who deals with us but as our natural parents: those that are able of body and mind he leaves to their deserts; to those of weaker merits he imparts a larger portion, and pieces out the defect of one by the excess of the other. Thus have we no just quarrel with nature for leaving us naked; or to envy the horns, hoofs, skins, and furs of other creatures, being provided with reason, that can supply them all.* We need not labour with so many arguments to confute judicial astrology; for if there be a truth therein, it doth not injure divinity: if to be born under Mercury disposeth us to be witty, under Jupiter to be wealthy, I do not owe a knee unto these, but unto that merciful hand that hath ordered my indifferent and uncertain nativity unto such benevolous aspects. Those

* He were a strange fool that should be angry because dogs and sheep need no shoes, and yet himself is full of care to get some: God hath supplied those needs to them by natural provisions, and to thee by an artificial: for He hath given thee reason to learn a trade, or some means to make or buy them, so that it only differs in the manner of our provision; and which had you rather want, shoes or reason? Taylor's Holy Living, p. 99.

So Anacreon:—

> φύσις κέρατα ταύροις
> ὁπλὰς δ' ἔδωκεν ἵπποις
> ποδωκίην λαγωοῖς,
> λέουσι χάσμ' ὀδόντων,
> τοῖς ἰχθύσιν τὸ νηκτὸν
> τοῖς ὀρνέοις πέτασθαι
> τοῖς ἀνδράσιν φρόνημα.

that hold that all things are governed by fortune, had not erred, had they not persisted there. The Romans that erected a temple to Fortune, acknowledged therein, though in a blinder way, somewhat of divinity; for in a wise supputation all things begin and end in the Almighty. There is a nearer way to heaven than Homer's chain;* an easy logic may conjoin heaven and earth in one argument, and with less than a *sorites* resolve all things into God. For though we christen effects by their most sensible and nearest causes, yet is God the true and infallible cause of all, whose concourse, though it be general, yet doth it subdivide itself into the particular actions of everything, and is that spirit, by which each singular essence not only subsists, but performs its operation.

Danger of confounding the First with Second causes.

XIX. The bad construction and perverse comment on these pair of second causes, or visible hands of God, have perverted the devotion of many unto atheism, who forgetting the honest advisoes of faith, have listened unto the conspiracy of passion and reason. I have, therefore, always endeavoured to compose those feuds and angry dissensions between affection, faith, and reason; for there is in our soul a kind of triumvirate, or triple government of three competitors, which distract the peace of this our

* Iliad, viii. 18.

commonwealth, not less than did that other the state of Rome.

Passion. Reason. Faith.

As reason is a rebel unto faith, so passion unto reason: as the propositions of faith seem absurd unto reason, so the theorems of reason unto passion, and both unto reason; yet a moderate and peaceable discretion may so state and order the matter, that they may be all kings, and yet make but one monarchy, every one exercising his sovereignty and prerogative in a due time and place, according to the restraint and limit of circumstance. There are, as in philosophy, so in divinity, sturdy doubts and boisterous objections, wherewith the unhappiness of our knowledge too nearly acquainteth us. More of these no man hath known than myself, which I confess I conquered, not in a martial posture, but on my knees. For our endeavours are not only to combat with doubts, but always to dispute with the devil: the villany of that spirit takes a hint of infidelity from our studies, and by demonstrating a naturality in one way, makes us mistrust a miracle in another. Thus having perused the *Archidoxes*, and read the secret sympathies of things, he would dissuade my belief from the miracle of the brazen serpent, make me conceit that image worked by sympathy, and was but an Egyptian trick to cure their diseases without a miracle. Again,

having seen some experiments of *bitumen*, and
having read far more of *naphtha*, he whispered
to my curiosity the fire of the altar might be
natural; and bid me mistrust a miracle in Elias, 1 Kings, xviii.
when he entrenched the altar round with water;
for that inflammable substance yields not easily
unto water, but flames in the arms of its antagonist.
And thus would he inveigle my belief
to think the combustion of Sodom might be Gen. xix. 24.
natural, and that there was an asphaltic and
bituminous nature in that lake before the fire
of Gomorrah. I know that manna is now
plentifully gathered in Calabria; and Josephus
tells me, in his days it was as plentiful in
Arabia; the devil therefore made the query,
Where was then the miracle in the days of Ex. xvi.
Moses? The Israelites saw but that in his
time, which the natives of those countries behold
in ours. Thus the devil played at chess
with me, and yielding a pawn, thought to gain
a queen of me, taking advantage of my honest
endeavours; and whilst I laboured to raise the
structure of my reason, he strived to undermine
the edifice of my faith.

Atheism can hardly exist.

XX. Neither had these, or any other, ever such advantage of me, as to incline me to any point of infidelity or desperate positions of atheism; for I have been these many years of opinion there was never any. Those that held religion was the difference of man from beasts, have spoken probably, and proceed upon a principle as inductive as the other. That doctrine of Epicurus, that denied the providence of God, was no atheism, but a magnificent and high-strained conceit of his majesty, which he deemed too sublime to mind the trivial actions of those inferior creatures. That fatal necessity of the stoics is nothing but the immutable law of his will. Those that heretofore denied the divinity of the Holy Ghost, have been condemned but as heretics; and those that now deny our Saviour, (though more than heretics,) are not so much as atheists; for though they deny two persons in the Trinity, they hold as we do, there is but one God.

That villain and secretary of hell, that composed that miscreant piece of the three impostors, though divided from all religions, and was neither Jew, Turk, nor Christian, was not a positive atheist. I confess every country hath its Machiavel, every age its Lucian, whereof common heads must not hear, nor more advanced judgments too rashly venture on: it is the rhetoric of Satan, and may pervert a loose or prejudicate belief.

Inconsistency of unbelief.

XXI. I confess I have perused them all, and can discover nothing that may startle a discreet belief; yet are their heads carried off with the wind and breath of such motives. I remember a Doctor in Physic of Italy, who could not perfectly believe the immortality of the soul, because Galen seemed to make a doubt thereof. With another I was familiarly acquainted in France, a divine, and a man of singular parts, that on the same point was so plunged and gravelled with three lines of Seneca, that all our antidotes, drawn from both Scripture and philosophy, could not expel the poison of his error. There are a set of heads that can credit the relations of mariners, yet question the testimonies of St. Paul; and peremptorily maintain the traditions of Ælian or Pliny, yet in histories of Scripture raise queries and objections, believing no more than they can parallel in human authors. I confess there are in Scripture stories that do exceed the fables of poets, and to a captious reader sound like Garagantua or Bevis: search all the legends of times past, and the fabulous conceits of these present, and it will be hard to find one that deserves to carry the buckler unto Samson; yet is all this of an easy possibility, if we conceive a divine concourse, or an influence but from the little finger of the Almighty. It is impossible that either in the discourse of man, or in the infallible voice of God, to the weakness of our apprehensions, there should not

Many questions may be raised not worthy of solution.

appear irregularities, contradictions, and antinomies: myself could show a catalogue of doubts, never yet imagined or questioned, as I know, which are not resolved at the first hearing; not fantastic queries or objections of air, for I cannot hear of atoms in divinity.* I can read the history of the pigeon that was sent out of the ark and returned no more, yet not question how she found out her mate that was left behind: that Lazarus was raised from the dead, yet not demand where in the interim his soul awaited; or raise a law-case, whether his heir might lawfully detain his inheritance bequeathed unto him by his death, and he, though restored to life, have no plea or title unto his former possessions. Whether Eve was framed out of the left side of Adam, I dispute not, because I stand not yet assured which is the right side of a man, or whether there be any such distinction in nature: that she was edified out of the rib of Adam I believe, yet raise no question who shall arise with that rib at the resurrection: whether Adam was an hermaphrodite, as the Rabbins contend upon the letter of the text, because it is contrary to

* "He who believes the Scripture to have proceeded from him who is the Author of Nature, may well expect to find the same sort of difficulties in it as are found in the Constitution of Nature." Origen, quoted by Butler in Introduct. to Anal.

reason that there should be an hermaphrodite before there was a woman, or a composition of two natures before there was a second composed. Likewise, whether the world was created in autumn, summer, or spring, because it was created in them all; for whatsoever sign the sun possesseth, those four seasons are actually existent. It is the nature of this luminary to distinguish the several seasons of the year, all which it makes at one time in the whole earth, and successive in any part thereof. There are a bundle of curiosities, not only in philosophy, but in divinity, proposed and discussed by men of most supposed abilities, which indeed are not worthy our vacant hours, much less our serious studies: pieces only fit to be placed in Pantagruel's library, or bound up with Tartaretus *de modo cacandi.*

And others which are often raised, may be easily solved.

XXII. These are niceties that become not those that peruse so serious a mystery. There are others more generally questioned and called to the bar, yet methinks of an easy and possible truth.

It is ridiculous to put off or drown the general flood of Noah, in that particular inundation of Deucalion: that there was a deluge once, seems not to me so great a miracle, as that there is not one always. How all the kinds of creatures, not only in their own bulks, but with a competency of food and sustenance, might be preserved in one ark, and within the extent of three hundred cubits, to a reason that rightly examines it, will appear very feasible. There is another secret not contained in the Scripture, which is more hard to comprehend, and put the honest Father to the refuge of a miracle; * and that is, not only how the distinct pieces of the world, and divided islands, should be first planted by men, but inhabited by tigers, panthers, and bears. How America abounded with beasts of prey and noxious animals, yet contained not in it that necessary creature, a horse, is very strange. By what passage those animals, not only birds, but dangerous and unwelcome beasts, came over; how there be creatures there which are not found in this triple continent; all which must needs be strange unto us, that hold but one ark, and that the creatures began their progress from the mountains of Ararat. They who to salve this would make the deluge particular, proceed upon a principle that I can no way grant; not only upon the negative of Holy Scriptures, but of mine own reason, whereby I can make it probable that

* St. Augustine (De Civ. Dei, xvi. 7) says that this might have been miraculously effected, but he does not say it could not have been done without a miracle. See Burnet's Sacred Theory of the Earth, lib. ii. c. 8.

the world was as well peopled in the time of Noah as in ours; and fifteen hundred years to people the world, as full a time for them, as four thousand years since have been to us. There are other assertions and common tenets drawn from Scripture, and generally believed as Scripture, whereunto, notwithstanding, I would never betray the liberty of my reason. 'T is a postulate to me that Methusalem was the long- Gen. v. 5.
est lived of all the children of Adam; and no 25-27.
man will be able to prove it, when from the process of the text I can manifest it may be otherwise.* That Judas perished by hanging himself, there is no certainty in Scripture; though in one place it seems to affirm it, and S. Matt.
by a doubtful word hath given occasion to trans- xxvii. 5.
late it; yet in another place, in a more punctual Acts, i. 18
description, it makes it improbable, and seems to overthrow it. That our fathers, after the flood, erected the tower of Babel, to preserve themselves against a second deluge, is generally opinioned and believed; yet is there another intention of theirs expressed in Scripture: be- Gen. xi. 4.
sides, it is improbable from the circumstance of the place, that is, a plain in the land of Shinar: these are no points of faith, and therefore may

* His meaning is, that as Adam was created a man in the prime of life, we may add forty years to the term of his actual existence.

admit a free dispute. There are yet others, and those familiarly concluded from the text, wherein (under favour) I see no consequence. The Church of Rome confidently proves the opinion of tutelary angels, from that answer when Peter knocked at the door, *It is not he, but his angel;* that is, might some say, his messenger, or somebody from him; for so the original signifies, and is as likely to be the doubtful family's meaning. This exposition I once suggested to a young divine, that answered upon this point; to which I remember the Franciscan opponent replied no more, but, *that it was a new, and no authentic interpretation.*

Acts, xii. 15.

The Bible the best of books.

XXIII. These are but the conclusions and fallible discourses of man upon the word of God, for such I do believe the Holy Scriptures; yet were it of man, I could not choose but say, it was the singularest and superlative piece that hath been extant since the creation. Were I a pagan I should not refrain the lecture of it; and cannot but commend the judgment of Ptolemy,* that thought not his library complete

* When Ptolemy Philadelphus, king of Egypt, founded the library at Alexandria, he placed it under the care of Demetrius Phalereus, an Athenian, who persuaded his royal master to add to it the books of the Jewish law. The king wrote to Eleazar, then high-priest, for them; who not only sent him the books, but with them seventy-two interpreters, skilled in both the Hebrew and Greek tongues, to translate them for him into Greek. Their labours produced the version called the Septuagint.

without it. The Alcoran of the Turks (I speak without prejudice) is an ill-composed piece, containing in it vain and ridiculous errors in philosophy, impossibilities, fictions, and vanities beyond laughter; maintained by evident and open sophisms, the policy of ignorance, deposition of universities, and banishment of learning: this hath gotten foot by arms and violence: that without a blow hath disseminated itself through the whole earth. It is not unremarkable what Philo first observed, that the law of Moses continued two thousand years without the least alteration; whereas, we see the laws of other commonweals do alter with occasions; and even those that pretended their original from some divinity, to have vanished without trace or memory. I believe, besides Zoroaster, there were divers that writ before Moses, who notwithstanding have suffered the common fate of time. Men's works have an age like themselves; and though they outlive their authors, yet have they a stint and period to their duration; this only is a work too hard for the teeth of time, and cannot perish but in the general flames, when all things shall confess their ashes.

XXIV. I have heard some with deep sighs lament the lost lines of Cicero; others with as many groans deplore the combustion of the

"Of making many books there is no end,"

Eccl. xii. 12. library of Alexandria;* for my own part, I think there be too many in the world, and could with patience behold the urn and ashes of the Vatican, could I, with a few others,
1 Kings iv. 32, 33. recover the perished leaves of Solomon. I would not omit a copy of Enoch's Pillars had they many nearer authors than Josephus,† or did not relish somewhat of the fable. Some men have written more than others have spoken: Pineda quotes more authors in one work, than are necessary in a whole world.‡ Of those three great inventions in Germany, there are two which are not without their incommodities.§ It is not a melancholy *utinam* of my

* See D'Israeli's Curiosities of Literature.

† For this, the story is, that Enoch, or his father Seth, having been informed by Adam, that the world was to perish once by water, and a second time by fire, did cause two pillars to be erected; the one of stone against the water, and another of brick against the fire; and that upon those pillars was engraven all such learning as had been delivered to, or invented by mankind; and that thence it came that all knowledge and learning was not lost by means of the flood, by reason that one of the pillars (though the other perished) did remain after the flood: and Josephus witnesseth, till his time, lib. i. Antiq. Judaic. cap. 3. K. This, though a tale, is truly moralized in the universities: Cambridge (of brick) and Oxford (of stone) wherein learning and religion are preserved, and where the worst college is more sightworthy than the best Dutch gymnasium. Fuller's Holy State, xliv.

‡ *Pineda*, in his *Monarchia Ecclesiastica*, quotes one thousand and forty authors.

§ In all probability he means printing, gunpowder, and the mariner's compass, or perhaps clocks: but it seems doubtful whether all these were not known to the Chinese before the generally received date of their invention.

own, but the desires of better heads, that there were a general synod; not to unite the incompatible difference of religion, but for the benefit of learning, to reduce it as it lay at first, in a few and solid authors; and to condemn to the fire those swarms and millions of rhapsodies begotten only to distract and abuse the weaker judgments of scholars, and to maintain the trade and mystery of typographers.

XXV. I cannot but wonder with what exceptions the Samaritans could confine their belief to the Pentateuch, or five books of Moses. I am ashamed at the rabbinical interpretation of the Jews, upon the Old Testament, as much as their defection from the New: and truly it is beyond wonder, how that contemptible and degenerate issue of Jacob, once so devoted to ethnic superstition, and so easily seduced to the idolatry of their neighbours, should now in such an obstinate and peremptory belief adhere unto their own doctrine, expect impossibilities, and, in the face and eye of the Church, persist without the least hope of conversion: this is a vice in them, that were a virtue in us; for obstinacy in a bad cause is but constancy in a good. And herein I must accuse those of my own religion, for there is not any of such a fugitive faith, such an unstable belief, as a Christian; none that do so often transform

Obstinacy of the Jews

and want of constancy among Christians.

themselves, not unto several shapes of Christianity, and of the same species, but unto more unnatural and contrary forms of Jew and Mahometan; that from the name of Saviour, can condescend to the bare term of prophet; and from an old belief that he is come, fall to a new expectation of his coming. It is the promise of Christ to make us all one flock; but how and when this union shall be, is as obscure to me as the last day. Of those four members of religion we hold a slender proportion;* there are, I confess, some new additions, yet small to those which accrue to our adversaries, and those only drawn from the revolt of Pagans, men but of negative impieties, and such as deny Christ, but because they never heard of him: but the religion of the Jews is expressly against the Christian, and the Mahometan against both; for the Turk in the bulk he now stands, is beyond all hope of conversion; if he fall asunder, there may be conceived hopes, but not without strong improbabilities. The Jew is obstinate in all fortunes; the persecution of fifteen hundred years hath but confirmed them in their error:

* The population of our globe has been divided thus: —

Christians	260,000,000
Jews	4,000,000
Mahometans	96,000,000
Idolaters of all sorts	500,000,000
Total population of the world . .	860,000,000

they have already endured whatsoever may be inflicted, and have suffered in a bad cause, even to the condemnation of their enemies. Persecution is a bad and indirect way to plant religion; it hath been the unhappy method of angry devotions, not only to confirm honest religion, but wicked heresies, and extravagant opinions. It was the first stone and basis of our faith; none can more justly boast of persecutions, and glory in the number and valour of martyrs; for, to speak properly, those are true and almost only examples of fortitude: those that are fetched from the field, or drawn from the actions of the camp, are not ofttimes so truly precedents of valour as audacity, and at the best attain but to some bastard piece of fortitude: if we shall strictly examine the circumstances and requisites which Aristotle requires to true and perfect valour, we shall find the name only in his master Alexander, and as little in that Roman worthy, Julius Cæsar; and if any, in that easy and active way, have done so nobly as to deserve that name, yet in the passive and more terrible piece, these have surpassed, and in a more heroical way may claim the honour of that title. It is not in the power of every honest faith to proceed thus far, or pass to heaven through the flames: every one hath it not in that full measure, nor in so

The blood of martyrs the seed of the Church.

audacious and resolute a temper, as to endure those terrible tests and trials; who, notwithstanding, in a peaceable way do truly adore their Saviour, and have, no doubt, a faith acceptable in the eyes of God.

Not all are martyrs who suffer in matters of religion.

XXVI. Now as all that die in the war are not termed soldiers; so neither can I properly term all those that suffer in matters of religion, martyrs. The Council of Constance condemns John Huss for an heretic; the stories of his own party style him a martyr. He must needs offend the divinity of both, that says he was neither the one nor the other.* There are many, (questionless,) canonized on earth, that shall never be saints in heaven; and have their names in histories and martyrologies, who in the eyes of God are not so perfect martyrs as was that wise heathen Socrates, that suffered on a fundamental point of religion, the unity of God. I have often pitied that miserable bishop that suffered in the cause of Antipodes;† yet cannot choose but accuse him of as much madness, for exposing his living on such a trifle, as those of ignorance and folly, that condemned him. I think my conscience will not give me

* The Bodleian MS. reads, Is it false divinity, if I say he was neither one or the other?

† This was Virgilius, Bishop of Saltzburg. He died November 27, 780. See Curiosities of Literature, and Whewell's History of the Inductive Sciences, vol. i. p. 256.

the lie, if I say there are not many extant that in a noble way fear the face of death less than myself; yet from the moral duty I owe to the commandment of God, and the natural respects that I tender unto the conservation of my essence and being, I would not perish upon a ceremony, politic points, or indifferency: nor is my belief of that untractable temper, as not to bow at their obstacles, or connive at matters wherein there are not manifest impieties; the leaven therefore and ferment of all, not only civil but religious actions, is wisdom; without which, to commit ourselves to the flames is homicide, and, I fear, but to pass through one fire into another.

Of miracles.

XXVII. That miracles are ceased, I can neither prove, nor absolutely deny, much less define the time and period of their cessation: that they survived Christ, is manifest upon record of Scripture; that they outlived the Apostles also, and were revived at the conversion of nations, many years after, we cannot deny, if we shall not question those writers whose testimonies we do not controvert in points that make for our own opinions; therefore that may have some truth in it that is reported by the Jesuits of their miracles in the Indies. I could wish it were true, or had any other testimony than their own pens: they may easily believe those miracles abroad, who daily conceive a greater at home, the transmutation of those visible elements into the body and blood of our Saviour: for the conversion of water into wine, which he wrought in Cana, or what the devil would have had him done in the wilderness, of stones into bread, compared to this, will

All equally easy to God.

scarce deserve the name of a miracle: though indeed, to speak properly, there is not one miracle greater than another, they being the extraordinary effects of the hand of God, to which all things are of an equal facility; and to create the world, as easy as one single creature; for this is also a miracle, not only to produce effects against or above nature, but before nature; and to create nature, as great a miracle as to contradict or transcend her. We do too narrowly define the power of God, restraining it to our capacities. I hold that God can do all things; how he should work contradictions I do not understand, yet dare not therefore deny. I cannot see why the angel of God

2 Esdr. iv. 5.

should question Esdras to recall the time past, if it were beyond his own power; or that God should pose mortality in that which he was not able to perform himself. I will not say God cannot, but he will not, perform many things, which we plainly affirm he cannot: this I am sure is the mannerliest proposition, wherein, notwithstanding, I hold no paradox. For strictly, his power is the same with his will, and they both with all the rest do make but one God.

XXVIII. Therefore that miracles have been, I do believe; that they may yet be wrought by the living, I do not deny; but have no confidence in those which are fathered on the dead; and this hath ever made me suspect the efficacy of relics, to examine the bones, question the habits and appurtenances of saints, and even of Christ himself. I cannot conceive why the cross that Helena found, and whereon Christ himself died, should have power to restore others unto life: I excuse not Constantine from a fall off his horse, or a mischief from his enemies, upon the wearing those nails on his bridle, which our Saviour bore upon the cross in his hands: I compute among your *piæ fraudes*, nor many degrees before consecrated swords and roses, that which Baldwyn king of Jerusalem returned the Genovese for their cost and pains in his war, to wit, the ashes of John the Baptist. Those that hold the sanctity of their souls doth leave behind a tincture and sacred faculty on their bodies, speak naturally of miracles, and do not salve the doubt. Now one reason I tender so little devotion unto relics is, I think, the slender and doubtful respect I have always

All relations of miracles not to be received alike.

held unto antiquities; for that indeed which I admire is far before antiquity, that is, eternity; and that is, God himself; who though he be styled the Ancient of Days, cannot receive the adjunct of antiquity, who was before the world, and shall be after it, yet is not older than it; for in his years there is no climacter; his duration is eternity, and far more venerable than antiquity.

Dan. vii. 9-22.

Oracles.

XXIX. But above all things, I wonder how the curiosity of wiser heads could pass that great and indisputable miracle, the cessation of oracles; and in what swoon their reasons lay, to content themselves, and sit down with such a far-fetched and ridiculous reason as Plutarch allegeth for it. The Jews, that can believe the supernatural solstice of the sun in the days of Joshua, have yet the impudence to deny the eclipse, which every pagan confessed at his death: but for this it is evident beyond all contradiction, the devil himself confessed it.* Certainly it is not a warrantable curiosity, to examine the verity of Scripture by the concordance of human history, or seek to confirm the chronology of Hester or Daniel, by the authority of Magasthenes or Herodotus; I confess, I have had an unhappy curiosity this way, till I laughed myself out of it with a piece of

* In his oracle to Augustus.

Justin,* where he delivers, that the children of Israel for being scabbed were banished out of Egypt. And truly since I have understood the occurrences of the world, and know in what counterfeiting shapes and deceitful vizards times present represent on the stage things past, I do believe them little more than things to come. Some have been of my opinion, and endeavoured to write the history of their own lives; wherein Moses hath outgone them all, and left not only the story of his life, but, as some will have it, of his death also.

XXX. It is a riddle to me, how this story of oracles hath not wormed out of the world that doubtful conceit of spirits and witches; how so many learned heads should so far forget their metaphysics, and destroy the ladder and scale of creatures, as to question the existence of spirits. For my part, I have ever believed, and do now know, that there are witches: they that doubt of these, do not only deny them, but spirits; and are obliquely, and upon consequence, a sort not of infidels, but atheists. Those that to confute their incredulity desire to see apparitions, shall questionless never behold any, nor have the power to be so much as witches; the devil hath them already in a heresy as capital as witchcraft; and to appear Witchcraft.

* Justin. Hist. lib. 36. Cf. Tacitus Hist. lib. v.

to them, were but to convert them. Of all the delusions wherewith he deceives mortality, there is not any that puzzleth me more than the legerdemain of changelings.* I do not credit those transformations of reasonable creatures into beasts, — or that the devil hath power to transpeciate a man into a horse, who tempted Christ (as a trial of his divinity) to convert but stones into bread. I could believe that spirits use with man the act of carnality, and that in both sexes; I conceive they may assume, steal, or contrive a body, wherein there may be action enough to content decrepit lust, or passion to satisfy more active veneries; yet in both, without a possibility of generation: † and therefore that opinion that Antichrist should be born of the tribe of Dan by conjunction with the devil, is ridiculous, and a conceit fitter for a rabbin than a Christian. I hold that the devil doth really possess some men, the spirit of melancholy others, the spirit of delusion others; that as the devil is concealed and denied

* "From thence a Faery thee unweeting reft,
There as thou slepst in tender swadling band,
And her base Elfin brood there for thee left:
Such men do Chaungelings call, so chaung'd by Faeries theft."
Faery Queene, i. x. 65.

See Mids. Night's Dream, ii. 1.

Luther's Divine Discourses, folio, p. 387.

† See Taylor's Holy Living, c. 2, S. 3, p. 64.

by some, so God and good angels are pretended by others, whereof the late defection * of the maid of Germany hath left a pregnant example.

Philosophy distinguished from magic.

XXXI. Again, I believe that all that use sorceries, incantations, and spells are not witches, or, as we term them, magicians. I conceive there is a traditional magic, not learned immediately from the devil, but at second hand from his scholars, who, having once the secret betrayed, are able, and do empirically practise without his advice, they both proceeding upon the principles of nature; where actives aptly conjoined to disposed passives will under any master produce their effects. Thus, I think at first a great part of philosophy was witchcraft, which being afterward derived to one another, proved but philosophy, and was indeed no more but the honest effects of nature: what invented by us, is philosophy, learned from him, is magic. We do surely owe the discovery of many secrets to the discovery of good and bad angels. I could never pass that sentence of Paracelsus, without an asterisk, or annotation: † *ascendens astrum multa revelat quærentibus magnalia naturæ*, i. e. *opera Dei*. I do think that many mysteries ascribed to our own inventions have

The suggestions of angels.

* *Defection*. MS. W. reads detection.

† Thereby is meant our good angel appointed us from our nativity.

been the courteous revelations of spirits; for those noble essences in heaven bear a friendly regard unto their fellow natures on earth; and therefore believe that those many prodigies and ominous prognostics, which forerun the ruins of states, princes, and private persons, are the charitable premonitions of good angels, which more careless inquiries term but the effects of chance and nature.

The Spirit of God diffused throughout the world.

XXXII. Now besides these particular and divided spirits there may be (for aught I know) an universal and common spirit to the whole world. It was the opinion of Plato, and it is yet of the Hermetical philosophers: if there be a common nature that unites and ties the scattered and divided individuals into one species, why may there not be one that unites them all? However, I am sure there is a common spirit that plays within us, yet makes no part of us; and that is, the Spirit of God, the fire and scintillation of that noble and mighty essence which is the life and radical heat of spirits, and those essences that know not the virtue of the sun; a fire quite contrary to the fire of hell: this is that gentle heat that brooded on the waters, and in six days hatched the world; this is that irradiation that dispels the mists of hell, the clouds of horror, fear, sorrow, despair; and preserves the region of the mind

Gen. i. 2.

in serenity: whosoever feels not the warm gale, and gentle ventilation of this spirit, (though I feel his pulse,) I dare not say he lives; for truly without this, to me there is no heat under the tropic; nor any light, though I dwelt in the body of the sun.

As when the labouring Sun hath wrought his track
Up to the top of lofty Cancer's back,
The icy ocean cracks, the frozen pole
Thaws with the heat of the celestial coal;
So when thy absent beams begin t' impart,
Again a solstice on my frozen heart,
My winter 's o'er, my drooping spirits sing,
And every part revives into a Spring.
But if thy quick'ning beams awhile decline,
And with their light bless not this orb of mine,
A chilly frost surpriseth every member,
And in the midst of June I feel December.
O how this earthly temper doth debase
The noble soul, in this her humble place.
Whose wingy nature ever doth aspire
To reach that place whence first it took its fire.
These flames I feel, which in my heart do dwell,
Are not thy beams, but take their fire from hell;
O quench them all, and let thy Light divine
Be as the Sun to this poor orb of mine;
And to thy sacred Spirit convert those fires,
Whose earthly fumes choke my devout aspires.

Of guardian and attendant spirits.

XXXIII. Therefore for spirits, I am so far from denying their existence, that I could easily believe, that not only whole countries, but particular persons, have their tutelary and guardian angels: it is not a new opinion of the Church of Rome, but an old one of Pythagoras and

Plato; there is no heresy in it; and if not manifestly defined in Scripture, yet is it an opinion of a good and wholesome use in the course and actions of a man's life, and would serve as an hypothesis to salve many doubts, whereof common philosophy affordeth no solution. Now if you demand my opinion and metaphysics of their natures, I confess them very shallow; most of them in a negative way, like that of God; or in a comparative, between ourselves and fellow-creatures; for there is in this universe a stair, or manifest scale of creatures, rising not disorderly, or in confusion, but with a comely method and proportion: between creatures of mere existence and things of life, there is a large disproportion of nature; between plants and animals or creatures of sense, a wider difference; between them and man, a far greater: and if the proportion hold on, between man and angels there should be yet a greater. We do not comprehend their natures, who retain the first definition of Porphyry,* and distinguish them from ourselves by immortality; for before his fall man also was immortal; yet must we needs affirm that he had a different essence from the angels: having therefore no certain knowledge of their natures, 't is no bad method of the schools, whatsoever perfection we find

* Essentiæ rationalis immortalis.

obscurely in ourselves, in a more complete and absolute way to ascribe unto them. I believe they have an extemporary knowledge, and upon the first motion of their reason do what we cannot without study or deliberation; that they know things by their forms, and define by specifical difference what we describe by accidents and properties; and therefore probabilities to us may be demonstrations unto them: that they have knowledge not only of the specifical, but numerical forms of individuals, and understand by what reserved difference each single hypostasis (besides the relation to its species) becomes its numerical self: that as the soul hath a power to move the body it informs, so there's a faculty to move any, though inform none; ours upon restraint of time, place, and
distance; but that invisible hand that conveyed Bel and the
Habakkuk to the lion's den, or Philip to Azo- Dragon 36. Acts viii.
tus, infringeth this rule, and hath a secret con- 40.
veyance, wherewith mortality is not acquainted: if they have that intuitive knowledge, whereby as in reflexion they behold the thoughts of one another, I cannot peremptorily deny but they know a great part of ours. They that, to refute the invocation of saints, have denied that they have any knowledge of our affairs below, have proceeded too far, and must pardon my opinion, till I can thoroughly answer that piece of Scrip-

St. Luke xv. 7, 10. ture, *at the conversion of a sinner, the angels in heaven rejoice.** I cannot with those in that father securely interpret the work of the first day, *fiat lux*, to the creation of angels; though I confess, there is not any creature that hath so near a glimpse of their nature as light in the sun and elements: we style it a bare accident; but where it subsists alone 't is a spiritual substance, and may be an angel: in brief, conceive light invisible, and that is a spirit.

Man a Microcosm, partaking of the Nature of all created Essences.

XXXIV. These are certainly the magisterial and master-pieces of the Creator, the flower, or (as we may say) the best part of nothing, actually existing, what we are but in hopes and probability: we are only that amphibious piece between corporal and spiritual essence, that middle form that links those two together, and makes good the method of God and nature, that jumps not from extremes, but unites the incompatible distances by some middle and participating natures. That we are the breath
Gen. i. 26, 27; ii. 7. and similitude of God, it is indisputable and upon record of Holy Scripture: but to call our-

* "Take any moral or religious book, and instead of understanding each sentence according to the main purpose and intention, interpret every phrase in its literal sense as conveying, and designed to convey, a metaphysical verity, or historical fact: — what a strange medley of doctrines should we not educe! And yet this is the way in which we are constantly in the habit of treating the books of the New Testament." — Coleridge.

selves a microcosm, or little world,* I thought it only a pleasant trope of rhetoric, till my near judgment and second thoughts told me there was a real truth therein: for first we are a rude mass, and in the rank of creatures which only are, and have a dull kind of being not yet privileged with life, or preferred to sense or reason; next we live the life of plants, the life of animals, the life of men, and at last the life of spirits, running on in one mysterious nature, those five kind of existences, which comprehend the creatures, not only of the world, but of the universe. Thus is man that great and true *amphibium*, whose nature is disposed to live not only like other creatures in divers elements, but in divided and distinguished worlds: for though there be but one world to sense, there are two to reason; the one visible, the other invisible, whereof Moses seems to have left description, and of the other so obscurely, that some parts thereof are yet in controversy. And truly for the first chapters of Genesis, I must confess a great deal of obscurity; though divines have to the power of human reason endeavoured to make all go in a literal meaning, yet those allegorical interpretations are also probable, and perhaps the mystical method of

* It was a saying of the Stoics: Βραχὺν μὲν κόσμον τὸν ἄνθρωπον, μέγαν δὲ ἄνθρωπον τὸν κόσμον εἶναι.

Moses bred up in the hieroglyphical schools of the Ægyptians.*

Of Creation. XXXV. Now for the immaterial world, methinks we need not wander so far as the first movable; for even in this material fabric the spirits walk as freely exempt from the affection of time, place, and motion, as beyond the extremest circumference: do but extract † from the corpulency of bodies, or resolve things beyond their first matter, and you discover the habitation of angels, which if I call the ubiquitary and omnipresent essence of God, I hope I shall not offend divinity: for before the creation of the world, God was really all things. For the angels he created no new world, or determinate mansion, and therefore they are every-

S^t. Matt. xviii. 10. where where is his essence, and do live at a distance even in himself: that God made all things for man, is in some sense true, yet not so far as to subordinate the creation of those purer creatures unto ours, though as ministering spirits they do and are willing to fulfil the will of God in these lower and sublunary affairs of

* "The second Chapter of Genesis from v. 4, and the third Chapter, are to my mind as evidently symbolical, as the first Chapter is literal. The first Chapter is manifestly by Moses himself; but the second and third seem to me of far higher antiquity, and have the air of being translated into words from graven stones." — Coleridge.

† *Abstract*, MS.

man. God made all things for himself, and it is impossible he should make them for any other end than his own glory; it is all he can receive, and all that is without himself: for honour being an external adjunct, and in the honourer rather than in the person honoured, it was necessary to make a creature, from whom he might receive this homage, and that is in the other world, angels, in this, man; which when we neglect, we forget the very end of our creation, and may justly provoke God, not only
to repent that he hath made the world, but that Gen. vi. 6;
he hath sworn he would not destroy it. That viii. 21, 22; ix. 9-17.
there is but one world, is a conclusion of Faith. Aristotle with all his philosophy hath not been able to prove it, and as weakly that the world was eternal; that dispute much troubled the pen of the ancient philosophers, but Moses decided that question, and all is salved with the new term of a creation, that is, a production of something out of nothing: and what is that? * whatsoever is opposite to something, or more exactly that which is truly contrary unto God: for he only is, all others have an existence with dependency, and are something but by a distinction; and herein is divinity conformant unto philosophy, and generation not only founded on contrarieties, but also creation; God being all things, is con-

* See Buckland's Bridgewater Treatise, vol. i. p. 22.

trary unto nothing, out of which were made all things, and so nothing became something, and omneity informed nullity into an essence.

Man the Master-piece of Creation.

Gen. i. 20-25.

Gen. ii. 7.

XXXVI. The whole creation is a mystery, and particularly that of man: at the blast of his mouth were the rest of the creatures made, and at his bare word they started out of nothing: but in the frame of man (as the text describes it) he played the sensible operator, and seemed not so much to create, as make him: when he had separated the materials of other creatures, there consequently resulted a form and soul; but having raised the walls of man, he has driven to a second and harder creation of substance like himself, an incorruptible and immortal soul. For these two affections we have the philosophy and opinion of the heathens, the flat affirmative of Plato, and not a negative from Aristotle. There is another scruple cast in by divinity (concerning its production) much disputed in the German auditories, and with that indifferency and equality of arguments, as leave the controversy undetermined. I am not of Paracelsus his mind,* that boldly delivers a receipt to make a man without conjunction; yet cannot but wonder at the multitude of heads that do deny traduction,

* D'Israeli's Curiosities of Literature.

having no other argument to confirm their belief, than that rhetorical sentence, and *anti-metathesis* of Augustine, *Creando infunditur, infundendo creatur:* either opinion will consist well enough with religion: yet I should rather incline to this, did not one objection haunt me, not wrong from speculations and subtilties, but from common sense, and observation; not picked from the leaves of any author, but bred amongst the weeds and tares of mine own brain; and this is a conclusion from the equivocal and monstrous productions in the copulation of a man with a beast: for if the soul of man be not transmitted, and transfused in the seed of the parents, why are not those productions merely beasts, but have also an impression and tincture of reason in as high a measure as it can evidence itself in those improper organs? Nor truly can I peremptorily deny that the soul in this her sublunary estate is wholly, and in all acceptions, inorganical, but that for the performance of her ordinary actions is required not only a symmetry and proper disposition of organs, but a crasis and temper correspondent to its operations; yet is not this mass of flesh and visible structure the instrument and proper corps of the soul, but rather of sense, and that the hand of reason. In our study of anatomy there is a mass of mysterious philosophy, and such as reduced the very heathens to divinity: yet amongst all these rare discoveries, and curious pieces I find in the fabric of man, I do not so much content myself, as in that I find not, — that is, no organ or instrument for the rational soul; for in the brain, which we term the seat of reason, there is not anything of moment more than I can discover in the crany of a beast: and this is a sensible, and no inconsiderable argument of the inorganity of the soul, at least in that sense we usually so receive it. Thus we are men, and we know not how: there is something in us that can be without us, and will be after us; though it is strange that it hath no history what it was before us, nor cannot tell how it entered in us.

Of the perishable body.

XXXVII. Now for these walls of flesh, wherein the soul doth seem to be immured before the resurrection, it is nothing but an elemental composition, and a fabric that must fall to ashes. *All flesh is grass*, is not only metaphorically, but literally true; for all those creatures we behold are but the herbs of the field, digested into flesh in them, or more remotely carnified in ourselves. Nay, further, we are what we all abhor, *anthropophagi* and cannibals, devourers not only of men, but of ourselves; and that not in an allegory, but a positive truth: for all this mass of flesh which we behold came

Is. xl. 6-8.

in at our mouths; this frame we look upon hath been upon our trenchers; in brief, we have devoured ourselves. I cannot believe the wisdom of Pythagoras did ever positively, and in a literal sense, affirm his metempsychosis, or impossible transmigration of the souls of men into beasts: of all metamorphoses, or transmigrations, I believe only one, that is of Lot's wife; Gen. xix. 26.
for that of Nebuchadnezzar proceeded not so far: Dan. iv. 33.
in all others I conceive there is no further verity than is contained in their implicit sense and morality. I believe that the whole frame of a beast doth perish, and is left in the same state after death as before it was materialled unto life: that the souls of men know neither contrary nor corruption; that they subsist beyond the body, and outlive death by the privilege of their proper natures, and without a miracle; that the souls of the faithful, as they leave earth, take possession of heaven: that those apparitions and ghosts of departed persons are not the wandering souls of men, but the unquiet walks of devils, prompting and suggesting us unto mischief, blood, and villany; instilling, and stealing into our hearts that the blessed spirits are not at rest in their graves, but wander solicitous of the affairs of the world: but that those phantasms appear often, and do frequent cemeteries, charnel-houses, and churches, it is

because those are the dormitories of the dead, where the devil, like an insolent champion, beholds with pride the spoils and trophies of his victory in Adam.

Death XXXVIII. This is that dismal conquest we
2 Esdr. vii. 48. all deplore, that makes us so often cry, *Adam, quid fecisti?* I thank God I have not those strait ligaments, or narrow obligations to the world, as to dote on life, or be convulsed and tremble at the name of death: not that I am insensible of the dread and horror thereof; or by raking into the bowels of the deceased, continual sight of anatomies, skeletons, or cadaverous reliques, like vespilloes, or grave-makers, I am become stupid, or have forgot the apprehension of mortality; but that marshalling all the horrors, and contemplating the extremi-
hath no terrors for a Christian. ties thereof, I find not anything therein able to daunt the courage of a man, much less a well resolved Christian; and therefore am not angry at the error of our first parents, or unwilling to bear a part of this common fate, and like the best of them to die, that is, to cease to breathe, to take a farewell of the elements, to be a kind of nothing for a moment, to be within one in-
1 Cor. xv. 19. stant of a spirit. When I take a full view and circle of myself without this reasonable moderator, and equal piece of justice, Death, I do conceive myself the miserablest person extant:

were there not another life that I hope for, all the vanities of this world should not intreat a a moment's breath from me: could the devil work my belief to imagine I could never die, I would not outlive that very thought. I have so abject a conceit of this common way of existence, this retaining to the sun and elements, I cannot think this to be a man, or to live according to the dignity of humanity. In expectation of a better, I can with patience embrace this life, yet in my best meditations do often defy death: I honour any man that contemns it, nor can I highly love any that is afraid of it: this makes me naturally love a soldier, and honour those tattered and contemptible regiments that will die at the command of a sergeant. For a Pagan there may be some motives to be in love with life; but for a Christian to be amazed at death, I see not how he can escape this dilemma, that he is too sensible of this life, or hopeless of the life to come.

Man has several separate states of existence.

XXXIX. Some divines count Adam thirty years old at his creation, because they suppose him created in the perfect age and stature of man. And surely we are all out of the computation of our age, and every man is some months elder than he bethinks him; for we live, move, have a being, and are subject to the actions of the elements, and the malice of diseases, in that

other world, the truest microcosm, the womb of our mother; for besides that general and common existence we are conceived to hold in our chaos, and whilst we sleep within the bosom of our causes, we enjoy a being and life in three distinct worlds, wherein we receive most manifest graduations. In that obscure world, and womb of our mother, our time is short, computed by the moon, yet longer than the days of many creatures that behold the sun; ourselves being not yet without life, sense, and reason; though for the manifestation of its actions, it awaits the opportunity of objects, and seems to live there but in its root and soul of vegetation. Entering afterwards upon the scene of the world, we rise up and become another creature, performing the reasonable actions of man, and obscurely manifesting that part of divinity in us; but not in complement and perfection, till we have once more cast our secondine, that is, this slough of flesh, and are delivered into the last
2 Cor. xii. 4. world, that is, that ineffable place of Paul, that proper *ubi* of spirits. The smattering I have of the philosopher's stone (which is something more than the perfect exaltation of gold) hath taught me a great deal of divinity, and instructed my belief, how that immortal spirit and incorruptible substance of my soul may lie obscure, and sleep a while within this house of

flesh.* Those strange and mystical transmigrations that I have observed in silkworms, turned my philosophy into divinity. There is in these works of nature, which seem to puzzle reason, something divine, and hath more in it than the eye of a common spectator doth discover.

Death to be ashamed of rather than feared.

XL. I am naturally bashful; nor hath conversation, age, or travel been able to effront or enharden me; yet I have one part of modesty which I have seldom discovered in another, that is, (to speak truly,) I am not so much afraid of death, as ashamed thereof: 't is the very disgrace and ignominy of our natures, that in a moment can so disfigure us, that our nearest friends, wife, and children, stand afraid and start at us. The birds and beasts of the field, that before in a natural fear obeyed us, forgetting all allegiance, begin to prey upon us. This very conceit hath in a tempest disposed and left me willing to be swallowed up in the abyss of waters, wherein I had perished unseen, unpitied, without wondering eyes, tears of pity, lectures of mortality, and none had said, *Quantum mutatus ab illo!* Not that I am ashamed of the anatomy of my parts, or can accuse nature for playing the bungler in any part of me, or my own vicious life for contracting any shame-

* Compare Wordsworth's Ode, "Intimations of Immortality," especially stanza v.

ful disease upon me, whereby I might not call myself as wholesome a morsel for the worms as any.

Posthumous fame not to be desired.

XLI. Some, upon the courage of a fruitful issue, wherein, as in the truest chronicle, they seem to outlive themselves, can with greater patience away with death. This conceit and counterfeit subsisting in our progenies seems to me a mere fallacy, unworthy the desires of a man that can but conceive a thought of the next world; who, in a nobler ambition, should desire to live in his substance in heaven, rather than his name and shadow in the earth. And therefore at my death I mean to take a total adieu of the world, not caring for a monument, history, or epitaph, not so much as the bare memory of my name to be found anywhere, but in the universal register of God. I am not yet so cynical as to approve the testament of Diogenes; * nor do altogether follow that *rodomontado* of Lucan:

—— *Cœlo tegitur, qui non habet urnam.*
Phars. vii. 819.

He that unburied lies wants not his herse,
For unto him a tomb 's the universe.

but commend, in my calmer judgment, those ingenuous intentions that desire to sleep by the

* Who willed his friend not to bury him, but hang him up with a staff in his hand to fright away the crows.

urns of their fathers, and strive to go the neatest way unto corruption. I do not envy the temper of crows and daws,* nor the numerous and weary days of our fathers before the flood. If there be any truth in astrology, I may outlive a jubilee; as yet I have not seen one revolution of Saturn, nor hath my pulse beat thirty years; and yet, excepting one, † have seen the ashes of and left under ground all the Kings of Europe; have been contemporary to three Emperors, four Grand Signiors, and as many Popes.‡ Methinks I have outlived myself, and begin to be weary of the sun: I have shaken hands with delight in my warm blood and canicular days: I perceive I do anticipate the vices of age; the world to me is but a dream or mock show, and we all therein but pantaloons and antics, to my severer contemplations.

XLII. It is not, I confess, an unlawful prayer to desire to surpass the days of our Saviour, or wish to outlive that age wherein he thought

Length of days not to be prayed for,

* As Theophrastus did, who, dying, accused nature for giving them, to whom it could be of no use, so long a life, while she granted so short a one to man. Cf. Cic. Tusc. Disp. iii. 69. An extreme longevity was ascribed to these birds.

† *Excepting one;* Christiern IV., King of Denmark, who died 1647.

‡ These were Rodolph II., Matthias, and Ferdinand II., Emperors of Germany; Achmet I., Mustapha I., Othman II., and Amurath IV., Grand Signiors; Leo XI.? Paul V., Gregory XV., and Urban VIII., Popes.

fittest to die; yet if (as divinity affirms) there shall be no gray hairs in heaven, but all shall rise in the perfect state of men, we do but outlive those perfections in this world, to be recalled unto them by a greater miracle in the next, and run on here but to be retrograde hereafter. Were there any hopes to outlive vice, or a point to be superannuated from sin, it were worthy our knees to implore the days of Methuselah. But age doth not rectify, but incurvate our natures, turning bad dispositions into worser habits, and (like diseases) brings on incurable vices; for every day as we grow weaker in age, we grow stronger in sin: and the number of our days doth but make our sins innumerable. The same vice committed at sixteen, is not the same, though it agrees in all other circumstances, as at forty, but swells and doubles from the circumstance of our ages; wherein, besides the constant and inexcusable habit of transgressing, the maturity of our judgement cuts off pretence unto excuse or pardon: every sin the oftener it is committed, the more it acquireth in the quality of evil; as it succeeds in time, so it proceeds in degrees of badness; for as they proceed they ever multiply, and, like figures in arithmetic, the last stands for more than all that went before it. And though I think that no man can live well once

for age doth but increase our vices.

but he that could live twice, yet for my own part I would not live over my hours past, or begin again the thread of my days: not upon Cicero's ground, because I have lived them well,* but for fear I should live them worse. I find my growing judgment daily instruct me how to be better, but my untamed affections and confirmed vitiosity makes me daily do worse: I find in my confirmed age the same sins I discovered in my youth; I committed many then, because I was a child; and because I commit them still, I am yet an infant. Therefore I perceive a man may be twice a child, before the days of dotage; and stand in need of Æson's bath † before threescore.

A special providence preserves our lives.

XLIII. And truly there goes a great deal of providence to produce a man's life unto threescore: there is more required than an able temper for those years; though the radical humour contain in it sufficient oil for seventy, yet I perceive in some it gives no light past thirty: men assign not all the causes of long life that write whole books thereof. They

* I suppose he alludes to an expression in an Epistle of Cicero, written in his exile, to his wife and children, where he hath these words to his wife: *Quod reliquum est, te sustenta, mea Terentia, ut potes; honestissime viximus, floruimus. Non vitium nostrum sed virtus nostra nos afflixit: peccatum est nullum, nisi quod non unà animam cum ornamentis amisimus.* L. xiii. Ep. 55. Cf. Cic. De Senectute, xxiii.

† Ovid, Met. vii. 176.

that found themselves on the radical balsam, or vital sulphur of the parts, determine not why Abel lived not so long as Adam. There is therefore a secret glome or bottom of our days: 't was His wisdom to determine them, but his perpetual and waking providence that fulfils and accomplisheth them, wherein the spirits, ourselves, and all the creatures of God in a secret and disputed way do execute his will. Let them not therefore complain of immaturity that die about thirty; they fall but like the whole world, whose solid and well-composed substance must not expect the duration and period of its constitution: when all things are completed in it, its age is accomplished; and the last and general fever may as naturally destroy it before six thousand, as me before forty. There is therefore some other hand that twines the thread of life than that of nature: we are not only ignorant in antipathies and occult qualities; our ends are as obscure as our beginnings; the line of our days is drawn by night, and the various effects therein by a pencil that is invisible, wherein, though we confess our ignorance, I am sure we do not err if we say it is the hand of God.

Tho' death is to be desired, yet suicide is unlawful.

XLIV. I am much taken with two verses of Lucan, since I have been able not only, as we do at school, to construe, but understand:

Victurosque Dei celant, ut vivere durent,
Felix esse mori. Pharsalia, iv. 519.

We 're all deluded, vainly searching ways
To make us happy by the length of days;
For cunningly to make 's protract this breath,
The gods conceal the happiness of death.

There be many excellent strains in that poet, wherewith his Stoical genius hath liberally supplied him; and truly there are singular pieces in the philosophy of Zeno, and doctrine of the Stoics, which I perceive delivered in a pulpit pass for current divinity: yet herein are they in extremes, that can allow a man to be his own assassin, and so highly extol the end and suicide of Cato; this is indeed not to fear death, but yet to be afraid of life. It is a brave act of valour to contemn death; but where life is more terrible than death, it is then the truest valour to dare to live: and herein religion hath taught us a noble example; for all the valiant acts of Curtius, Scævola, or Codrus do not parallel or match that one of Job; and sure there is no torture to the rack of a disease, nor any poniards in death itself, like those in the way or prologue unto it. *Emori nolo, sed me esse mortuum nihil æstumo.** I would not die, but care not to be dead. Were I of Cæsar's religion, I should be of his desires, and wish

* Cic. Tusc. Disp. i. 8.

rather to go off at one blow, than to be sawed in pieces by the grating torture of a disease. Men that look no farther than their outsides, think health an appurtenance unto life, and quarrel with their constitutions for being sick; but I that have examined the parts of man, and know upon what tender filaments that fabric hangs, do wonder that we are not always so; and considering the thousand doors that lead to death, do thank my God that we can die but once.* 'T is not only the mischief of diseases, and the villany of poisons, that make an end of us: we vainly accuse the fury of guns, and the new inventions of death; it is in the power of every hand to destroy us, and we are beholding unto every one we meet, he doth not kill us. There is therefore but one comfort left, that though it be in the power of the weakest arm to take away life, it is not in the strongest to deprive us of death; God would not exempt himself from that; the misery of immortality in the flesh He undertook not, that was, in it, immortal. Certainly there is no happiness within this circle of flesh, nor is it in the optics of these eyes to behold felicity. The first day

* "Strange that a harp of thousand strings
Should keep in tune so long!"

Ps. cxxxix. 14. "I will praise thee; for I am fearfully and wonderfully made."

of our jubilee is death; the devil hath therefore failed of his desires: we are happier with death than we should have been without it: there is no misery but in himself, where there is no end of misery; and so indeed, in his own sense, the Stoic is in the right. He forgets that he can die who complains of misery; we are in the power of no calamity while death is in our own.

Death the gate thro' which we pass to immortality.

XLV. Now besides this literal and positive kind of death, there are others whereof divines make mention, and those I think not merely metaphorical, as mortification, dying unto sin and the world; therefore, I say, every man hath a double horoscope, one of his humanity, his birth; another of his Christianity, his baptism; and from this do I compute or calculate my nativity, not reckoning those *horæ combustæ* and odd days, or esteeming myself anything, before I was my Saviour's, and inrolled in the register of Christ: whosoever enjoys not this life, I count him but an apparition, though he wear about him the sensible affections of flesh. In these moral acceptions, the way to be immortal is to die daily; nor can I think I have the true theory of death, when I contemplate a skull, or behold a skeleton, with those vulgar imaginations it casts upon us: I have therefore enlarged that common *memento mori* into a more Christian memorandum, *memento quatuor novissima*, those four inevitable points of us all, Death, Judgment, Heaven, and Hell. Neither did the contemplations of the heathens rest in their graves, without a further thought of Rhadamanth or some judicial proceeding after death, though in another way, and upon suggestion of their natural reasons. I cannot but marvel from what sibyl or oracle they stole the prophecy of the world's destruction by fire, or whence Lucan learned to say,

> *Communis mundo superest rogus, ossibus astra*
> *Mixturus* —— Pharsalia, vii. 814.
>
> There yet remains to th' world one common fire,
> Wherein our bones with stars shall make one pyre.

I believe the world grows near its end, yet is neither old nor decayed, nor will ever perish upon the ruins of its own principles.* As the work of creation was above nature, so its adversary, annihilation; without which the world hath not its end, but its mutation. Now what

* The Author of nature has not given laws to the universe, which, like the institutions of men, carry in themselves the elements of their own destruction. He has not permitted in his works any symptom of infancy or old age, or any sign by which we may estimate either their future or their past duration. He may put an end, as he no doubt gave a beginning, to the present system at some determinate period of time; but we may rest assured that this great catastrophe will not be brought about by the laws now existing, and that it is not indicated by anything which we perceive. — Playfair's Works, vol. iv. p. 55.

force should be able to consume it thus far, without the breath of God, which is the truest consuming flame, my philosophy cannot inform me. Some believe there went not a minute to the world's creation, nor shall there go to its destruction; those six days so punctually de- Gen. i.
scribed make not to them one moment, but rather seem to manifest the method and idea of that great work in the intellect of God, than the manner how he proceeded in its operation. I cannot dream that there should be at the last day any such judicial proceeding, or calling to the bar, as indeed the Scripture seems to imply, and the literal commentators do conceive: for unspeakable mysteries in the Scriptures are often delivered in a vulgar and illustrative way; and being written unto man, are delivered, not as they truly are, but as they may be understood; wherein, notwithstanding, the different interpretations according to different capacities may stand firm with our devotion, nor be any way prejudicial to each single edification.

XLVI. Now to determine the day and year of this inevitable time is not only convincible and statute-madness, but also manifest impiety. How shall we interpret Elias's six thousand years, or imagine the secret communicated to a rabbi, which God hath denied unto his angels? St. Matt. xxiv. 36.
It had been an excellent quære to have posed

the devil of Delphos, and must needs have
forced him to some strange amphibology: it
hath not only mocked the predictions of sundry
astrologers in ages past, but the prophecies of
many melancholy heads in these present; who,
neither understanding reasonably things past or
present, pretend a knowledge of things to come:
heads ordained only to manifest the incredible
St Matt. effects of melancholy, and to fulfil old prophecies
xxiv. 11-24. rather than be authors of new. *In those days*
St. Matt. *there shall come wars and rumours of wars*, to me
xxiv. 6. St. Mark seems no prophecy, but a constant truth in all
xiii. 7. times verified since it was pronounced. *There*
St. Luke *shall be signs in the moon and stars;* how comes
xxi. 25. he then like a thief in the night, when he gives
an item of his coming? That common sign
drawn from the revelation of antichrist is as
obscure as any: in our common compute he
hath been come these many years: for my own
part, to speak freely, I am half of opinion that
antichrist is the philosopher's stone in divinity,
for the discovery and invention whereof, though
there be prescribed rules and probable induc-
tions, yet hath hardly any man attained the
perfect discovery thereof. That general opinion that the world grows near its end, hath
possessed all ages past as nearly as ours: I am
afraid that the souls that now depart, cannot
escape that lingering expostulation of the saints

under the altar, *Quousque Domine?* How long, O Lord; and groan in the expectation of the great jubilee. Rev. vi. 9, 10.

XLVII. This is the day that must make good that great attribute of God, his justice; that must reconcile those unanswerable doubts that torment the wisest understandings; and reduce those seeming inequalities and respective distributions in this world to an equality and recompensive justice in the next. This is that one day, that shall include and comprehend all that went before it; wherein, as in the last scene, all the actors must enter to complete and make up the catastrophe of this great piece. This is the day whose memory hath only power to make us honest in the dark, and to be virtuous without a witness. *Ipsa suæ pretium virtus sibi*—that virtue is her own reward, is but a cold principle, and not able to maintain our variable resolutions in a constant and settled way of goodness. I have practised that honest artifice of Seneca, and in my retired and solitary imaginations, to detain me from the foulness of vice, have fancied to myself the presence of my dear and worthiest friends, before whom I should lose my head, rather than be vicious: yet herein I found that there was naught but moral honesty, and this was not to be virtuous for His sake who must reward us at the last. I have

The day of judgment.

tried if I could reach that great resolution of his, to be honest without a thought of heaven or hell: and indeed I found upon a natural inclination, and inbred loyalty unto virtue, that I could serve her without a livery; yet not in that resolved and venerable way, but that the frailty of my nature, upon an easy temptation, might be induced to forget her. The life therefore and spirit of all our actions is the resurrection, and a stable apprehension that our ashes shall enjoy the fruit of our pious endeavours: without this, all religion is a fallacy, and those impieties of Lucian, Euripides, and Julian are no blasphemies, but subtle verities, and atheists have been the only philosophers.

The resurrection of the dead. 1 Cor. xv. 35.

XLVIII. How shall the dead arise? is no question of my faith; to believe only possibilities is not faith, but mere philosophy: many things are true in divinity, which are neither inducible by reason nor confirmable by sense; and many things in philosophy confirmable by sense, yet not inducible by reason. Thus it is impossible by any solid or demonstrative reasons to persuade a man to believe the conversion of the needle to the north; though this be possible, and true, and easily credible, upon a single experiment unto the sense. I believe that our estranged and divided ashes shall unite again; that our separated dust, after so many pilgrimages and transformations into the parts of minerals, plants, animals, elements, shall at the voice of God return into their primitive shapes, and join again to make up their primary and predestinate forms. As at the creation there was a separation of that confused mass into its species; so at the destruction thereof there shall be a separation into its distinct individuals. As at the creation of the world, all the distinct species that we behold lay involved in one mass, till the fruitful voice of God separated this united multitude into its several species; so at the last day, when these corrupted reliques shall be scattered in the wilderness of forms, and seem to have forgot their proper habits, God by a powerful voice shall command them back into their proper shapes, and call them out by their single individuals: then shall appear the fertility of Adam, and the magic of that sperm that hath dilated into so many millions.* I have often beheld as a miracle that artificial resurrection and revivification of Mercury, how, being mortified into a thousand shapes, it assumes again

Types of the resurrection.

* What is made to be immortal, nature cannot, nor will the voice of God, destroy. Those bodies that we behold to perish, were in their created natures immortal, and liable unto death only accidentally, and upon forfeit; and therefore they owe not that natural homage unto death as other bodies do, but may be restored to immortality with a lesser miracle, and by a bare and easy revocation of course, return immortal. Edits. 1642.

its own, and returns into its numerical self. Let us speak naturally and like philosophers: the forms of alterable bodies in these sensible corruptions perish not; nor, as we imagine, wholly quit their mansions, but retire and contract themselves into their secret and unaccessible parts, where they may best protect themselves from the action of their antagonist. A plant or vegetable consumed to ashes, to a contemplative and school-philosopher seems utterly destroyed, and the form to have taken his leave forever; but to a sensible artist the forms are not perished, but withdrawn into their incombustible part, where they lie secure from the action of that devouring element. This is made good by experience, which can from the ashes of a plant revive the plant, and from its cinders recall it into its stalk and leaves again.* What

* Sir Kenelm Digby thus describes the beautiful experiment, called, from the Greek, Palingenesis: —

" *Quercetanus*, the famous physician of King Henry the Fourth, tells us a wonderful story of a *Polonian* doctor, that showed him a dozen glasses hermetically sealed, in each of which was a different plant: for example, a rose in one, a tulip in another, a clove gilly-flower in a third, and so of the rest. When he offered these glasses to your first view, you saw nothing in them but a heap of ashes in the bottom. As soon as he held some gentle heat under any of them, presently there arose out of the ashes the idea of a flower and the stalk belonging to those ashes, and it would shoot up and spread abroad to the due height and just dimensions of such a flower, and had perfect colour, shape, magnitude, and all other accidents, as if it really were that very the art of man can do in these inferior pieces, what blasphemy is it to affirm the finger of God cannot do in these more perfect and sensible structures! This is that mystical philosophy, from whence no true scholar becomes an atheist, but from the visible effects of nature grows up a real divine, and beholds not in a dream, as Ezekiel, but in an ocular and visible object, the types of his resurrection.

Heaven, or Hell, not to be defined.

XLIX. Now the necessary mansions of our restored selves are those two contrary and incompatible places we call heaven and hell: to define them, or strictly to determine what and where these are, surpasseth my divinity. That elegant apostle which seemed to have a glimpse of heaven, hath left but a negative description thereof: *which neither eye hath seen, nor ear hath heard, nor can enter into the heart of man:* he was translated out of himself to behold it; but being returned into himself could not express it. St. John's description by emeralds, chrysolites, and precious stones, is too weak to express the

1 Cor. ii. 9. Is. lxiv. 4.

Rev. xxi. 19-21.

flower. But whenever you drew the heat from it, would this flower sink down by little and little, till at length it would bury itself in its bed of ashes. And thus it would do as often as you exposed it to moderate heat, or withdrew it from it. I confess it would be no small delight to me to see this experiment, with all the circumstances that *Quercetan* sets down. *Athanasius Kircherus*, at Rome, assured me that he had done it; and gave me the process of it. But no industry of mine could effect it." — *Treatise on the Vegetation of Plants.*

material heaven we behold. Briefly, therefore, where the soul hath the full measure and complement of happiness; where the boundless appetite of that spirit remains completely satisfied, that it can neither desire addition nor alteration; that, I think, is truly Heaven: and this can only be in the enjoyment of that essence, whose infinite goodness is able to terminate the desires of itself, and the unsatiable wishes of ours: wherever God will thus manifest himself, there is heaven, though within the circle of this sensible world. Thus the soul of man may be in heaven anywhere, even within the limits of his own proper body; and when it ceaseth to live in the body, it may remain in its own soul, that is, its Creator. And thus we may say
2 Cor. xii. 2-4. that St. Paul, whether in the body or out of
the body, was yet in heaven. To place it in the empyreal, or beyond the tenth sphere, is to forget the world's destruction; for when this sensible world shall be destroyed, all shall then be here as it is now there, an empyreal heaven, a *quasi* vacuity; when to ask where heaven is, is to demand where the presence of God is, or where we have the glory of that happy vision. Moses, that was bred up in all the learning of the Ægyptians, committed a gross absurdity in
Ex. xxxiii. 12-23. philosophy, when with these eyes of flesh he
desired to see God, and petitioned his Maker,

that is, Truth itself, to a contradiction. Those that imagine heaven and hell neighbours, and conceive a vicinity between those two extremes, upon consequence of the parable, where Dives discoursed with Lazarus in Abraham's bosom, do too grossly conceive of those glorified creatures, whose eyes shall easily outsee the sun, and behold without a perspective the extremest distances: for if there shall be in our glorified eyes the faculty of sight and reception of objects, I could think the visible species there to be in as unlimitable a way, as now the intellectual. I grant that two bodies placed beyond the tenth sphere, or in a vacuity, according to Aristotle's philosophy, could not behold each other, because there wants a body or medium to hand and transport the visible rays of the object unto the sense; but when there shall be a general defect of either medium to convey, or light to prepare and dispose that medium, and yet a perfect vision, we must suspend the rules of our philosophy, and make all good by a more absolute piece of optics.

St. Luke xvi. 19-31.

L. I cannot tell how to say that fire is the essence of hell: I know not what to make of purgatory, or conceive a flame that can either prey upon, or purify the substance of a soul: those flames of sulphur mentioned in the Scriptures, I take not to be understood of this present

Of Fire as an agent in destruction.

hell, but of that to come, where fire shall make up the complement of our tortures, and have a body or subject wherein to manifest its tyranny. Some who have had the honour to be textuary in divinity, are of opinion it shall be the same specifical fire with ours. This is hard to conceive; yet can I make good how even that may prey upon our bodies, and yet not consume us: for in this material world there are bodies that persist invincible in the powerfullest flames; and though by the action of fire they fall into ignition and liquation, yet will they never suffer a destruction. I would gladly know how Moses
Exod. xxxii. 20. with an actual fire calcined or burnt the golden calf unto powder: for that mystical metal of gold, whose solary and celestial nature I admire, exposed unto the violence of fire, grows only hot and liquefies, but consumeth* not; so when the consumable and volatile pieces of our bodies shall be refined into a more impregnable and fixed temper, like gold, though they suffer from the actions of flames, they shall never perish, but lie immortal in the arms of fire. And surely, if this frame must suffer only by the action of this element, there will many bodies escape; and not only heaven but earth will not be at an end, but rather a beginning. For

* Moses is not said to have *consumed* it, but to have ground it to powder.

at present it is not earth, but a composition of fire, water, earth, and air; but at that time, spoiled of these ingredients, it shall appear in a substance more like itself, its ashes. Philosophers that opinioned the world's destruction by fire, did never dream of annihilation, which is beyond the power of sublunary causes; for the last and proper action of that element is but vitrification, or a reduction of a body into glass; and therefore some of our chymicks facetiously affirm, that at the last fire all shall be crystallized and reverberated into glass, which is the utmost action of that element. Nor need we fear this term, annihilation, or wonder that God will destroy the works of his creation; for man subsisting, who is, and will then truly appear, a microcosm, the world cannot be said to be destroyed. For the eyes of God, and perhaps also of our glorified selves, shall as really behold and contemplate the world in its epitome or contracted essence, as now it doth at large and in its dilated substance. In the seed of a plant to the eyes of God, and to the understanding of man, there exists, though in an invisible way, the perfect leaves, flowers, and fruit thereof; for things that are in *posse* to the sense, are actually existent to the understanding. Thus God beholds all things, who contemplates as fully his works in their epitome as in their full volume; and beheld as amply the whole world in that little compendium of the sixth day, as in the scattered and dilated pieces of those five before.

The heart of man is his own torment.

LI. Men commonly set forth the torments of hell by fire, and the extremity of corporal afflictions, and describe hell in the same method that Mahomet doth heaven. This indeed makes a noise, and drums in popular ears: but if this be the terrible piece thereof, it is not worthy to stand in diameter with heaven, whose happiness consists in that part that is best able to comprehend it, that immortal essence, that translated divinity and colony of God, the soul. Surely though we place hell under earth, the devil's walk and purlieu is about it: men speak too popularly who place it in those flaming mountains, which to grosser apprehensions represent hell. The heart of man is the place the devil dwells in: I feel sometimes a hell within myself: * Lucifer keeps his court in my breast, Legion is revived in me. There are as many hells, as Anaxarchus conceited worlds: there

* So Milton, Paradise Lost, i. 254, —

> "The mind is its own place, and in itself
> Can make a heaven of hell, a hell of heaven," —

and iv. 18. So also, Tasso, c. xii. st. 77.

> "Swift from myself I run, myself I fear,
> Yet still my hell within myself I bear."

was more than one hell in Magdalene, when there were seven devils, for every devil is an hell unto himself; he holds enough of torture in his own *ubi*, and needs not the misery of circumference to afflict him; and thus a distracted conscience here is a shadow or introduction unto hell hereafter. Who can but pity the merciful intention of those hands that do destroy themselves? the devil, were it in his power, would do the like; which being impossible, his miseries are endless, and he suffers most in that attribute wherein he is impassible, his immortality.

Contemplation of heaven.

LII. I thank God, and with joy I mention it, I was never afraid of hell, nor never grew pale at the description of that place; I have so fixed my contemplations on heaven, that I have almost forgot the idea of hell, and am afraid rather to lose the joys of the one, than endure the misery of the other: to be deprived of them is a perfect hell, and needs, methinks, no addition to complete our afflictions. That terrible term hath never detained me from sin, nor do I owe any good action to the name thereof. I fear God, yet am not afraid of him: his mercies make me ashamed of my sins, before his judgments afraid thereof: these are the forced and secondary method of his wisdom, which he useth but as the last remedy, and upon provo-

Heb. xii. 2.

2 Esdr. ix. 13.

cation: a course rather to deter the wicked, than incite the virtuous to his worship. I can hardly think there was ever any scared into heaven; they go the fairest way to heaven that would serve God without a hell; other mercenaries, that crouch unto him in fear of hell, though they term themselves the servants, are indeed but the slaves of the Almighty.*

The judgments of God to be regarded as proofs of affection.

LIII. And to be true, and speak my soul, when I survey the occurrences of my life, and call into account the finger of God, I can perceive nothing but an abyss and mass of mercies, either in general to mankind, or in particular to myself: and whether out of the prejudice of my affection, or an inverting and partial conceit of his mercies, I know not; but those which others term crosses, afflictions, judgments, misfortunes, to me who inquire farther into them than their visible effects, they both appear, and in event have ever proved, the secret and dissembled favours of his affection. It is a singular piece of wisdom to apprehend truly, and without passion, the works of God, and so well to distinguish his justice from his mercy, as not to

* Excellent throughout! The fear of hell may indeed in some desperate cases, like the *moxa*, give the first rouse from a moral lethargy, or like the green venom of copper, by evacuating poison or a dead load from the inner man, prepare it for nobler ministrations and medicines from the realm of light and life, that nourish while they stimulate. Coleridge.

miscall those noble attributes: yet it is likewise an honest piece of logic, so to dispute and argue the proceedings of God, as to distinguish even his judgments into mercies. For God is merciful unto all, because better to the worst than the best deserve; and to say he punisheth none in this world, though it be a paradox, is no absurdity. To one that hath committed murder, if the judge should only ordain a fine, it were a madness to call this a punishment, and to repine at the sentence, rather than admire the clemency of the judge: thus our offences being mortal, and deserving not only death, but damnation, if the goodness of God be content to traverse and pass them over with a loss, misfortune, or disease, what phrensy were it to term this a punishment, rather than an extremity of mercy, and to groan under the rod of his judgments, rather than admire the sceptre of his mercies! Therefore to adore, honour, and admire him is a debt of gratitude due from the obligation of our nature, states, and conditions; and with these thoughts, He that knows them best will not deny that I adore him. That I obtain heaven, and the bliss thereof, is accidental, and not the intended work of my devotion; it being a felicity I can neither think to deserve, nor scarce in modesty to expect. For these two ends of us all, either as rewards or punishments, are mercifully ordained and disproportionably disposed unto our actions; the one being so far beyond our deserts, the other so infinitely below our demerits.

Salvation through Christ alone.

LIV. There is no salvation to those that believe not in Christ, that is, say some, since his nativity, and, as divinity affirmeth, before also; which makes me much apprehend the end of those honest worthies and philosophers which died before his incarnation. It is hard to place those souls in hell whose worthy lives do teach us virtue on earth; methinks, amongst those many subdivisions of hell, there might have been one limbo left for these. What a strange vision will it be to see their poetical fictions converted into verities, and their imagined and fancied furies into real devils! How strange to them will sound the history of Adam, when they shall suffer for him they never heard of! when they that derive their genealogy from the gods, shall know they are the unhappy issue of sinful man! It is an insolent part of reason, to controvert the works of God, or question the justice of his proceedings. Could humility teach others, as it hath instructed me, to contemplate the infinite and incomprehensible distance betwixt the Creator and the creature; or did we seriously perpend that one simile of St. Paul,
Rom. ix. 20. *Shall the vessel say to the potter, Why hast thou*

made me thus? it would prevent these arrogant disputes of reason; nor would we argue the definitive sentence of God, either to heaven or hell. Men that live according to the right rule and law of reason, live but in their own kind, as beasts do in theirs; who justly obey the prescript of their natures, and therefore cannot reasonably demand a reward of their actions, as only obeying the natural dictates of their reason. It will, therefore, and must at last appear, that all salvation is through Christ; which verity, I fear, these great examples of virtue must con firm, and make it good, how the perfectest actions of earth have no title or claim unto heaven.

Our practice inconsistent with our theory.

LV. Nor truly do I think the lives of these, or of any other, were ever correspondent, or in all points conformable unto their doctrines. It is evident that Aristotle transgressed the rule of his own ethics: the Stoics that condemn passion, and command a man to laugh in Phalaris his bull, could not endure without a groan a fit of the stone or colic. The sceptics, that affirmed they knew nothing, even in that opinion confute themselves, and thought they knew more than all the world beside. Diogenes I hold to be the most vainglorious man of his time, and more ambitious in refusing all honours, than Alexander in rejecting none. Vice and the devil put a fallacy upon our reasons, and, provoking us too hastily to run from it, entangle and profound us deeper in it. The duke of Venice, that weds himself unto the sea by a ring of gold, I will not argue of prodigality, because it is a solemnity of good use and consequence in the state: but the philosopher that threw his money into the sea to avoid avarice, was a notorious prodigal.* There is no road or ready way to virtue: it is not an easy point of art to disentangle ourselves from this riddle, or web of sin. To perfect virtue, as to religion, there is required a *panoplia*, or complete armour; that whilst we lie at close ward against one vice, we lie not open to the veny of another: and indeed wiser discretions that have the thread of reason to conduct them, offend without a pardon; whereas, underheads may stumble without dishonour. There are so many circumstances to piece up one good action, that it is a lesson to be good, and we are

* The Doge performs this ceremony every year, in token of the sovereignty of the state of Venice over the Adriatic, and to commemorate the celebrated declaration of Pope Alexander III.: "Que la mer vous soit soumise comme l'épouse l'est à son époux, puisque vous en avez acquis l'empire par la victoire." Apollonius Thyaneus threw his gold into the sea, saying these words: *Pessundo divitias, ne pessundarer ab illis.* Polycrates, the tyrant of Samos, cast the best jewel he had into the sea, that thereby he might learn to compose himself against the vicissitudes of fortune.

forced to be virtuous by the book. Again, the practice of men holds not an equal pace; yea, and often runs counter to their theory: we naturally know what is good, but naturally pursue what is evil: the rhetoric wherewith I persuade another, cannot persuade myself: there is a depraved appetite in us, that will with patience hear the learned instructions of reason, but yet perform no farther than agrees to its own irregular humour. In brief, we all are monsters, that is, a composition of man and beast, wherein we must endeavour to be as the poets fancy that wise man Chiron, that is, to have the region of man above that of beast, and sense to sit but at the feet of reason. Lastly, I do desire with God, that all, but yet affirm with men, that few shall know salvation: that the bridge is narrow, the passage strait unto life: yet those who do confine the Church of God either to particular nations, churches, or families, have made it far narrower than our Saviour ever meant it.

1 Tim. ii. 3, 4. 2 Pet. iii. 9.

The Church of God not circumscribed.

LVI. The vulgarity of those judgments that wrap the Church of God in Strabo's cloak,* and

* 'T is *Strabonis tunica* in the translation, but *chlamydi* would do better, which is the proper expression of the word that Strabo useth: it is not Europe, but the known part of the world, that Strabo resembleth to a cloak, and that is it the author here alludeth to; but we have no reason to think that the resemblance of Strabo is very proper.

restrain it unto Europe, seem to me as bad geographers as Alexander, who thought he had conquered all the world, when he had not subdued the half of any part thereof: for we cannot deny the Church of God both in Asia and Africa, if we do not forget the peregrinations of the apostles, the deaths of the martyrs, the sessions of many, and, even in our reformed judgment, lawful councils, held in those parts in the minority and nonage of ours: nor must a few differences, more remarkable in the eyes of man than perhaps in the judgment of God, excommunicate from heaven one another; much less those Christians who are in a manner all martyrs, maintaining their faith in the noble way of persecution, and serving God in the fire, whereas we honour him but in the sunshine.

A sectarian spirit hostile to charity.

'Tis true we all hold there is a number of elect, and many to be saved; yet take our opinions together, and from the confusion thereof there will be no such thing as salvation, nor shall any one be saved. For first, the Church of Rome condemneth us, we likewise them; the sub-reformists and sectaries sentence the doctrine of our Church as damnable; the atomist, or familist,* reprobates all these; and all these, them again. Thus whilst the mercies

* The *atomists*, or *familists*, were religionists who sprung up about the year 1575. See Hist. of the Puritans, i. 273.

of God do promise us heaven, our conceits and opinions exclude us from that place. There must be, therefore, more than one St. Peter: particular churches and sects usurp the gates of heaven, and turn the key against each other, and thus we go to heaven against each other's wills, conceits, and opinions, and, with as much uncharity as ignorance, do err, I fear, in points not only of our own, but one another's salvation.

"Judge not, that ye be not judged."

LVII. I believe many are saved, who to man seem reprobated; and many are reprobated, who, in the opinion and sentence of man, stand elected. There will appear at the last day, strange and unexpected examples, both of his justice and his mercy; and therefore to define either is folly in man, and insolency even in the devils: those acute and subtile spirits, in all their sagacity, can hardly divine who shall be saved; which if they could prognostic, their labour were at an end, nor need they compass the earth seeking whom they may devour. Those who, upon a rigid application of the law, sentence Solomon unto damnation, condemn not only him, but themselves, and the whole world: for by the letter and written word of God, we are without exception in the state of death; but there is a prerogative of God and an arbitrary pleasure above the letter of his own law, by which alone we can pretend unto salvation, and through which Solomon might be as easily saved as those who condemn him.

LVIII. The number of those who pretend unto salvation, and those infinite swarms who think to pass through the eye of this needle, have much amazed me. That name and compellation of *little flock*, doth not comfort, but deject my devotion; especially when I reflect upon mine own unworthiness, wherein, according to my humble apprehensions, I am below them all. I believe there shall never be an anarchy in heaven; but as there are hierarchies amongst the angels, so shall there be degrees of priority amongst the saints. Yet is it (I protest) beyond my ambition to aspire unto the first ranks; my desires only are, and I shall be happy therein, to be but the last man, and bring up the rear in heaven.

St. Luke xii. 32.

Our confidence can only be in God's mercy.

LIX. Again, I am confident, and fully persuaded, yet dare not take my oath of my salvation. I am as it were sure, and do believe without all doubt, that there is such a city as Constantinople: yet for me to take my oath thereon were a kind of perjury, because I hold no infallible warrant from my own sense to confirm me in the certainty thereof. And truly, though many pretend an absolute certainty of their salvation, yet when an humble soul shall contemplate her own unworthiness, she shall meet with many doubts, and suddenly find how little we stand in need of the precept of St. Paul, *work out your salvation with fear and trembling.* That which is the cause of my election, I hold to be the cause of my salvation, which was the mercy and *beneplacit* of God, before I was, or the foundation of the world. "Before Abraham was, I am," is the saying of Christ; yet is it true in some sense, if I say it of myself; for I was not only before myself, but Adam, that is, in the idea of God, and the decree of that synod held from all eternity: and in this sense, I say, the world was before the creation, and at an end before it had a beginning; and thus was I dead before I was alive: though my grave be England, my dying place was paradise: and Eve miscarried of me, before she conceived of Cain.

Phil. ii. 12.

St. John viii. 58.

LX. Insolent zeals, that do decry good works and rely only upon faith, take not away merit: for depending upon the efficacy of their faith, they enforce the condition of God, and in a more sophistical way do seem to challenge heaven. It was decreed by God, that only those that lapt in the water like dogs, should have the honour to destroy the Midianites; yet could none of those justly challenge, or imagine he

Faith.

Judges vii 4-7.

deserved that honour thereupon. I do not deny, but that true faith, and such as God requires, is not only a mark or token, but also a means of our salvation; but where to find this, is as obscure to me as my last end. And
St. Matt. xvii. 20. if our Saviour could object unto his own disciples and favourites, a faith, that, to the quantity of a grain of mustard-seed, is able to remove mountains; surely, that which we boast of is not anything, or at the most but a remove from nothing. This is the tenor of my belief; wherein, though there be many things singular, and to the humour of my irregular self, yet if they square not with maturer judgments, I disclaim them, and do no further favour them, than the learned and best judgments shall authorize them.

THE SECOND PART.

OW for that other virtue of charity, Charity.
without which faith is a mere no- 1 Cor. xiii
tion, and of no existence, I have 2.
ever endeavoured to nourish the merciful disposition and humane inclination I borrowed from my parents, and regulate it to the written and prescribed laws of charity: and if I hold the true anatomy of myself, I am delineated and naturally framed to such a piece of virtue; for I am of a constitution so general, that it consorts and sympathizeth with all things: I have no antipathy, or rather idio-syncrasy, in diet, humour, air, anything. I wonder not at the French for their dishes of frogs, snails, and toadstools; nor at the Jews for locusts and grasshoppers; but being amongst them, make them my common viands, and I find they agree with my stomach as well as theirs. I could digest a salad gath-

ered in a churchyard, as well as in a garden. I cannot start at the presence of a serpent, scorpion, lizard, or salamander: at the sight of a toad or viper, I find in me no desire to take up a stone to destroy them. I feel not in myself those common antipathies that I can discover in others: those national repugnances do not touch me, nor do I behold with prejudice the French, Italian, Spaniard, or Dutch: but where I find their actions in balance with my countrymen's, I honour, love, and embrace them in the same degree. I was born in the eighth climate, but seem for to be framed and constellated unto all: I am no plant that will not prosper out of a garden; all places, all airs, make unto me one country; I am in England, everywhere, and under any meridian; I have been shipwrecked, yet am not enemy with the sea or winds; I can study, play, or sleep in a tempest. In brief, I am averse from nothing: my conscience would give me the lie if I should absolutely detest or hate any essence but the devil; or so at least abhor anything, but that we might come to composition. If there be any among those common objects of hatred I do contemn and laugh at, it is that great enemy of reason, virtue, and religion, the multitude: that numerous piece of monstrosity, which, taken asunder, seem men, and the reasonable creatures of God; but confused together, make but one great beast, and a monstrosity more prodigious than Hydra: it is no breach of charity to call these fools; it is the style all holy writers have afforded them, set down by Solomon in canonical Scripture, and a point of our faith to believe so. Neither in the name of multitude do I only include the base and minor sort of people;* there is a rabble even amongst the gentry, a sort of plebeian heads, whose fancy moves with the same wheel as these; men in the same level with mechanics, though their fortunes do somewhat gild their infirmities, and their purses compound for their follies. But as in casting account, three or four men together come short in account of one man placed by himself below them; so neither are a troop of these ignorant *Doradoes*† of that true esteem and value, as many a forlorn person, whose condition doth place him below their feet. Let us speak like politicians: there is a nobility without heraldry, a natural dignity, whereby one man is ranked with another, another filed before him, according to the quality of his

* "Do not imagine that I consider as *vulgar* those only of the poor and humble classes; but all who are *ignorant*, even be they lords or princes, they must be classed under the denomination *vulgar*." — Cervantes.

† *Dorado*, Spanish. Gilt-head.

desert, and pre-eminence of his good parts.* Though the corruption of these times and the bias of present practice wheel another way, thus it was in the first and primitive commonwealths, and is yet in the integrity and cradle of well-ordered polities, till corruption getteth ground; ruder desires labouring after that which wiser considerations contemn, every one having a liberty to amass and heap up riches, and they a license or faculty to do or purchase anything.

Charity must spring from a proper motive.

II. This general and indifferent temper of mine doth more nearly dispose me to this noble virtue. It is a happiness to be born and framed unto virtue, and to grow up from the seeds of nature, rather than the inoculation and forced grass of education: yet if we are directed only by our particular natures, and regulate our inclinations by no higher rule than that of our reasons, we are but moralists; divinity will still call us heathens. Therefore this great work of charity must have other motives, ends, and impulsions. I give no alms to satisfy the hun-

* "Nobilitas sola est atque unica, virtus."
Juvenal.

"Howe'er it be, it seems to me,
'T is only noble to be good;
Kind hearts are more than coronets,
And simple faith than Norman blood."
Tennyson.

ger of my brother, but to fulfil and accomplish the will and command of my God: I draw not my purse for his sake that demands it, but His that enjoined it: I relieve no man upon the rhetoric of his miseries, nor to content mine own commiserating disposition; for this is still but moral charity, and an act that oweth more to passion than reason. He that relieves another upon the bare suggestion and bowels of pity, doth not this so much for his sake as for his own; for by compassion we make others' misery our own, and so, by relieving them, we relieve ourselves also. It is as erroneous a conceit to redress other men's misfortunes upon the common considerations of merciful natures, that it may be one day our own case; for this is a sinister and politic kind of charity, whereby we seem to bespeak the pities of men in the like occasions. And truly I have observed that those professed eleemosynaries, though in a crowd or multitude, do yet direct and place their petitions on a few and selected persons: there is surely a physiognomy, which those experienced and master mendicants observe, whereby they instantly discover a merciful aspect, and will single out a face wherein they spy the signatures and marks of mercy. For there are mystically in our faces certain characters which carry in them the motto of our

The nature of created beings signified in their outward forms.

souls, wherein he that cannot read A B C may read our natures. I hold, moreover, that there is a phytognomy, or physiognomy, not only of men, but of plants and vegetables: and in every one of them some outward figures which hang as signs or bushes of their inward forms.* The finger of God hath left an inscription upon all his works, not graphical or composed of letters, but of their several forms, constitutions, parts, and operations, which, aptly joined together, do make one word that doth express their natures.
Ps. cxlvii. 4. By these letters God calls the stars by their names; and by this alphabet Adam assigned to
Gen. ii. 19, 20. every creature a name peculiar to its nature.
Now there are, besides these characters in our
Of chiromancy. faces, certain mystical figures in our hands, which I dare not call mere dashes, strokes *à la volée*, or at random, because delineated by a pencil that never works in vain; and hereof I take more particular notice, because I carry that in mine own hand which I could never read of nor discover in another. Aristotle, I confess, in his acute and singular book of physiognomy, hath made no mention of chiromancy; yet I believe the Egyptians, who were nearer ad-

* Vintners were wont to hang up *bushes*, or garlands of ivy, over their doors. See Epilogue to *As you like it:* "If it be true that good wine needs no bush, 't is true that a good play needs no epilogue."

dicted to those abstruse and mystical sciences, had a knowledge therein, to which those vagabond and counterfeit Egyptians did after pretend, and perhaps retained a few corrupted principles, which sometimes might verify their prognostics.

Variety of outward forms in nature.

It is the common wonder of all men, how among so many millions of faces there should be none alike. Now, contrary, I wonder as much how there should be any: he that shall consider how many thousand several words have been carelessly and without study composed out of twenty-four letters; withal, how many hundred lines there are to be drawn in the fabric of one man, shall easily find that this variety is necessary; and it will be very hard that they shall so concur as to make one portrait like another. Let a painter carelessly limn out a million of faces, and you shall find them all different; yea, let him have his copy before him, yet after all his art there will remain a sensible distinction; for the pattern or example of everything is the perfectest in that kind, whereof we still come short, though we transcend or go beyond it, because herein it is wide, and agrees not in all points unto its copy. Nor doth the similitude of creatures disparage the variety of nature, nor any way confound the works of God. For even in things alike there is diversity; and those that do seem to accord do manifestly disagree. And thus is man like God; for in the same things that we resemble him, we are utterly different from him. There was never anything so like another as in all points to concur: there will ever some reserved difference slip in, to prevent the identity, without which two several things would not be alike, but the same, which is impossible.

The souls of our fellow-creatures as much the object of charity as their bodies.

III. But to return from philosophy to charity: I hold not so narrow a conceit of this virtue, as to conceive that to give alms is only to be charitable, or think a piece of liberality can comprehend the total of charity. Divinity hath wisely divided the act thereof into many branches, and hath taught us in this narrow way many paths unto goodness; as many ways as we may do good, so many ways we may be charitable: there are infirmities not only of body, but of soul, and fortunes, which do require the merciful hand of our abilities. I cannot contemn a man for ignorance, but behold him with as much pity as I do Lazarus. It is no greater charity to clothe his body, than apparel the nakedness of his soul. It is an honourable object to see the reasons of other men wear our liveries, and their borrowed understandings do homage to the bounty of ours: it is the cheapest way of beneficence, and, like the natural charity of the sun, illuminates another without obscuring itself. To be reserved and caitiff in this part of goodness, is the sordidest piece of covetousness, and more contemptible than pecuniary avarice. To this (as calling myself a scholar) I am obliged by the duty of my condition: I make not therefore my head a grave, but a treasury of knowledge: I intend no monopoly, but a community in learning: I study not for my own sake only, but for theirs that study not for themselves. I envy no man that knows more than myself, but pity them that know less. I instruct no man as an exercise of my knowledge, or with an intent rather to nourish and keep it alive in mine own head than beget and propagate it in his: and in the midst of all my endeavours, there is but one thought that dejects me, that my acquired parts must perish with myself, nor can be legacied among my honoured friends.

The duty of imparting knowledge.

I cannot fall out or contemn a man for an error, or conceive why a difference in opinion should divide an affection; for controversies, disputes, and argumentations, both in philosophy and in divinity, if they meet with discreet and peaceable natures, do not infringe the laws of charity. In all disputes, so much as there is of passion, so much there is of nothing to the purpose; for

Differences of opinion need not divide affection.

then reason, like a bad hound, spends upon a false scent, and forsakes the question first started. And in this is one reason why controversies are never determined; for though they be amply proposed, they are scarce at all handled; they do so swell with unnecessary digressions, and the parenthesis on the party is often as large as the main discourse upon the subject. The foundations of religion are already established, and the principles of salvation subscribed unto by all: there remain not many controversies worth a passion; and yet never any disputed without, not only in divinity, but inferior arts. What a *βατραχομυομαχία* and hot skirmish is betwixt S and T in Lucian?* How do grammarians hack and slash for the genitive case in Jupiter!† How they do break their own pates to salve that of Priscian! *Si foret in terris, rideret Democritus.* Yea, even amongst wiser militants, how many wounds have been given, and credits slain, for the poor victory of an opinion, or beggarly conquest of a distinction! Scholars are men of peace, they bear no arms, but their tongues are sharper than Actius his razor; ‡

* In his dialogue, *judicium vocalium*, where there is a large oration made to the vowels, being judges, by Sigma against Tau, complaining that Tau has bereaved him of many words, which should begin with Sigma.

† Whether *Jovis* or *Jupitris*.

‡ Accius Nævius is reported by Livy, Lib. i. cap. 36, to have

their pens carry farther, and give a louder report than thunder: I had rather stand in the shock of a basilisco,* than in the fury of a merciless pen. It is not mere zeal to learning, or devotion to the Muses, that wiser princes patron the arts, and carry an indulgent aspect unto scholars; but a desire to have their names eternized by the memory of their writings, and a fear of the revengeful pen of succeeding ages; for these are the men that, when they have played their parts, and had their *exits*, must step out and give the moral of their scenes, and deliver unto posterity an inventory of their virtues and vices. And surely there goes a great deal of conscience to the compiling of an history: there is no reproach to the scandal of a story; it is such an authentic kind of falsehood that with authority belies our good names to all nations and posterity.

IV. There is another offence unto charity, which no author hath ever written of, and few take notice of; and that's the reproach, not of whole professions, mysteries, and conditions, but of whole nations, wherein by opprobrious epithets we miscall each other, and by an uncharitable logic, from a disposition in a few, conclude

National want of charity.

cut a whetstone through with a razor, at the challenge of the King, Tarquinius Priscus.

* *Basilisco*, a kind of cannon.

a habit in all. St. Paul, that calls the Cretans liars, doth it but indirectly, and upon quotation of their own poet.* It is as bloody a thought in one way, as Nero's was in another; † for by a word we wound a thousand, and at one blow assassine the honour of a nation. It is as complete a piece of madness to miscall and rave against the times, or think to recall men to reason by a fit of passion. Democritus, that thought to laugh the times into goodness, seems to me as deeply hypochondriac as Heraclitus that bewailed them. It moves not my spleen to behold the multitude in their proper humours, that is, in their fits of folly and madness; as well understanding that wisdom is not profaned unto the world, and 't is the privilege of a few to be virtuous. They that endeavour to abolish vice, destroy also virtue; for contra-

* That is, Epimenides; the place is Tit. i. v. 12, where St. Paul useth this verse, taken out of Epimenides:

Κρῆτες ἀεὶ ψεῦσται, κακὰ θηρία, γαστέρες ἀργαί.

† I suppose he alludes to that passage in Sueton. 38, in the life of Nero, where he relates that a certain person upon a time spoke in his hearing these words,

Ἐμοῦ θανόντος γαῖα μιχθήτω πυρί,

i. e. When I am dead let earth be mingled with fire. Whereupon the Emperor uttered these words, Ἐμοῦ ζῶντος, i. e. Yea, whilst I live: there, by one word, he expressed a cruel thought which I think is the thing he meant. This is more cruel than the wish of Caligula, that the people of Rome had but one neck, that he might destroy them all at a blow.

ries, though they destroy one another, are yet the life of one another. Thus virtue (abolish vice) is an idea. Again, the community of sin doth not disparage goodness; for when vice gains upon the major part, virtue, in whom it remains, becomes more excellent; and being lost in some, multiplies its goodness in others which remain untouched, and persists entire in the general inundation. I can therefore behold vice without a satire, content only with an admonition, or instructive reprehension; for noble natures, and such as are capable of goodness, are railed into vice, that might as easily be admonished into virtue; and we should be all so far the orators of goodness, as to protect her from the power of vice, and maintain the cause of injured truth. No man can justly censure or condemn another, because indeed no man truly knows another. This I perceive in myself; for I am in the dark to all the world, and my nearest friends behold me but in a cloud: those that know me but superficially, think less of me than I do of myself; those of my near acquaintance think more. God, who truly knows me, knows that I am nothing; for He only beholds me and all the world, who looks not on us through a derived ray, or a trajection of a sensible species, but beholds the substance without the help of accidents, and the

Man most ignorant in the knowledge of himself.

forms of things as we their operations. Further, no man can judge another, because no man knows himself: for we censure others but as they disagree from that humour which we fancy laudable in ourselves, and commend others but for that wherein they seem to quadrate and consent with us. So that in conclusion, all is but that we all condemn, self-love. 'Tis the general complaint of these times, and perhaps of those past, that charity grows cold; which I perceive most verified in those which most do manifest the fires and flames of zeal; for it is a virtue that best agrees with coldest natures, and such as are complexioned for humility. But how shall we expect charity towards others, when we are uncharitable to ourselves? *Charity begins at home*, is the voice of the world; yet is every man his greatest enemy, and as it were his own executioner. *Non occides*, is the commandment of God, yet scarce observed by any man; for I perceive every man is his own Atropos, and lends a hand to cut the thread of his own days. Cain was not therefore the first murderer, but Adam, who brought in death; whereof he beheld the practice and example in his own son Abel, and saw that verified in the experience of another, which faith could not persuade him in the theory of himself.

V. There is, I think, no man that apprehendeth his own miseries less than myself, and no man that so nearly apprehends another's. I could lose an arm without a tear, and with few groans, methinks, be quartered into pieces; yet can I weep most seriously at a play, and receive with a true passion the counterfeit griefs of those known and professed impostures. It is a barbarous part of inhumanity to add unto any afflicted party's misery, or endeavour to multiply in any man a passion whose single nature is already above his patience: this was the greatest affliction of Job; and those oblique expostulations of his friends, a deeper injury than the downright blows of the devil. It is not the tears of our own eyes only, but of our friends also, that do exhaust the current of our sorrows; which falling into many streams, runs more peaceably, and is contented with a narrower channel. It is an act within the power of charity, to translate a passion out of one breast into another, and to divide a sorrow almost out of itself; for an affliction, like a dimension, may be so divided, as, if not invisible, at least to become insensible. Now with my friend I desire not to share or participate, but to engross his sorrows, that, by making them mine own I may more easily discuss them; for in mine own reason, and within myself, I can com-

Of sympathy.

Job xix.

mand that which I cannot intreat without myself, and within the circle of another. I have often thought those noble pairs and examples of friendship not so truly histories of what had been, as fictions of what should be; but I now perceive nothing in them but possibilities, nor anything in the heroic examples of Damon and Pythias, Achilles and Patroclus, which methinks upon some grounds I could not perform within the narrow compass of myself. That a man should lay down his life for his friend, seems strange to vulgar affections, and such as confine themselves within that worldly principle, *Charity begins at home.* For mine own part, I could never remember the relations that I held unto myself, nor the respect that I owe unto my own nature, in the cause of God, my country, and my friends.* Next to these three, I do embrace myself. I confess I do not observe that order that the schools ordain our affections, to love our parents, wives, children, and then our friends; for excepting the injunc-

* Cf. Pope's Essay on Man:

"Self-love but serves the virtuous mind to wake,
As the small pebble stirs the peaceful lake;
The centre moved, a circle straight succeeds,
Another still, and still another spreads;
Friend, parent, neighbour, next it will embrace,
His country next, and next all human race;
Wide and more wide the o'erflowings of the mind
Take every creature in of every kind."

tions of religion, I do not find in myself such a necessary and indissoluble sympathy to all those of my blood. I hope I do not break the fifth commandment, if I conceive I may love my friend before the nearest of my blood, even those to whom I owe the principles of life; I never yet cast a true affection on a woman; but I have loved my friend as I do virtue, my soul, my God. From hence methinks I do conceive how God loves man, what happiness there is in the love of God. Omitting all other, there are three most mystical unions; two natures in one person; three persons in one nature; one soul in two bodies. For though indeed they be really divided, yet are they so united as they seem but one, and make rather a duality than two distinct souls.

The mystery of true affection.

VI. There are wonders in true affection: it is a body of enigmas, mysteries, and riddles; wherein two so become one, as they both become two. I love my friend before myself, and yet methinks I do not love him enough: some few months hence, my multiplied affection will make me believe I have not loved him at all: when I am from him, I am dead till I be with him; when I am with him, I am not satisfied, but would still be nearer him. United souls are not satisfied with embraces, but desire to be truly each other; which being impossible, their desires are infinite, and must proceed without a possibility of satisfaction. Another misery there is in affection, that whom we truly love like our ownselves, we forget their looks, nor can our memory retain the idea of their faces; and it is no wonder, for they are ourselves, and our affection makes their looks our own. This noble affection falls not on vulgar and common constitutions, but on such as are marked for virtue: he that can love his friend with this noble ardour, will in a competent degree affect all. Now if we can bring our affections to look beyond the body, and cast an eye upon the soul, we have found out the true object, not only of friendship, but charity; and the greatest happiness that we can bequeath the soul is that wherein we all do place our last felicity, salvation; which though it be not in our power to bestow, it is in our charity and pious invocations to desire, if not procure and further. I cannot contentedly frame a prayer for myself in particular, without a catalogue for my friends; nor request a happiness wherein my sociable disposition doth not desire the fellowship of my neighbour. I never hear the toll of a passing bell, though in my mirth, without my prayers and best wishes for the departing spirit: I cannot go to cure the body of my patient, but I forget my profession, and call unto God for his soul: I cannot see one say his prayers, but, instead of imitating him, I fall into a supplication for him, who perhaps is no more to me than a common nature: and if God hath vouchsafed an ear to my supplications, there are surely many happy that never saw me, and enjoy the blessing of mine unknown devotions. To pray for enemies, that is, for their salvation, is no harsh precept, but the practice of our daily and ordinary devotions. I cannot believe the story of the Italian: our bad wishes and uncharitable desires proceed no further than this life; it is the devil, and the uncharitable votes of hell, that desire our misery in the world to come.

To forgive is the sweetest revenge.

VII. To do no injury, nor take none, was a principle, which to my former years, and impatient affections, seemed to contain enough of morality; but my more settled years, and Christian constitution, have fallen upon severer resolutions. I can hold there is no such thing as injury; that if there be, there is no such injury as revenge, and no such revenge as the contempt of an injury; that to hate another, is to malign himself; that the truest way to love another, is to despise ourselves. I were unjust unto mine own conscience, if I should say I am at variance with anything like myself. I find there are many pieces in this one fabric of man;

this frame is raised upon a mass of antipathies: I am one, methinks, but as the world; wherein notwithstanding, there are a swarm of distinct essences, and in them another world of contrarieties; we carry private and domestic enemies within, public and more hostile adversaries without. The devil, that did but buffet St. Paul, plays methinks at sharp with me: let me be nothing, if within the compass of myself I do not find the battle of Lepanto, passion against reason, reason against faith, faith against the devil, and my conscience against all. There is another man within me, that's angry with me, rebukes, commands, and dastards me. I have no conscience of marble to resist the hammer of more heavy offences; nor yet so soft and waxen, as to take the impression of each single peccadillo or scape of infirmity: I am of a strange belief, that it is as easy to be forgiven some sins, as to commit some others. For my original sin, I hold it to be washed away in my baptism: * for my actual transgressions, I compute and reckon with God but from my last repentance, sacrament, or general absolution; and therefore am not terrified with the sins or

* This is most true as far as the imputation of the same is concerned. For where the means of avoiding its consequences have been afforded, each after transgression is actual, by a neglect of those means. Coleridge.

madness of my youth. I thank the goodness of God, I have no sins that want a name; I am not singular in offences, my transgressions are epidemical, and from the common breath of our corruption. For there are certain tempers of body which, matched with an humorous depravity of mind, do hatch and produce vitiosities, whose newness and monstrosity of nature admits no name: this was the temper of that lecher that carnalled with a statua, and the constitution of Nero in his spintrian recreations. For the heavens are not only fruitful in new and unheard-of stars, the earth in plants and animals, but men's minds also in villany and vices: now the dulness of my reason, and the vulgarity of my disposition, never prompted my invention, nor solicited my affection unto any of these; yet even those common and quotidian infirmities that so necessarily attend me, and do seem to be my very nature, have so dejected me, so broken the estimation that I should have otherwise of myself, that I repute myself the most abjectest piece of mortality. Divines prescribe a fit of sorrow to repentance: there goes indignation, anger, sorrow, hatred, into mine; passions of a contrary nature, which neither seem to suit with this action, nor my proper constitution. It is no breach of charity to ourselves, to be at variance with our vices: nor to abhor that part of us which is an enemy to the ground of charity, our God; wherein we do but imitate our great selves the world, whose divided antipathies and contrary faces do yet carry a charitable regard unto the whole by their particular discords, preserving the common harmony, and keeping in fetters those powers, whose rebellions once masters, might be the ruin of all.

Of Pride and Conceit.

VIII. I thank God, amongst those millions of vices I do inherit and hold from Adam, I have escaped one, and that a mortal enemy to charity, the first and father-sin, not only of man, but of the devil, pride: a vice whose name is comprehended in a monosyllable, but in its nature not circumscribed with a world: I have escaped it in a condition that can hardly avoid it: those petty acquisitions and reputed perfections that advance and elevate the conceits of other men, add no feathers unto mine. I have seen a grammarian tower and plume himself over a single line in Horace, and show more pride in the construction of one ode, than the author in the composure of the whole book. For my own part, besides the jargon and *patois* of several provinces, I understand no less than six languages; yet I protest I have no higher conceit of myself, than had our fathers before the confusion of Babel, when there was but one language in the world, and none to boast himself either linguist or critic. I have not only seen several countries, beheld the nature of their climes, the chorography of their provinces, topography of their cities, but understood their several laws, customs, and policies; yet cannot all this persuade the dulness of my spirit unto such an opinion of myself, as I behold in nimbler and conceited heads that never looked a degree beyond their nests. I know the names, and somewhat more, of all the constellations in my horizon; yet I have seen a prating mariner, that could only name the pointers and the north star, out-talk me, and conceit himself a whole sphere above me. I know most of the plants of my country, and of those about me; yet methinks I do not know so many as when I did but know a hundred, and had scarcely ever simpled further than Cheapside:* for, indeed, heads of capacity, and such as are not full with a handful or easy measure of knowledge, think they know nothing till they know all; which being impossible, they fall upon the opinion of Socrates, and only know they know not anything. I cannot think that Homer pined away upon the riddle of the fishermen; or that Aristotle, who understood the

* ". . . . these lisping hawthorn buds, that come like women in men's apparel, and smell like Bucklersbury in simple-time." — Merry Wives of Windsor, iii. 3.

uncertainty of knowledge, and confessed so often the reason of man too weak for the works of nature, did ever drown himself upon the flux and reflux of *Euripus.* We do but learn to-day, what our better advanced judgments will unteach to-morrow; and Aristotle doth but instruct us, as Plato did him; that is, to confute himself. I have run through all sorts, yet find no rest in any: though our first studies and junior endeavours may style us Peripatetics, Stoics, or Academics; yet I perceive the wisest heads prove, at last, almost all Sceptics, and stand like Janus in the field of knowledge. I have therefore one common and authentic philosophy I learned in the schools, whereby I discourse and satisfy the reason of other men; another more reserved, and drawn from experience, whereby I content mine own. Solomon, that complained of ignorance in the height of knowledge, hath not only humbled my conceits, but discouraged my endeavours. There is yet another conceit that hath sometimes made me shut my books, which tells me it is a vanity to waste our days in the blind pursuit of knowledge; it is but attending a little longer, and we shall enjoy that by instinct and infusion, which we endeavour at here by labour and inquisition: it is better to sit down in a modest ignorance, and rest contented with the natural blessing of our own reasons, than buy the uncertain knowledge of this life with sweat and vexation, which death gives every fool gratis, and is an accessary of our glorification.

Of marriage and harmony.

IX. I was never yet once [married], and commend their resolutions who never marry twice: not that I disallow of second marriage; as neither in all cases of polygamy, which, considering some times, and the unequal number of both sexes, may be also necessary. The whole world was made for man, but the twelfth part of man for woman: man is the whole world, and the breath of God; woman the rib, and crooked piece of man. I could be content that we might procreate like trees without conjunction, or that there were any way to perpetuate the world without this trivial and vulgar way of coition: it is the foolishest act a wise man commits in all his life; nor is there anything that will more deject his cooled imagination, when he shall consider what an odd and unworthy piece of folly he hath committed. I speak not in prejudice, nor am averse from that sweet sex, but naturally amorous of all that is beautiful: I can look a whole day with delight upon a handsome picture, though it be but of an horse. It is my temper, and I like it the better, to affect all harmony; and sure there is music even in the beauty, and the silent note which Cupid strikes, far sweeter than the sound of an instrument:* for there is music wherever there is harmony, order, or proportion: and thus far we may maintain *the music of the spheres;* for those well-ordered motions, and regular paces, though they give no sound unto the ear, yet to the understanding they strike a note most full of harmony.† Whatsoever is harmonically composed, delights in harmony; which makes me much distrust the symmetry of those heads which declaim against all church music. For myself, not only from my obedience, but my particular genius, I do embrace it: for even that vulgar and tavern music, which makes one man merry, another mad, strikes in me a deep fit of devotion, and a profound contemplation of the First Composer; there is something in it of divinity more than the ear discovers: it is an

* So Daniell (Complaint of Rosamond):

"Ah Beauty! Syren faire, enchanting Good,
Sweet silent Rhetorick of persuading eyes;
Dumbe eloquence, whose power doth move the blood,
More than the words or wisdom of the wise;
Still Harmony, whose diapason lies
Within a brow; the Key which passions move
To ravish sense and play a world in love."

"When Love speaks, the voice of all the gods
Makes heaven drowsy with the harmony."

Love's Labour 's Lost, iv. 3.

† See Merchant of Ven., v. 1. Milton's Arcades.

hieroglyphical and shadowed lesson of the whole world, and creatures of God; such a melody to the ear, as the whole world, well understood, would afford the understanding.* In brief, it is a sensible fit of that harmony which intellectually sounds in the ears of God. It unties the ligaments of my frame, takes me to pieces, dilates me out of myself, and by degrees, methinks, resolves me into Heaven. I will not say, with Plato, the soul is an harmony, but harmonical, and hath its nearest sympathy unto music: thus some, whose temper of body agrees and humours the constitution of their souls, are born poets, though indeed all are naturally inclined unto rhythm.† This made Tacitus, in the very first line of his story, fall upon a

* "Is not God's Universe a Symbol of the Godlike; is not Immensity a Temple; is not Man's History, and Men's History, a perpetual Evangel? Listen, and for Organ-music thou wilt ever, as of old, hear the Morning Stars sing together." — Sartor Resartus, p. 299.

† "The old musician, who, rather figuratively we may suppose, than with philosophical seriousness, declared the *soul itself to be nothing but harmony,* provoked the sprightly remark of Cicero, *that he drew his philosophy from the Art which he professed;* but if, without departing from his own art, he had merely described the human frame as the noblest and sweetest of musical instruments, endued with a natural disposition to resonance and sympathy, alternately affecting and affected by the soul which pervades it, his description might, perhaps, have been physically just, and certainly ought not to have been hastily ridiculed." — Asiatic Researches, vol. iii. p. 56.

verse;* and Cicero, the worst of poets, but declaiming for a poet, falls in the very first sentence upon a perfect hexameter.† I feel not in me those sordid and unchristian desires of my profession; I do not secretly implore and wish for plagues, rejoice at famines, revolve ephemerides and almanacks in expectation of malignant aspects, fatal conjunctions, and eclipses: I rejoice not at unwholesome springs, nor unseasonable winters: my prayer goes with the husbandman's; I desire everything in its proper season, that neither men nor the times be out of temper. Let me be sick myself, if sometimes the malady of my patient be not a disease unto me; I desire rather to cure his infirmities than my own necessities: where I do him no good, methinks it is scarce honest gain; though I confess 't is but the worthy salary of our well-intended endeavours. I am not only ashamed, but heartily sorry, that, besides death, there are diseases incurable: yet not for my own sake, or that they be beyond my art, but for the general cause and sake of humanity, whose common cause I apprehend as mine own. And to speak more generally, those three noble professions which all civil commonwealths do honour are raised upon the

Our Physician hath the general cause of humanity at heart.

* *Urbem Romam in principio reges habuere.* Annales, i. 1.

† *In qua me non inficior mediocriter esse.* Pro Archia.

fall of Adam, and are not exempt from their infirmities; there are not only diseases incurable in physic, but cases indissolvable in laws, vices incorrigible in divinity. If general councils may err, I do not see why particular courts should be infallible: their perfectest rules are raised upon the erroneous reasons of man; and the laws of one do but condemn the rules of another; as Aristotle ofttimes the opinions of his predecessors, because, though agreeable to reason, yet were they not consonant to his own rules, and the logic of his proper principles. Again, to speak nothing of the sin against the Holy Ghost, whose cure not only, but whose nature, is unknown; I can cure the gout or stone in some, sooner than Divinity, pride or avarice in others. I can cure vices by physic when they remain incurable by divinity; and they shall obey my pills when they contemn their precepts. I boast nothing, but plainly say, we all labour against our own cure; for death is the cure of all diseases. There is no *catholicon* or universal remedy I know, but this; which, though nauseous to queasie stomachs, yet to prepared appetites is nectar, and a pleasant potion of immortality.

St. Matt. xii. 31. St. Mark iii. 28.

X. For my conversation, it is like the sun's, with all men, and with a friendly aspect to good and bad. Methinks there is no man bad, and

Our Physician thinketh no man so bad but

that there is good in him,—

the worst, best; that is, while they are kept within the circle of those qualities wherein they are good: there is no man's mind of such discordant and jarring a temper, to which a tunable disposition may not strike a harmony. *Magnæ virtutes, nec minora vitia*: it is the posie * of the best natures, and may be inverted on the worst. There are in the most depraved and venomous dispositions, certain pieces that remain untouched, which by an *antiperistasis* become more excellent, or by the excellency of their antipathies are able to preserve themselves from the contagion of their enemy vices, and persist entire beyond the general corruption. For it is also thus in Nature. The greatest balsams do lie enveloped in the bodies of the most powerful corrosives: I say, moreover, and I ground upon experience, that poisons contain within themselves their own antidote, and that which preserves them from the venom of themselves, without which they were not deleterious to others only, but to themselves also.

and feareth his own corruption more than contagion from others.

But it is the corruption that I fear within me, not the contagion of commerce without me. 'T is that unruly regiment within me, that will destroy me; 't is I that do infect myself; the man without a navel yet lives in me; † I feel

* *Posie.* The motto on a ring. Cf. Hamlet, iii. 2. Mer. of Ven., v. 1.

† *That is*, the old Adam.

that original canker corrode and devour me; and therefore *defenda me Dios de me*, Lord, deliver me from myself, is a part of my litany, and the first voice of my retired imaginations. There is no man alone, because every man is a microcosm, and carries the whole world about him; *Nunquam minus solus quam cum solus*, though it be the apophthegm of a wise man,* is yet true in the mouth of a fool; for indeed, though in a wilderness, a man is never alone, not only because he is with himself and his own thoughts, but because he is with the devil, who ever consorts with our solitude, and is that unruly rebel that musters up those disordered motions which accompany our sequestered imaginations: and to speak more narrowly, there is no such thing as solitude, nor anything that can be said to be alone and by itself, but God, who is his own circle, and can subsist by himself; all others, besides their dissimilary and heterogeneous parts, which in a manner multiply their natures, cannot subsist without the concourse of God, and the society of that hand which doth uphold their natures. In brief, there can be nothing truly alone and by itself, which is not truly one; and such is only God: all others do transcend an unity, and so by consequence are many.

* *Publius Scipio.* Cic. de Off., lib. iii.

Man's life a constant miracle.

XI. Now for my life, it is a miracle of thirty years, which to relate, were not a history, but a piece of poetry, and would sound to common ears like a fable: for the world, I count it not an inn, but an hospital; and a place not to live, but to die in. The world that I regard is myself; it is the microcosm of mine own frame that I cast mine eye on; for the other, I use it but like my globe, and turn it round sometimes for my recreation. Men that look upon my outside, perusing only my condition and fortunes, do err in my altitude; for I am above Atlas his shoulders. The Earth is a point not only in respect of the heavens above us, but of that heavenly and celestial part within us: that mass of flesh that circumscribes me, limits not my mind: that surface that tells the heavens it hath an end, cannot persuade me I have any: I take my circle to be above three hundred and sixty; though the number of the arc do measure my body, it comprehendeth not my mind: whilst I study to find how I am a microcosm, or little world, I find myself something more than the great. There is surely a piece of divinity in us, something that was before the elements, and owes no homage unto the sun. Nature tells me
Gen. i. 27. I am the image of God, as well as Scripture: he that understands not thus much, hath not his introduction or first lesson, and is yet to

begin the alphabet of man. Let me not injure the felicity of others, if I say I am as happy as any: *Ruat cœlum, fiat voluntas tua*, salveth all; so that whatsoever happens, it is but what our daily prayers desire. In brief, I am content; and what should Providence add more? Surely this is it we call happiness, and this do I enjoy; with this I am happy in a dream, and as content to enjoy a happiness in a fancy, as others in a more apparent truth and reality. There is surely a nearer apprehension of anything that delights us in our dreams, than in our waked senses: without this I were unhappy; for my awaked judgment discontents me, ever whispering unto me, that I am from my friend; but my friendly dreams in the night requite me, and make me think I am within his arms. I thank God for my happy dreams, as I do for my good rest, for there is a satisfaction in them unto reasonable desires, and such as can be content with a fit of happiness: and surely it is not a melancholy conceit to think we are all asleep in this world, and that the conceits of this life are as mere dreams to those of the next; as the phantasms of the night, to the conceits of the day. There is an equal delusion in both, and the one doth but seem to be the emblem or picture of the other: we are somewhat more than ourselves in our sleeps, and

Of Dreams.

the slumber of the body seems to be but the waking of the soul. It is the ligation of sense, but the liberty of reason; and our waking conceptions do not match the fancies of our sleeps. At my nativity my ascendant was the watery sign of Scorpius; I was born in the planetary hour of Saturn, and I think I have a piece of that leaden planet in me.* I am no way facetious, nor disposed for the mirth and galliardize of company; yet in one dream I can compose a whole comedy, behold the action, and apprehend the jests, and laugh myself awake at the conceits thereof. Were my memory as faithful as my reason is then fruitful, I would never study but in my dreams; and this time also would I choose for my devotions: but our grosser memories have then so little hold of our abstracted understandings, that they forget the story, and can only relate to our awaked souls a confused and broken tale of that that hath passed. Aristotle, who hath written a singular tract of sleep, hath not, methinks, thoroughly defined it; nor yet Galen, though he seem to have corrected it; for those noctambuloes and night-walkers, though in their sleep, do yet enjoy the action of their senses: we must therefore say that there is something in us that is not in the jurisdiction of Morpheus; and that

* Cf. Hor. Od. ii. xvii. 17.

those abstracted and ecstatic souls do walk about in their own corps, as spirits with the bodies they assume, wherein they seem to hear, see, and feel, though indeed the organs are destitute of sense, and their natures of those faculties that should inform them. Thus it is observed, that men sometimes, upon the hour of their departure, do speak and reason above themselves. For then the soul, beginning to be freed from the ligaments of the body, begins to reason like herself, and to discourse in a strain above mortality.*

XII. We term sleep a death; and yet it is Of sleep.

* That the soul is endowed with clearer faculties just before its separation from the body, is an opinion of great antiquity. See Bishop *Newton's* fourth Dissertation on Prophecy, and compare *Daniell* (Civil Wars, iii. 62), 1562.

> Whether the soul receives intelligence,
> By her near Genius, of the body's end,
> And so imparts a sadness to the sense,
> Foregoing ruin, whereto it doth tend;
> Or whether Nature else hath conference
> With profound Sleep, and so doth warning send,
> By prophetizing dreams, what hurt is near,
> And gives the heavy careful heart to fear."

And *Waller:*

> The soul's dark cottage, battered and decayed,
> Lets in new light thro' chinks that time hath made:
> Stronger by weakness, wiser men become,
> As they draw near to their eternal home.
> Leaving the old, both worlds at once they view,
> That stand upon the threshold of the new."

Compare *Shakspeare's* King Richard II., ii. 1.

waking that kills us, and destroys those spirits that are the house of life. 'T is indeed a part of life that best expresseth death; for every man truly lives, so long as he acts his nature, or some way makes good the faculties of himself. Themistocles, therefore, that slew his soldier in his sleep, was a merciful executioner: 'tis a kind of punishment the mildness of no laws hath invented: I wonder the fancy of Lucan and Seneca did not discover it. It is that death by which we may be literally said to die daily; a death which Adam died before his mortality; a death whereby we live a middle and moderating point between life and death: in fine, so like death, I dare not trust it without my prayers, and an half adieu unto the world, and take my farewell in a colloquy with God.

The night is come; like to the day,
Depart not thou, great God, away.
Let not my sins, black as the night,
Eclipse the lustre of thy light.
Keep still in my horizon: for to me
The sun makes not the day, but Thee.
Thou whose nature cannot sleep,
On my temples sentry keep:
Guard me 'gainst those watchful foes,
Whose eyes are open while mine close.
Let no dreams my head infest,
But such as Jacob's temples blest.
Whilst I do rest, my soul advance;
Make my sleep a holy trance:

That I may, my rest being wrought,
Awake into some holy thought.
And with as active vigour run
My course, as doth the nimble sun.
Sleep is a death, O make me try,
By sleeping, what it is to die:
And as gently lay my head
On my grave, as now my bed.
Howe'er I rest, great God, let me
Awake again at last with Thee.
And thus assured, behold I lie
Securely, or to wake or die.
These are my drowsy days; in vain
I do now wake to sleep again:
O come that hour, when I shall never
Sleep thus again, but wake for ever.

This is the dormitive I take to bedward; I need no other laudanum than this to make me sleep; after which I close mine eyes in security, content to take my leave of the sun, and sleep unto the resurrection.

Justice.

XIII. The method I should use in distributive justice, I often observe in commutative, and keep a geometrical proportion in both, whereby becoming equable to others, I become unjust to myself, and supererogate in that common principle, *Do unto others as thou wouldst be done unto thyself*. I was not born unto riches, neither is it, I think, my star to be wealthy; or if it were, the freedom of my mind, and frankness of my disposition, were able to contradict and cross my fates: for to me, avarice seems not so much a vice, as a deplorable piece of

Avarice a ridiculous vice.

madness;* to conceive ourselves urinals, or be persuaded that we are dead, is not so ridiculous, nor so many degrees beyond the power of hellebore,† as this. The opinions of theory, and positions of men, are not so void of reason, as their practised conclusions: some have held that snow is black, that the earth moves, that the soul is air, fire, water; but all this is philosophy, and there is no delirium, if we do but speculate the folly and indisputable dotage of avarice.‡ To that subterraneous idol, and god of the earth, I do confess I am an atheist; I cannot persuade myself to honour that the world adores; whatsoever virtue its prepared substance may have within my body, it hath no influence nor operation without: I would not entertain a base design, or an action that should call me villain, for the Indies; and for this only do I love and honour my own soul, and have methinks two arms too few to embrace myself. §Aristotle is too severe, that

Poor men

* "That a man who is Deputy Lieutenant of the whole world, should not act like a Prince within his territories, is a thing to be counted more a matter of prodigy than proof." — Religio Jurisprudentis.

† *Hellebore* was thought to be a specific against madness.

‡ i. e. There is nothing worthy of the name delirium when compared with the folly, &c.

§ There is an error here. Aristotle distinctly says (Eth. iv. 2) that true liberality consists not in the magnitude of the gift, but will not allow us to be truly liberal without wealth, and the bountiful hand of fortune: if this be true, I must confess I am charitable only in my liberal intentions, and bountiful well-wishes. But if the example of the mite be not only an act of wonder, but an example of the noblest charity, surely poor men may also build hospitals, and the rich alone have not erected cathedrals. I have a private method which others observe not; I take the opportunity of myself to do good; I borrow occasion of charity from my own necessities, and supply the wants of others, when I am in most need myself;* for it is an honest stratagem to take advantage of ourselves, and so to husband the acts of virtue, that where they were defective in one circumstance, they may repay their want, and multiply their goodness in another.† I have not Peru in my desires, but a competence and ability to perform those good works, to which the Almighty hath inclined my nature. He is rich, who hath enough to be charitable; and it is hard to be so poor, that a noble mind may not find a way to this piece of goodness. *He*

may be liberal,

St. Luke xxi. 1-4.

and may even build Hospitals and Cathedrals.

in the disposition of the giver: but he says (Eth. iv. 5) that a man with slender means cannot be *munificent.*

* When I am reduced to the last tester, I love to divide it with the poor. MSS. and Ed. 1642.

† Essays of Elia, 1st part.

Prov. xix. 17. *that giveth to the poor lendeth to the Lord:* * there is more rhetoric in that one sentence, than in a library of sermons; and indeed if those sentences were understood by the reader, with the same emphasis as they are delivered by the Author, we need not those volumes of instructions, but might be honest by an epitome. Upon this motive only I cannot behold a beggar without relieving his necessities with my purse, or his soul with my prayers; these scenical and accidental differences between us, cannot make me forget that common and untouched part of us both: there is under these *centoes* and Job xxxi. 13–15. miserable outsides, these mutilate and semi-bodies, a soul of the same alloy with our own, whose genealogy is God as well as ours, and in as fair a way to salvation as ourselves.† Statists that labour to contrive a commonwealth

* In St. George's Church, Doncaster, is to be seen this epitaph:—

How now, who is here?
I, Robin of Doncastere
And Margaret my fere.

That I spent, that I had:
That I gave, that I have:
That I left, that I lost.

A. D. 1579.

Quoth Robertus Byrks, who in this world did reign
3 score years and 7, and yet lived not one.

† So Herbert:

"Man is God's image; but a poor man is
Christ's stamp to boot: both images regard.
God reckons for him, counts the favour His:
Write, So much given to God: thou shalt be heard."

without poverty, take away the object of charity, not only not understanding the commonwealth of a Christian, but forgetting the prophecy of Christ.

St. Matt. xxvi. 11. Cf. Deut. xv. 11.

God alone loved for his own sake; and our neighbour for God's.

XIV. Now there is another part of charity, which is the basis and pillar of this, and that is the love of God, for whom we love our neighbour; for this I think charity, to love God for himself, and our neighbour for God.* All that is truly amiable is God, or as it were a divided piece of him, that retains a reflex or shadow of himself. Nor is it strange that we should place affection on that which is invisible: all that we truly love is thus; what we adore under affection of our senses, deserves not the honour of so pure a title. Thus we adore virtue, though to the eyes of sense she be invisible: thus that part of our noble friends that we love, is not that part that we embrace, but that insensible part that our arms cannot embrace. God being all goodness, can love nothing but himself; he loves us but for that part which is as it were himself, and the traduction of his Holy Spirit.† Let us call to assize the loves

* "Flatter not thyself in thy faith to God, if thou wantest charity for thy neighbour: and think not thou hast charity for thy neighbour, if thou wantest faith to God: where they are not both together, they are both wanting; they are both dead if once divided." — Quarles's Enchiridion, Cent. ii. 11. 1650.

† "Every true Virtue is a part of that Love with which God loveth himself." — Spinosa.

of our parents, the affection of wives and children, and they are all dumb shows and dreams, without reality, truth, or constancy: for first, there is a strong bond of affection between us and our parents; yet how easily dissolved! we betake ourselves to a woman, forget our mother in a wife, and the womb that bare us, in that that shall bear our image: this woman blessing us with children, our affection leaves the level it held before, and sinks from our bed unto our issue and picture of posterity, where affection holds no steady mansion. They growing up in years, desire our ends; or applying themselves to a woman, take a lawful way to love another better than ourselves. Thus I perceive a man may be buried alive, and behold his grave in his own issue.

Our Physician concludeth and declareth his belief that there is no happiness but in God.

XV. I conclude therefore and say, there is no happiness under (or, as Copernicus will have it, above) the sun, nor any crambe in that repeated verity and burthen of all the wisdom of Solomon, All is vanity and vexation of spirit; there is no felicity in that the world adores. Aristotle, whilst he labours to refute the ideas of Plato, falls upon one himself: for his *summum bonum* is a chimera, and there is no such thing as his felicity. That wherein God himself is happy, the holy angels are happy, in whose defect the devils are unhappy; that dare

I call happiness: whatsoever conduceth unto this, may with an easy metaphor deserve that name; whatsoever else the world terms happiness, is to me a story out of Pliny, an apparition, or neat delusion, wherein there is no more of happiness than the name. Bless me in this life with but peace of my conscience, command of my affections, the love of Thyself and my dearest friends, and I shall be happy enough to pity Cæsar. These are, O Lord, the humble desires of my most reasonable ambition, and all I dare call happiness on earth; wherein I set no rule or limit to thy hand or providence: dispose of me according to the wisdom of thy pleasure: thy will be done, though in my own undoing.

A
Letter to a Friend

Upon occasion of the Death of his intimate Friend.

Letter to a Friend.

IVE me leave to wonder that news of this nature should have such heavy wings that you should hear so little concerning your dearest Friend, and that I must make that unwilling repetition to tell you, *ad portam rigidos calces extendit*, that he is dead and buried, and by this time no puny among the mighty nations of the dead; for though he left this world not very many days past, yet every hour you know largely addeth unto that dark society; and considering the incessant mortality of mankind, you cannot conceive there dieth in the whole earth so few as a thousand an hour.

Although at this distance you had no early account or particular of his death, yet your affection may cease to wonder that you had not some secret sense or intimation thereof

by dreams, thoughtful whisperings, mercurisms, airy nuncios, or sympathetical insinuations, which many seem to have had at the death of their dearest friends: for since we find in that famous story,* that spirits themselves were fain to tell their fellows at a distance that the great *Antonio* was dead, we have a sufficient excuse for our ignorance in such particulars, and must rest content with the common road, and *Appian* way of knowledge by information. Though the uncertainty of the end of this world hath confounded all human predictions, yet they who
St. Matt. xxiv. 29. shall live to see the sun and moon darkened, and the stars to fall from heaven, will hardly be deceived in the advent of the last day; and therefore strange it is, that the common fallacy of consumptive persons, who feel not themselves dying, and therefore still hope to live, should also reach their friends in perfect health and judgment: that you should be so little acquainted with Plautus his sick complexion, or that almost an Hippocratical face should not alarum you to higher fears, or rather despair, of his continuation in such an emaciated state, wherein medical predictions fail not, as sometimes in acute diseases, and wherein 't is as dangerous to be sentenced by a Physician as a Judge.

* In *Plutarch* his *Defect of Oracles*, wherein he relates that a voice was heard crying to mariners at sea, *Great Pan is dead.*

Upon my first visit I was bold to tell them who had not let fall all hopes of his recovery, that in my sad opinion he was not like to behold a grasshopper, much less to pluck another fig; and in no long time after, seemed to discover that odd mortal symptom in him not mentioned by Hippocrates, that is, to lose his own face, and look like some of his near relations: for he maintained not his proper countenance, but looked like his uncle, the lines of whose face lay deep and invisible in his healthful visage before: for as from our beginning we run through variety of looks, before we come to consistent and settled faces, so before our end, by sick and languishing alterations, we put on new visages, and in our retreat to earth may fall upon such looks, which from community of seminal originals were before latent in us.

He was fruitlessly put in hope of advantage by change of air, and imbibing the pure aerial nitre of these parts; and therefore, being so far spent, he quickly found Sardinia in Tivoli,* and the most healthful air of little effect, where

* The unwholesome atmosphere of *Sardinia* was as proverbial as the salubrity of *Tivoli*.

> "Nullo fata loco possis excludere: cum mors
> Venerit, in medio Tibure Sardinia est."
>
> Mart. iv. lx. 5.

Cf. Tac. Annal. ii. 85.

Death had set her broad arrow; * for he lived not unto the middle of May, and confirmed the observation of Hippocrates of that mortal time of the year, when the leaves of the fig-tree resemble a daw's claw. He is happily seated who lives in places whose air, earth, and water promote not the infirmities of his weaker parts, or is early removed into regions that correct them. He that is tabidly inclined were unwise to pass his days in Portugal: cholical persons will find little comfort in Austria or Vienna: he that is weak-legged must not be in love with Rome, nor an infirm head with Venice or Paris. Death hath not only particular stars in heaven, but malevolent places on earth, which single out our infirmities and strike at our weaker parts; in which concern, passager and migrant birds have the great advantages, who are naturally constituted for distant habitations, whom no seas nor places limit, but in their appointed seasons will visit us from Greenland and Mount Atlas, and as some think, even from the Antipodes.

Though we could not have his life, yet we missed not our desires in his soft departure, which was scarce an expiration; and his end not unlike his beginning, when the *salient point*

* In the Queen's forests the mark of a broad arrow is set upon such trees as are to be cut down.

scarce affords a sensible motion, and his departure so like unto sleep, that he scarce needed the civil ceremony of closing his eyes; contrary unto the common way, wherein death draws up, sleep lets fall the eyelids. With what strife and pains we come into the world we know not, but 't is commonly no easy matter to get out of it: yet if it could be made out, that such who have easy nativities have commonly hard deaths, and contrarily; his departure was so easy, that we might justly suspect his birth was of another nature, and that some *Juno* sat cross-legged at his nativity. Besides his soft death, the incurable state of his disease might somewhat extenuate your sorrow, who know that monsters but seldom happen, miracles more rarely, in Physick. Angelus Victorius gives a serious account of a consumptive, hectical, phthisical woman, who was suddenly cured by the intercession of Ignatius. We read not of any in Scripture who in this case applied unto our Saviour, though some may be contained in that large expression, that He went about Galilee healing all manner of sickness, and all manner of diseases. Amulets, spells, sigils, and incantations, practised in other diseases, are seldom pretended in this; and we find no sigil in the *Archidoxis* of Paracelsus to cure an extreme consumption or marasmus, which, if other

Garden of Cyrus, cap. v.

Vide Consultationes.

St. Matt. iv. 23.

diseases fail, will put a period unto long livers, and at last makes dust of all. And therefore the Stoics could not but think that the fiery principle would wear out all the rest, and at last make an end of the world; which notwithstanding, without such a lingering period, the Creator may effect at his pleasure, and to make an end of all things on earth, and our planetical system of the world, He need but put out the sun.

Religio Medici, xlv.

I was not so curious to entitle the stars unto any concern of his death, yet could not but take notice that he died when the moon was in motion from the meridian: at which time, an old Italian long ago would persuade me, that the greatest part of men died: but herein I confess I could never satisfy my curiosity, although from the time of tides in places upon or near the sea, there may be considerable deductions, and Pliny hath an odd and remarkable passage concerning the death of men and animals upon the recess or ebb of the sea.* However, certain it is, he died in the dead and deep part of the night, when *Nox* might be most apprehensibly said to be the daughter of *Chaos*, the mother of *Sleep* and *Death*, according to old genealogy; and so went out of this world

Hesiod, Theog. 756.

* Cf. Plin. Hist. Nat. ii. 98. Mead *de Imperio Solis atque Lunæ.* Shaks. Henry Vth, ii. 3.

about that hour when our blessed Saviour entered it, and about what time many conceive he will return again unto it. Cardan hath a peculiar and no hard observation from a man's hand, to know whether he was born in the day or night, which I confess holdeth in my own; and Scaliger to that purpose hath another from the tip of the ear. Most men are begotten in the night, animals in the day; but whether more persons have been born in the night or the day, were a curiosity undecidable, though more have perished by violent deaths in the day, yet in natural dissolutions both times may hold an indifferency, at least but contingent inequality. The whole course of time runs out in the nativity and death of things; which whether they happen by succession or coincidence, are best computed by the natural, not artificial, day.

That Charles the Fifth was crowned upon the day of his nativity, it being in his own power so to order it, makes no singular animadversion; but that he should also take King Francis prisoner upon that day was an unexpected coincidence, which made the same remarkable. Antipater, who had an anniversary feast every year upon his birthday, needed no astrological revolution to know what day he should die on. When the fixed stars have made a revolution unto the points from whence they first set out, some of the ancients thought the world would have an end, which was a kind of dying upon the day of its nativity. Now the disease prevailing and swiftly advancing about the time of his nativity, some were of opinion that he would leave the world on the day he entered into it: but this being a lingering disease, and creeping softly on, nothing critical was found or expected, and he died not before fifteen days after. Nothing is more common with infants than to die on the day of their nativity, to behold the worldly hours, and but the fractions thereof; and even to perish before their nativity in the hidden world of the womb, and before their good angel is conceived to undertake them. But in persons who outlive many years, and when there are no less than three hundred and sixty-five days to determine their lives every year, — that the first day should make the last, that the tail of the snake should return into its mouth precisely at that time, and they should wind up upon the day of their nativity, — is indeed a remarkable coincidence, which, though astrology hath taken witty pains to salve, yet hath it been very wary in making predictions of it.* In this consumptive condition, and remarkable extenuation, he came to be almost

* This remarkable coincidence happened in our author's case: he himself died on the seventy-sixth anniversary of his birthday.

half himself, and left a great part behind him which he carried not to the grave. And though that story of Duke John Ernestus Mansfield be not so easily swallowed that at his death his heart was not found to be so big as a nut; yet if the bones of a good skeleton weigh little more than twenty pounds, his inwards and flesh remaining could make no bouffage, but a light bit for the grave. I never more lively beheld the starved characters of Dante in any living face;* an *aruspex* might have read a lecture upon him without exenteration, his flesh being so consumed, that he might in a manner have discerned his bowels without opening of him: so that to be carried, *sextâ cervice*, to the grave, was but a civil unnecessity; and the complements of the coffin might outweigh the subject of it. Omnibonus Ferrarius, in mortal dysenteries of children, looks for a spot behind the ear; in consumptive diseases some eye the complexion of moles; Cardan eagerly views the nails, some the lines of the hand, the *thenar* or muscle of the thumb; some are so curious as

Turkish History, p. 1483.

De arte medica infantium.

* Dante, describing a very emaciated countenance, says:

"Who reads the name
Of man upon his forehead, there the M
Had traced most plainly."
Purg. c. xxiii. 28.

Alluding to the conceit that the letters O M O may be traced in the human face. Cf. Hydriotaphia, cap. 3.

to observe the depth of the throat-pit, how the proportion varieth of the small of the legs unto the calf, or the compass of the neck unto the circumference of the head: but all these, with many more, were so drowned in a mortal visage, and last face of Hippocrates, that a weak physiognomist might say at first eye, this was

Aul. Gell. iii. 33.

a face of earth, and that *Morta* had set her hard seal upon his temples, easily perceiving what *caricatura* draughts Death makes upon pined faces, and unto what an unknown degree a man may live backward.

Physiologia barbæ humanæ.

Though the beard be only made a distinction of sex, and sign of masculine heat by Ulmus, yet the precocity and early growth thereof in him was not to be liked in reference unto long life. Lewis, that virtuous but unfortunate King of Hungary, who lost his life at the battle of Mohacz, was said to be born without a skin, to have bearded at fifteen, and to have shown some gray hairs about twenty; from whence the diviners conjectured, that he would be spoiled of his kingdom and have but a short life: but hairs make fallible predictions, and many temples early gray have outlived the Psalmist's

Ps. xc. 10.

period. Hairs which have most amused me have not been in the face or head, but on the back, and not in men but children, as I long ago observed in that endemial distemper of little children in Languedoc, called the *Morgellons*, wherein they critically break out with harsh hairs on their backs, which takes off the unquiet symptoms of the disease, and delivers them from coughs and convulsions. See Picotus de Rheumatismo.

The Egyptian mummies that I have seen have had their mouths open, and somewhat gaping, which affordeth a good opportunity to view and observe their teeth, wherein 't is not easy to find any wanting or decayed; and therefore in Egypt, where one man practised but one operation, or the diseases but of single parts, it must needs be a barren profession to confine unto that of drawing of teeth, and little better than to have been tooth-drawer unto King Pyrrhus, who had but two in his head.* How the Bannyans of India maintain the integrity of those parts, I find not particularly observed; who notwithstanding have an advantage of their preservation by abstaining from all flesh, and employing their teeth in such food unto which they may seem at first framed, from their figure and conformation: but sharp and corroding rheums had so early mouldered those rocks and hardest parts of his fabric, that a man might well conceive that his years were never like

* "Pyrrhus had an air of majesty rather terrible than august. Instead of teeth in his upper jaw he had one continued bone, marked with small lines resembling the divisions of a row of teeth." — Plutarch.

to double, or twice tell over his teeth. Corruption had dealt more severely with them than sepulchral fires and smart flames with those of burnt bodies of old; for in the burnt fragments of urns which I have enquired into, although I seem to find few incisors or shearers, yet the dog teeth and grinders do notably resist those fires. In the years of his childhood he had languished under the disease of his country, the *rickets;* after which notwithstanding, many have become strong and active men; but whether any have attained unto very great years, the disease is scarce so old as to afford good observation. Whether the children of the English plantations be subject unto the same infirmity, may be worth the observing. Whether lameness and halting do still increase among the inhabitants of Rovigno in Istria, I know not; yet scarce twenty years ago Monsieur du Loyr observed, that a third part of that people halted: but too certain it is that the rickets increaseth among us; the small-pox grows more pernicious than the great; the king's purse knows that the king's evil grows more common. Quartan agues are become no strangers in Ireland, more common and mortal in England: and though the ancients gave that disease very good words,* yet now that bell

* *ἀσφαλέστατος δὲ πάντων καὶ ῥήϊστος καὶ μακρότατος ὁ τεταρταῖος.* Hippoc. Epidem. i. 86.

makes no strange sound which rings out for the effects thereof.

Some think there were few consumptions in the old world, when men lived much upon milk; and that the ancient inhabitants of this island were less troubled with coughs when they went naked and slept in caves and woods, than men now in chambers and feather-beds. Plato will tell us that there was no such disease as a catarrh in Homer's time, and that it was but new in Greece in his age. Polydore Virgil delivereth that pleurisies were rare in England, who lived in the days of Henry the Eighth. Some will allow no diseases to be new, others think that many old ones are ceased, and that such which are esteemed new, will have but their time: however, the mercy of God hath scattered the great heap of diseases, and not loaded any one country with all: some may be new in one country which have been old in another: new discoveries of the earth discover new diseases: for besides the common swarm, there are endemial and local infirmities proper unto certain regions, which in the whole earth make no small number: and if Asia, Africa, and America should bring in their list, *Pandora's* box would swell, and there must be a strange Pathology.

Most men expected to find a consumed kell,

empty and bladder-like guts, livid and marbled lungs, and a withered pericardium in this exsuccous corpse: but some seemed too much to wonder that two lobes of his lungs adhered unto his side: for the like I have often found in bodies of no suspected consumptions or difficulty of respiration. And the same more often happeneth in man than other animals, and some think in women than in men; but the most remarkable I have met with was in a man, after a cough of almost fifty years, in whom all the lobes adhered unto the Pleura, and each lobe unto another; who having also been much troubled with the gout, brake the rule of Cardan, and died of the stone in the bladder.* Aristotle makes a query, why some animals cough, as man; some not, as oxen. If coughing be taken as it consisteth of a natural and voluntary motion, including expectoration and spitting out, it may be as proper unto man as bleeding at the nose; otherwise we find that Vegetius and rural writers have not left so many medicines in vain against the coughs of cattle; and men who perish by coughs die the death of sheep, cats, and lions: and though birds have no midriff, yet we meet with divers reme-

* *Cardan* in his *Encomium Podagræ* reckoneth this among the *dona Podagræ*, that they are delivered thereby from Phthisis and Calculus.

dies in Arrianus against the cough of hawks. And though it might be thought that all animals who have lungs do cough, yet in cetaceous fishes, who have large and strong lungs, the same is not observed, nor yet in oviparous quadrupeds: and in the greatest thereof, the crocodile, although we read much of their tears, we find nothing of that motion.

From the thoughts of sleep, when the soul was conceived nearest unto divinity, the ancients erected an art of divination, wherein while they too widely expatiated in loose and inconsequent conjectures, Hippocrates wisely considered dreams as they presaged alterations in the body, and so offered hints toward the preservation of health and prevention of diseases: and therein was so serious as to advise alteration of diet, exercise, sweating, bathing, and vomiting; and also so religious, as to order prayers and supplications unto respective deities; in good dreams unto *Sol*, *Jupiter cœlestis*, *Jupiter opulentus*, *Minerva*, *Mercurius*, and *Apollo:* in bad, unto *Tellus*, and the Heroes. And therefore I could not but take notice how his female friends were irrationally curious so strictly to examine his dreams, and in this low state to hope for the phantasms of health. He was now past the healthful dreams of the sun, moon, and stars, in their clarity and proper

De Insomniis.

courses. 'T was too late to dream of flying, of limpid fountains, smooth waters, white vestments, and fruitful green trees, which are the visions of healthful sleeps, and at good distance from the grave.

And they were also too deeply dejected that he should dream of his dead friends, inconsequently divining, that he would not be long from them; for strange it was not that he should sometimes dream of the dead, whose thoughts run always upon death; besides, to dream of the dead, so they appear not in dark habits, and take nothing away from us, in Hippocrates his sense, was of good signification: for we live by the dead, and everything is or must be so before it becomes our nourishment. And Cardan, who dreamed that he discoursed with his dead Father in the moon, made thereof no mortal interpretation: and even to dream that we are dead, was no condemnable phantasm in old *Oneirocriticism*, as having a signification of liberty, vacuity from cares, exemption and freedom from troubles unknown unto the dead.

Some dreams I confess may admit of easy and feminine exposition; he who dreamed that he could not see his right shoulder, might easily fear to lose the sight of his right eye; he that before a journey dreamed that his feet were cut off, had a plain warning not to undertake his intended journey. But why to dream of lettuce should presage some ensuing disease, why to eat figs should signify foolish talk, why to eat eggs great trouble, and to dream of blindness should be so highly commended, according to the oneirocritical verses of Astrampsychus and Nicephorus, I shall leave unto your divination.

He was willing to quit the world alone and altogether, leaving no earnest behind him for corruption or after-grave, having small content in that common satisfaction to survive or live in another, but amply satisfied that his disease should die with himself, nor revive in a posterity to puzzle physic, and make sad mementos of their parent hereditary. Leprosy awakes not sometimes before forty, the gout and stone often later; but consumptive and tabid roots sprout more early, and at the fairest make seventeen years of our life doubtful before that age. They that enter the world with original diseases as well as sin, have not only common mortality, but sick traductions, to destroy them, make commonly short courses, and live not at length but in figures: so that a sound *cæsarean* nativity may outlast a natural birth, and a knife may sometimes make way for a more lasting fruit than a midwife; which makes so few infants now able to endure the old test of the river,* and many to have feeble children who could scarce have been married at Sparta, and those provident states who studied strong and healthful generations; which happen but contingently in mere pecuniary matches, or marriages made by the candle, wherein notwithstanding there is little redress to be hoped from an Astrologer or a Lawyer, and a good discerning Physician were like to prove the most successful counsellor.

Julius Scaliger, who in a sleepless fit of the gout could make two hundred verses in a night, would have but five plain words upon his tomb.† And this serious person, though no minor wit, left the poetry of his epitaph unto others, either unwilling to commend himself, or to be judged by a distich, and perhaps considering how unhappy great Poets have been in versifying their own epitaphs: wherein Petrarcha, Dante, and Ariosto have so unhappily failed, that if their tombs should outlast their works, posterity would find so little of Apollo on them, as to mistake them for *Ciceronian* Poets.

In this deliberate and creeping progress unto the grave, he was somewhat too young, and of

* "Durum ab stirpe genus, natos ad flumina primum
Deferimus, sævoque gelu duramus et undis."
Virg. Æn. ix. 603.

† IVLII CÆSARIS SCALIGERI QVOD FVIT.

too noble a mind, to fall upon that stupid symptom observable in divers persons near their journey's end, and which may be reckoned among the mortal symptoms of their last disease: that is, to become more narrow-minded, miserable, and tenacious, unready to part with anything, when they are ready to part with all, and afraid to want when they have no time to spend; meanwhile Physicians, who know that many are mad but in a single depraved imagination, and one prevalent decipiency, and that beside and out of such single deliriums a man may meet with sober actions and good sense in Bedlam, cannot but smile to see the heirs and concerned relations gratulating themselves on the sober departure of their friends; and though they behold such mad covetous passages, content to think they die in good understanding, and in their sober senses.

Avarice, which is not only infidelity but idolatry, either from covetous progeny or questuary education, had no root in his breast, who made good works the expression of his faith, and was big with desires unto public and lasting charities; and surely where good wishes and charitable intentions exceed ability, theorical beneficency may be more than a dream. They build not castles in the air who would build churches on earth; and though they leave no

Coloss. iii. 5.

Rel. Med. Pt. ii. c. xiii.

such structures here, may lay good foundations in Heaven.* In brief, his life and death were such, that I could not blame them who wished the like, and almost, to have been himself; almost, I say, for though we may wish the prosperous appurtenances of others, or to be another in his happy accidents, yet so intrinsical is every man unto himself, that some doubt may be made, whether any would exchange his being, or substantially become another man.

He had wisely seen the world at home and abroad, and thereby observed under what variety men are deluded in the pursuit of that which is not here to be found. And although he had no opinion of reputed felicities below, and apprehended men widely out in the estimate of such happiness, yet his sober contempt of the world wrought no *Democratism* or *Cynicism*, no laughing or snarling at it, as well understanding there are not felicities in this world to satisfy a serious mind; and therefore to soften the stream of our lives, we are fain to take in the reputed contentations of this world, to unite with the crowd in their beatitudes, and to make ourselves happy by consor-

* So Wordsworth (Eccles. Sonnet, King's Coll. Chapel):

"They dreamt not of a perishable home
Who thus could build."

tion, opinion, or co-existimation: for strictly to separate from received and customary felicities, and to confine unto the rigour of realities, were to contract the consolation of our beings unto too uncomfortable circumscriptions.

Not to fear death, nor desire it, was short of his resolution: to be dissolved, and be with Christ, was his dying ditty. He conceived his thread too long, in no long course of years, and when he had scarce outlived the second life of Lazarus; * esteeming it enough to approach the years of his Saviour, who so ordered his own human state, as not to be old upon earth. But to be content with death may be better than to desire it: a miserable life may make us wish for death, but a virtuous one to rest in it; which is the advantage of those resolved Christians, who looking on death not only as the sting, but the period and end of sin, the horizon and isthmus between this life and a better, and the death of this world but as a nativity of another, do contentedly submit unto the common necessity, and envy not Enoch or Elias.

2 Cor. v. 1. Phil. i. 23.

Gen. v. 24. Heb. xi. 5. 2 Kings ii.

Not to be content with life is the unsatisfactory state of those who destroy themselves; who

* S. Epiphanius mentions a tradition that Lazarus had died at the age of thirty when he was raised from the dead by our Lord, and that he lived thirty years afterwards. Epiphan. Hæres. lxvi. c. 39.

being afraid to live, run blindly upon their own death, which no man fears by experience; and the Stoics had a notable doctrine to take away the fear thereof, that is, in such extremities, to desire that which is not to be avoided, and wish what might be feared, and so made evils voluntary, and to suit with their own desires, which took off the terror of them. But the ancient martyrs were not encouraged by such fallacies; who, though they feared not death, were afraid to be their own executioners, and therefore thought it more wisdom to crucify their lusts than their bodies, to circumcise than stab their hearts, and to mortify than kill themselves.

Rel. Med. xliv.

His willingness to leave this world about that age when most men think they may best enjoy it, though paradoxical unto worldly ears, was not strange unto mine, who have so often observed that many, though old, oft stick fast unto the world, and seem to be drawn like Cacus his oxen, backward, with great struggling and reluctancy, unto the grave.* The long habit of living makes meer men more hardly to part with life, and all to be nothing but what is to come. To live at the rate of the old world, when some could scarce remember themselves

* *Cacus* was a robber, who having stolen Hercules his oxen on Mount Aventine, dragged them backwards into his cave, that their tracks might not be discovered. Livy, i. 7. Virg. Æn. viii. 209.

young, may afford no better digested death than a more moderate period. Many would have thought it an happiness to have had their lot of life in some notable conjunctures of ages past: but the uncertainty of future times hath tempted few to make a part in ages to come. And surely, he that hath taken the true altitude of things, and rightly calculated the degenerate state of this age, is not like to envy those that shall live in the next, much less three or four hundred years hence, when no man can comfortably imagine what face this world will carry: and therefore, since every age makes a step unto the end of all things and the Scripture affords so hard a character of the last times, quiet minds will be content with their generations, and rather bless ages past, than be ambitious of those to come.

Though Age had set no seal upon his face, yet a dim eye might clearly discover fifty in his actions; and therefore, since wisdom is the gray hair, and an unspotted life old age, although his years came short, he might have been said to have held up with longer livers, and to have been Solomon's old man. And Wisd. v. 7-14.
surely if we deduct all those days of our life which we might wish unlived, and which abate the comfort of those we now live, if we reckon up only those days which God hath accepted

of our lives, a life of good years will hardly be a span long, the son in this sense may outlive the father, and none be climacterically old. He that early arriveth unto the parts and prudence of age, is happily old without the uncomfortable attendants of it: and 't is superfluous to live unto gray hairs, when in a precocious temper we anticipate the virtues of them. In brief, he cannot be accounted young who outliveth the old man. He that hath early arrived unto the measure of a perfect stature in Christ, hath already fulfilled the prime and longest intention of his being: and one day lived after the perfect rule of piety is to be preferred before sinning immortality. Although he attained not unto the years of his predecessors, yet he wanted not those preserving virtues which confirm the thread of weaker constitutions. Cautelous Chastity and crafty Sobriety were far from him; those jewels were paragon, without flaw, hair, ice, or cloud in him: which affords me a hint to proceed in these good wishes, and few *mementos* unto you.

Ephes. iv. 13.

TRUE CHRISTIAN MORALS.

To the Right Honourable

DAVID, EARL OF BUCHAN,

Viscount Auchterhouse, Lord Cardross and Glendovachie, one of the Lords Commissioners of Police, and Lord Lieutenant of the Counties of Stirling and Clackmannan in North Britain.

My Lord, —

THE honour you have done our family obligeth us to make all just acknowledgments of it; and there is no form of acknowledgment in our power, more worthy of your Lordship's acceptance, than this dedication of the last Work of our honoured and learned Father. Encouraged hereunto by the knowledge we have of your Lordship's judicious relish of universal learning and sublime virtue, we beg the favour of your acceptance of it, which will very much oblige our family in general, and her in particular, who is,

My Lord,

Your Lordship's most humble servant,

ELIZABETH LITTLETON.

PREFACE TO THE FIRST EDITION.

IF any one, after he has read RELIGIO MEDICI, and the ensuing DISCOURSE, can make doubt whether the same person was the Author of them both, he may be assured by the testimony of Mrs. Littleton, Sir Thomas Browne's daughter, who lived with her father when it was composed by him, and who, at the time, read it written by his own hand; and also by the testimony of others (of whom I am one) who read the manuscript of the Author immediately after his death, and who have since read the same, from which it hath been faithfully and exactly transcribed for the press. The reason why it was not printed sooner is, because it was unhappily lost, by being mislaid among other manuscripts, for which search was lately made in the presence of the Lord Archbishop of Canterbury, of which his Grace by letter informed Mrs. Littleton, when he sent the manuscript to her. There is nothing printed in the Discourse, or in the short notes, but what is found in the original manuscript of the Author, except only where an oversight had made the addition or transposition of some words necessary.

JOHN JEFFERY,

ARCHDEACON OF NORWICH.

Christian Morals.

PART I.

READ softly and circumspectly in this funambulatory track and narrow path of goodness: pursue virtue virtuously: leaven not good actions, nor render virtues disputable. Stain not fair acts with foul intentions: maim not uprightness by halting concomitances, nor circumstantially deprave substantial goodness.

Consider whereabout thou art in Cebes his table, or that old philosophical *pinax* of the life of man: * whether thou art yet in the road of uncertainties; whether thou hast yet entered the narrow gate, got up the hill and asperous way, which leadeth unto the house of sanity; or taken that purifying potion from the hand

* The Pinax, or tablet, of Cebes, a Theban philosopher, in which the life of man is represented in a beautiful allegory.

of sincere erudition, which may send thee clear and pure away unto a virtuous and happy life.

Milton, Par. Lost, xi 840.

In this virtuous voyage of thy life hull not about like the ark, without the use of rudder, mast, or sail, and bound for no port. Let not disappointment cause despondency, nor difficulty despair. Think not that you are sailing from Lima to Manilla, when you may fasten up the rudder, and sleep before the wind; but expect rough seas, flaws, and contrary blasts; and it is well if by many cross tacks and veerings you arrive at the port; for we sleep in lions' skins in our progress unto virtue, and we slide not, but climb unto it.

ὁ κυμινοπρίστης. Arist. Eth. iv. 1.

Sit not down in the popular forms and common level of virtues. Offer not only peace-offerings, but holocausts unto God; where all is due make no reserve, and cut not a cumin-seed with the Almighty: to serve him singly to serve ourselves were too partial a piece of piety, not like to place us in the illustrious mansions of glory.

II. Rest not in an ovation, but a triumph over thy passions. Let anger walk hanging down the head; let malice go manacled, and envy fettered, after thee. Behold within thee the long train of thy trophies, not without thee. Make the quarrelling Lapithytes sleep, and Centaurs within lie quiet. Chain up the unruly legion of thy breast. Lead thine own captivity captive, and be Cæsar within thyself.

III. He that is chaste and continent not to impair his strength, or honest for fear of contagion, will hardly be heroically virtuous. Adjourn not this virtue until that temper, when Cato could lend out his wife, and impotent satyrs write satires upon lust.

IV. Show thy art in honesty, and lose not thy virtue by the bad managery of it. Be temperate and sober: not to preserve your body in an ability for wanton ends; not to avoid the infamy of common transgressors that way, and thereby to hope to expiate or palliate obscure and closer vices; not to spare your purse, nor simply to enjoy health; but in one word, that thereby you may truly serve God, which every sickness will tell you you cannot well do without health. The sick man's sacrifice is but a lame oblation. Pious treasures laid up in healthful days, plead for sick non-performances, without which we must needs look back with anxiety upon the lost opportunities of health, and may have cause rather to envy than pity the ends of penitent public sufferers, who go with healthful prayers unto the last scene of their lives, and in the integrity of their faculties return their spirit unto God that gave it.

V. Be charitable before wealth make thee

St. Mark xii. 41–44. covetous, and lose not the glory of the mite.
If riches increase, let thy mind hold pace with
them; and think it not enough to be liberal,
St. Matt. x. 42. but munificent. Though a cup of cold water
St. Mark ix. 41. from some hand may not be without its reward,
St. Luke x. 34. yet stick not thou for wine and oil for the
wounds of the distressed; and treat the poor,
St. John vi. 12, 13. as our Saviour did the multitude, to the reliques
of some baskets. Diffuse thy beneficence early, and while thy treasures call thee master: there may be an Atropos of thy fortunes before that of thy life, and thy wealth cut off before that hour when all men shall be poor; for the justice of death looks equally upon the dead, and Charon expects no more from Alexander than from Irus.*

Eccl. xi. 2. VI. Give not only unto seven, but also unto eight, that is, unto more than many. Though
St. Matt. v. 42. to give unto every one that asketh may seem severe advice, yet give thou also before asking; that is, where want is silently clamorous, and men's necessities, not their tongues, do loudly call for thy mercies. For though sometimes necessitousness be dumb, or misery speak not out; yet true charity is sagacious, and will find out hints for beneficence. Acquaint thyself

* *Irus*, a beggar (Odyss. xviii. 233) whose poverty became proverbial:

"*Irus et est subito, qui modo Crœsus erat.*" — Ovid.

with the physiognomy of want, and let the dead colours and first lines of necessity suffice to tell thee there is an object for thy bounty. Spare not where thou canst not easily be prodigal, and fear not to be undone by mercy; for since he who hath pity on the poor lendeth unto the Almighty rewarder, who observes no ides* but every day for his payments, charity becomes pious usury, Christian liberality the most thriving industry, and what we adventure in a cock-boat may return in a carrack unto us. He who thus casts his bread upon the water shall surely find it again; for though it falleth to the bottom, it sinks but like the axe of the prophet, to rise again unto him.

Prov. xix. 17.

Eccl. xi. 1.

2 Kings vi. 5-7.

VII. If avarice be thy vice, yet make it not thy punishment. Miserable men commiserate not themselves; bowelless unto others, and merciless unto their own bowels. Let the fruition of things bless the possession of them, and think it more satisfaction to live richly than die rich. For since thy good works, not thy goods, will follow thee; since wealth is an appurtenance of life, and no dead man is rich; to famish in plenty, and live poorly to die rich, were a multiplying improvement in madness, and use upon use in folly.

Rev. xiv. 13.

* *Ides*, the middle day of the Roman month, on which money put out to interest was commonly repaid.

VIII. Trust not to the omnipotency of gold,
Job xxxi. 24-27. and say not unto it, Thou art my confidence.
Kiss not thy hand to that terrestrial sun, nor
Ex. xxi. 6. bore thy ear unto its servitude. A slave unto
St. Matt. vi. 24. mammon makes no servant unto God. Covet-
St. Luke xvi. 13. ousness cracks the sinews of faith, numbs the
apprehension of anything above sense; and only affected with the certainty of things present, makes a peradventure of things to come; lives but unto one world, nor hopes but fears another; makes their own death sweet unto others, bitter unto themselves; brings formal sadness, scenical mourning, and no wet eyes at the grave.

IX. Persons lightly dipped, not grained in generous honesty, are but pale in goodness, and faint-hued in integrity. But be thou what thou virtuously art, and let not the ocean wash away thy tincture. Stand magnetically upon that axis, when prudent simplicity hath fixed there; and let no attraction invert the poles of thy honesty. That vice may be uneasy and even monstrous unto thee, let repeated good acts and long confirmed habits make virtue almost natural, or a second nature in thee. Since virtuous superstructions have commonly generous foundations, dive into thy inclinations, and early discover what nature bids thee to be, or tells thee thou mayest be. They who thus timely descend into themselves, and cultivate the good seeds which nature hath set in them, prove not shrubs but cedars in their generation. And to be in the form of the best of the bad, or the worst of the good, will be no satisfaction unto them.

X. Make not the consequence of virtue the ends thereof. Be not beneficent for a name or cymbal of applause; nor exact and just in commerce for the advantages of trust and credit, which attend the reputation of true and punctual dealing: for these rewards, though unsought for, plain virtue will bring with her. To have other by-ends in good actions sours laudable performances, which must have deeper roots, motives, and instigations, to give them the stamp of virtues.

St. Matt. vi. 1, 2.

XI. Let not the law of thy country be the *non ultra* of thy honesty; nor think that always good enough which the law will make good. Narrow not the law of charity, equity, mercy. Join gospel righteousness with legal right. Be not a mere Gamaliel in the faith, but let the Sermon on the Mount be thy Targum unto the law of Sinai.

St. Matt. v. vi. vii. Ex. xx.

XII. Live by old ethics and the classical rules of honesty. Put no new names or notions upon authentic virtues and vices. Think not that morality is ambulatory; that vices in

Cf. Thucyd. iii. 82.

one age are not vices in another; or that virtues, which are under the everlasting seal of right reason, may be stamped by opinion. And therefore, though vicious times invert the opinions of things, and set up new ethics against virtue, yet hold thou unto old morality; and
Ex. xxiii. 2. rather than follow a multitude to do evil, stand like Pompey's pillar conspicuous by thyself, and single in integrity. And since the worst of times afford imitable examples of virtue; since no deluge of vice is like to be so general but more than eight will escape; eye well those heroes who have held their heads above water, who have touched pitch and not been defiled, and in the common contagion have remained uncorrupted.

XIII. Let age, not envy, draw wrinkles on thy cheeks; be content to be envied, but envy not. Emulation may be plausible and indignation allowable, but admit no treaty with that passion which no circumstance can make good. A displacency at the good of others because they enjoy it, though not unworthy of it, is an absurd depravity, sticking fast unto corrupted nature, and often too hard for humility and charity, the great suppressors of envy. This surely is a lion not to be strangled but by Hercules himself, or the highest stress of our
Phil. iii. 21. minds, and an atom of that power which subdueth all things unto itself.

XIV. Owe not thy humility unto humiliation from adversity, but look humbly down in that state when others look upwards upon thee. Think not thy own shadow longer than that of others, nor delight to take the altitude of thyself. Be patient in the age of pride, when men live by short intervals of reason under the dominion of humour and passion, when it is in the power of every one to transform thee out of thyself, and run thee into the short madness. If you cannot imitate Job, yet come not short of Socrates, and those patient Pagans who tired the tongues of their enemies, while they perceived they spit their malice at brazen walls and statues.

Hor. Ep. i. ii. 62.

Juv. Sat. xiii. 185.

XV. Let not the sun in Capricorn * go down upon thy wrath, but write thy wrongs in ashes. Draw the curtain of night upon injuries, shut them up in the tower of oblivion,† and let them be as though they had not been. To forgive our enemies, yet hope that God will punish them, is not to forgive enough. To forgive them ourselves, and not to pray God to forgive them, is a partial piece of charity. Forgive thine enemies totally, and without any reserve, that however, God will revenge thee.

Eph. iv. 26.

* Even when the days are shortest.

† Alluding unto the Tower of Oblivion mentioned by Procopius, as a place of imprisonment among the Persians: whoever was put therein was, as it were, buried alive, and it was death for any but to name him.

XVI. While thou so hotly disclaimest the devil, be not guilty of diabolism. Fall not into one name * with that unclean spirit, nor act his nature whom thou so much abhorrest; that is, to accuse, calumniate, backbite, whisper, detract, or sinistrously interpret others. Degenerous depravities, and narrow-minded vices! not only below St. Paul's noble Christian, but Aristotle's † true gentleman. Trust not with some that the Epistle of St. James is apocryphal, and so read with less fear that stabbing
St. James, i. 26. truth, that in company with this vice thy re-
Ex. xxxii. 19. ligion is in vain. Moses broke the tables without breaking of the law; but where charity is broke, the law itself is shattered, which can-
Rom. xiii. 10. not be whole without Love, which is the fulfilling of it. Look humbly upon thy virtues; and though thou art rich in some, yet think thyself poor and naked without that crowning grace,
1 Cor. xiii. which thinketh no evil, which envieth not, which beareth, hopeth, believeth, endureth all things. With these sure graces, while busy tongues are
St. Luke xvi. 24. crying out for a drop of cold water, mutes
Rev. iv. 8. may be in happiness, and sing the *Trisagion* in heaven.

XVII. However thy understanding may waver in the theories of true and false, yet fasten

* *One name*, ὁ διάβολος, the calumniator.

† Compare Arist. Ethics, iv. 7, and Romans xiii.

the rudder of thy will, steer straight unto good, and fall not foul on evil. Imagination is apt to rove, and conjecture to keep no bounds. Some have run out so far, as to fancy the stars might be but the light of the crystalline heaven shot through perforations on the bodies of the orbs. Others more ingeniously doubt whether there hath not been a vast tract of land in the Atlantic Ocean, which earthquakes and violent causes have long ago devoured. Speculative misapprehensions may be innocuous, but immorality pernicious; theorical mistakes and physical deviations may condemn our judgments, not lead us into judgment. But perversity of will, immoral and sinful enormities, walk with *Adraste* and *Nemesis* at their backs, pursue us unto judgment, and leave us viciously miserable.

XVIII. Bid early defiance unto those vices which are of thine inward family, and having a root in thy temper plead a right and propriety in thee. Raise timely batteries against those strong-holds built upon the rock of nature, and make this a great part of the militia of thy life. Delude not thyself into iniquities from participation or community, which abate the sense but not the obliquity of them. To conceive sins less, or less of sins, because others also transgress, were morally to commit that natural fallacy of man, to take comfort from society, and think adversities less because others also suffer them. The politic nature of vice must be opposed by policy; and, therefore, wiser honesties project and plot against it: wherein, notwithstanding, we are not to rest in generals, or the trite stratagems of art. That may succeed with one, which may prove successless with another: there is no community or common weal of virtue: every man must study his own economy, and adapt such rules unto the figure of himself.

XIX. Be substantially great in thyself, and more than thou appearest unto others; and let the world be deceived in thee, as they are in the lights of heaven. Hang early plummets upon the heels of pride, and let ambition have but an *epicycle* and narrow circuit in thee. Measure not thyself by thy morning shadow, but by the extent of thy grave; and reckon thyself above the earth, by the line thou must be contented with under it. Spread not into boundless expansions either of designs or desires. Think not that mankind liveth but for a few; and that the rest are born but to serve those ambitions which make but flies of men and wildernesses of whole nations. Swell not into vehement actions which embroil and confound the earth; but be one of those violent ones
St. Matt. xi. 12. which force the kingdom of heaven. If thou

must needs rule, be Zeno's king,* and enjoy that empire which every man gives himself. He who is thus his own monarch contentedly sways the sceptre of himself, not envying the glory of crowned heads and elohim of the earth. Could the world unite in the practice of that despised train of virtues, which the divine ethics of our Saviour hath so inculcated upon us, the furious face of things must disappear; Eden would be yet to be found, and the angels might look down, not with pity, but joy upon us.

XX. Though the quickness of thine ear were able to reach the noise of the moon, which some think it maketh in its rapid revolution; though the number of thy ears should equal Argus his eyes: yet stop them all with the wise man's wax,† and be deaf unto the suggestions of talebearers, calumniators, pick-thank or malevolent delators, who, while quiet men sleep, sowing St. Matt.
the tares of discord and division, distract the xiii. 25.
tranquillity of charity and all friendly society.

* The Stoics illustrated their doctrines by describing an ideal personage whom they called "The wise man"; and he (they said) "was the only King, the only Dictator, the only Rich Man." Cic. de Finibus, iii. 22. Hor. Sat. i. iii.

"The way to subject all things to thy selfe, is to subject thyselfe to reason: thou shalt govern many, if reason govern thee: wouldst thou be crowned the monarch of a little world? command thy selfe." — Quarles's Enchir., ii. 19.

† *Wise man's wax.* Ulysses adopted this plan to escape the enchantment of the Sirens. Odyss. M. 173.

St. James iii. 6. These are the tongues that set the world on
2 Tim. ii. 17. fire, cankers of reputation, and, like that of
Jonah iv. 6, 7. Jonas his gourd, wither a good name in a night. Evil spirits may sit still, while these spirits walk about and perform the business of hell. To speak more strictly, our corrupted hearts are the factories of the devil, which may be at work without his presence; for when that circumventing spirit hath drawn malice, envy, and all unrighteousness unto well-rooted habits in his disciples, iniquity then goes on upon its own legs; and if the gate of hell were shut up for a time, vice would still be fertile and produce the fruits of hell. Thus, when God forsakes us, Satan also leaves us: for such offenders he looks upon as sure and sealed up, and his temptations then needless unto them.

XXI. Annihilate not the mercies of God by the oblivion of ingratitude: for oblivion is a kind of annihilation; and for things to be as though they had not been, is like unto never being. Make not thy head a grave, but a repository of God's mercies. Though thou hadst the memory of Seneca, or Simonides, and conscience, the punctual memorist within us, yet trust not to thy remembrance in things which need phylacteries. Register not only strange, but merciful occurrences. Let ephemerides, not olympiads, give thee account of His mercies;* let thy diaries stand thick with dutiful mementos and asterisks of acknowledgment. And to be complete and forget nothing, date not his mercy from thy nativity; look beyond the world, and before the æra of Adam.

XXII. Paint not the sepulchre of thyself, and strive not to beautify thy corruption. Be not an advocate for thy vices, nor call for many hour-glasses to justify thy imperfections.† Think not that always good which thou thinkest thou canst always make good, nor that concealed
which the sun doth not behold; that which the St. Luke
sun doth not now see will be visible when the viii. 17.
sun is out, and the stars are fallen from heaven.
Meanwhile there is no darkness unto conscience, 1 Cor. iv. 5.
which can see without light, and in the deepest obscurity give a clear draught of things, which the cloud of dissimulation hath concealed from all eyes. There is a natural standing court within us, examining, acquitting, and condemning at the tribunal of ourselves; wherein iniquities have their natural *thetas* ‡ and no nocent is absolved by the verdict of himself.§ And

* *Let ephemerides*, &c., that is, Take note of God's mercies day by day, not merely every four years.

† In the Athenian Courts the time allowed to each pleader was measured by a kind of hour-glass, called *clepshydra*.

‡ *Theta*, Θ, was the symbol used in condemnation to capital punishment, being the initial letter of Θάνατος.

§ "*Se judice, nemo nocens absolvitur.*"—Juv. Sat. xiii. 2.

therefore, although our transgressions shall be tried at the last bar, the process need not be long: for the Judge of all knoweth all, and every man will nakedly know himself; and when so few are like to plead *not guilty*, the assize must soon have an end.

XXIII. Comply with some humours, bear with others, but serve none. Civil complacency consists with decent honesty. Flattery is a juggler, and no kin unto sincerity. But while thou maintainest the plain path, and scornest to flatter others, fall not into self-adulation, and become not thine own parasite. Be deaf unto thyself, and be not betrayed at home. Self-credulity, pride, and levity lead unto self-idolatry. There is no Damocles* like unto self-opinion, nor any Siren to our own fawning conceptions. To magnify our minor things, or hug ourselves in our apparitions; to afford a credulous ear unto the clawing suggestions of fancy; to pass our days in painted mistakes of ourselves, and though we behold our own blood to think ourselves the sons of Jupiter: are blandishments of self-love, worse than outward delusion. By this imposture, wise men sometimes are mistaken in their elevation, and look above themselves. And fools, which are *antipodes* unto the wise, conceive themselves to

* *Damocles*, the parasite and flatterer of Dionysius.

be but their *periœci*, and in the same parallel with them.

XXIV. Be not a *Hercules Furens* abroad, and a poltroon within thyself. To chase our enemies out of the field, and be led captive by our vices; to beat down our foes, and fall down to our concupiscences; are solecisms in moral schools, and no laurel attends them. To well manage our affections, and wild horses of Plato, are the highest Circenses:* and the noblest digladiation is in the theatre of ourselves; for therein our inward antagonists, not only like common gladiators, with ordinary weapons and downright blows make at us, but also like retiary and laqueary combatants, with nets, frauds, and entanglements, fall upon us. Weapons for such combats are not to be forged at Lipara;† Vulcan's art doth nothing in this internal militia, wherein, not the armour of Achilles, but the armature of St. Paul, gives the glorious Eph. vi. 11-17.
day, and triumphs, not leading up into capitols, but up into the highest heavens. And, therefore, while so many think it the only valour to command and master others, study thou the

* Plato speaks of man as a charioteer driving two refractory steeds, given to quarrel; one being immortal and heavenly, the other mortal and of the earth. Χαλεπὴ δὴ καὶ δύσκολος ἐξ ἀνάγκης ἡ περὶ ἡμᾶς ἡνιόχησις. Phædrus, XXV.

† *Lipara*, where Vulcan's stithy was said to be.

dominion of thyself, and quiet thine own commotions. Let right reason be thy Lycurgus, and lift up thy hand unto the law of it: move by the intelligences of the superior faculties, not by the rapt of passion, nor merely by that of temper and constitution. They who are merely carried on by the wheel of such inclinations, without the hand and guidance of sovereign reason, are but the automatous part of mankind, rather lived than living, or at least underliving themselves.

XXV. Let not fortune, which hath no name in Scripture, have any in thy divinity. Let Providence, not chance, have the honour of thy acknowledgments, and be thy Œdipus in contingencies. Mark well the paths and winding ways thereof; but be not too wise in the construction, or sudden in the application. The hand of Providence writes often by abbreviatures, hieroglyphics, or short characters, which,
Dan. v. like the Laconism on the wall, are not to be made out but by a hint or key from that Spirit which indited them. Leave future occurrences to their uncertainties, think that which is present thine own: and since it is easier to foretell an eclipse than a foul day at some distance, look for little regular below. Attend with patience the uncertainty of things, and what lieth yet unexerted in the chaos of futurity. The uncer-

tainty and ignorance of things to come, makes the world new unto us by unexpected emergencies; whereby we pass not our days in the trite road of affairs affording no novity; for the novelizing spirit of man lives by variety, and the new faces of things.

XXVI. Though a contented mind enlargeth the dimension of little things; and unto some it is wealth enough not to be poor; and others are well content if they be but rich enough to be honest, and to give every man his due: yet fall not into that obsolete affectation of bravery, to throw away thy money, and to reject all honours or honourable stations in this courtly and splendid world. Old generosity is superannuated, and such contempt of the world out of date. No man is now like to refuse the favour of great ones, or be content to say unto princes, Stand out of my sun. And if there be any of such antiquated resolutions, they are not like to be tempted out of them by great ones: and 't is fair if they escape the name of hypochondriacs from the genius of latter times; unto whom contempt of the world is the most contemptible opinion, and to be able, like Bias, to carry all they have about them, were to be the eighth wise man. However, the old tetric philosophers looked always with indignation upon such a face of things; and, observing the unnatural current of riches, power, and honour in the world, and withal the imperfection and demerit of persons often advanced unto them, were tempted unto angry opinions, that affairs were ordered more by stars than reason, and that things went on rather by lottery than election.

XXVII. If thy vessel be but small in the ocean of this world, if meanness of possessions be thy allotment upon earth, forget not those virtues which the great Disposer of all bids thee to entertain from thy quality and condition; that is, submission, humility, content of mind, and industry. Content may dwell in all stations. To be low, but above contempt, may be high enough to be happy. But many of low degree may be higher than computed, and some cubits above the common commensuration; for in all states virtue gives qualifications and allowances, which make out defects. Rough diamonds are sometimes mistaken for pebbles; and meanness may be rich in accomplishments, which riches in vain desire. If our merits be above our stations, if our intrinsical value be greater than what we go for, or our value than our valuation, and if we stand higher in God's than in the censor's book,* it may make some equitable balance in the inequalities of this

* *Censor's book*, in which the name and estate of every Roman citizen was registered.

world, and there may be no such vast chasm or gulf between disparities as common measures determine. The Divine eye looks upon high and low differently from that of man. They who seem to stand upon Olympus, and high mounted unto our eyes, may be but in the valleys and low ground unto his; for he looks upon those as highest who nearest approach his divinity, and upon those as lowest who are farthest from it.

XXVIII. When thou lookest upon the imperfections of others, allow one eye for what is laudable in them, and the balance they have from some excellency, which may render them considerable. While we look with fear or hatred upon the teeth of the viper, we may behold his eye with love. In venomous natures something may be amiable: poisons afford anti-poisons: nothing is totally, or altogether uselessly bad. Notable virtues are sometimes dashed with notorious vices, and in some vicious tempers have been found illustrious acts of virtue; which makes such observable worth in some actions of King Demetrius, Antonius, and Ahab, as are not to be found in the same kind in Aristides, Numa, or David. Constancy, generosity, clemency, and liberality have been highly conspicuous in some persons not marked out in other concerns for example or imitation.

Cf. Rel. Med. Pt. 2, x.

But since goodness is exemplary in all, if others have not our virtues, let us not be wanting in theirs; nor, scorning them for their vices whereof we are free, be condemned by their virtues wherein we are deficient. There is dross, alloy, and embasement in all human tempers; and he flieth without wings, who thinks to find ophir or pure metal in any. For perfection is not, like light, centred in any one body; but, like the dispersed seminalities of vegetables at the creation, scattered through the whole mass of the earth, no place producing all, and almost all some. So that 't is well, if a perfect man can be made out of many men, and, to the perfect eye of God, even out of mankind. Time, which perfects some things, imperfects also others. Could we intimately apprehend the ideated man, and as he stood in the intellect of God upon the first exertion by creation, we might more narrowly comprehend our present degeneration, and how widely we are fallen from the pure exemplar and idea of our nature: for after this corruptive elongation from a primitive and pure creation, we are almost lost in degeneration; and Adam hath not only fallen from his Creator, but we ourselves from Adam, our Tycho and primary generator.

XXIX. Quarrel not rashly with adversities not yet understood, and overlook not the mercies often bound up in them; for we consider not sufficiently the good of evils, nor fairly compute the mercies of Providence in things afflictive at first hand. The famous Andreas Doria being invited to a feast by Aloysio Fieschi with design to kill him, just the night before fell mercifully into a fit of the gout, and so escaped that mischief. When Cato intended to kill himself, from a blow which he gave his servant, who would not reach his sword unto him, his hand so swelled that he had much ado to effect his design. Hereby any one but a resolved Stoic might have taken a fair hint of consideration, and that some merciful genius would have contrived his preservation. To be sagacious in such intercurrences is not superstition, but wary and pious discretion; and to contemn such hints were to be deaf unto the speaking hand of God, wherein Socrates and Cardan would hardly have been mistaken.

XXX. Break not open the gate of destruction, and make no haste or bustle unto ruin. Post not heedlessly on unto the *non ultra* of folly, or precipice of perdition. Let vicious ways have their tropics and deflexions, and swim in the waters of sin but as in the Asphaltic lake, though smeared and defiled, not to sink to the bottom. If thou hast dipped thy foot in the brink, yet venture not over Rubi-

con.* Run not into extremities from whence there is no regression. In the vicious ways of the world it mercifully falleth out that we become not extempore wicked, but it taketh some time and pains to undo ourselves. We
Iliad A. 590. fall not from virtue, like Vulcan from heaven, in a day. Bad dispositions required some time to grow into bad habits; bad habits must undermine good, and often repeated acts make us habitually evil; so that by gradual depravations, and while we are but staggeringly evil, we are not left without parentheses of considerations, thoughtful rebukes, and merciful interventions to recall us unto ourselves.† For the wisdom of God hath methodized the course of things unto the best advantage of goodness, and thinking considerators overlook not the tract thereof.

XXXI. Since men and women have their proper virtues and vices, and even twins of different sexes have not only distinct coverings in the womb, but differing qualities and virtuous habits after, transplace not their proprieties, and confound not their distinctions. Let mas-

* The river, by crossing which, Cæsar declared war against the Senate. Sueton. Jul. Cæs. 32. Lucan. Phars. i. 184.

† "Shame leaves us by degrees, not at first coming;
For nature checks a new offence with loathing,
But use of sin doth make it seem as nothing."
Daniell.

culine and feminine accomplishments shine in their proper orbs, and adorn their respective subjects. However, unite not the vices of both sexes in one; be not monstrous in iniquity, nor hermaphroditically vicious.

XXXII. If generous honesty, valour, and plain dealing be the cognizance of thy family, or characteristic of thy country, hold fast such inclinations sucked in with thy first breath, and which lay in the cradle with thee. Fall not into transforming degenerations, which under the old name create a new nation. Be not an alien in thine own nation; bring not Orontes into Tiber; learn the virtues, not the vices, of thy foreign neighbours, and make thy imitation by discretion, not contagion. Feel something of thyself in the noble acts of thy ancestors, and find in thine own genius that of thy predecessors. Rest not under the expired merits of others, shine by those of thine own. Flame not like the central fire which enlighteneth no eyes, which no man seeth, and most men think there is no such thing to be seen. Add one ray unto the common lustre; add not only to the number, but the note of thy generation; and prove not a cloud, but an asterisk in thy region.

Juv. Sat. iii. 62.

XXXIII. Since thou hast an alarum in thy breast, which tells thee thou hast a living spirit in thee above two thousand times in an hour, dull not away thy days in slothful supinity and the tediousness of doing nothing. To strenuous minds there is an inquietude in overquietness, and no laboriousness in labour; and to tread a mile after the slow pace of a snail, or the heavy measures of the lazy of Brazilia, were a most tiring penance, and worse than a race of some furlongs at the Olympics. The rapid courses of the heavenly bodies are rather imitable by our thoughts, than our corporeal motions: yet the solemn motions of our lives amount unto a greater measure than is commonly apprehended. Some few men have surrounded the globe of the earth; yet many in the set locomotions and movements of their days have measured the circuit of it, and twenty thousand miles have been exceeded by them. Move circumspectly, not meticulously, and rather carefully solicitous than anxiously solicitudinous. Think not there is a lion in the way, nor walk with leaden sandals in the paths of goodness; but in all virtuous motions let prudence determine thy measures. Strive not to run, like Hercules, a furlong in a breath: festination may prove precipitation; deliberating delay may be wise cunctation, and slowness no slothfulness.

Prov. xxii. 13.

XXXIV. Since virtuous actions have their

own trumpets, and, without any noise from thyself, will have their resound abroad, busy not Ps. cviii. 1.
thy best member in the encomium of thyself. Praise is a debt we owe unto the virtues of others, and due unto our own from all, whom malice hath not made mutes, or envy struck dumb. Fall not, however, into the common prevaricating way of self-commendation and boasting, by denoting the imperfections of others. Dante, Purg. xvii. 112.
He who discommendeth others, obliquely commendeth himself. He who whispers their infirmities, proclaims his own exemption from them; and consequently says, I am not as this St. Luke xviii. 11.
publican, or *hic niger*, whom I talk of. Open Hor. Sat. i. iv. 85.
ostentation and loud vainglory is more tolerable than this obliquity, as but containing some froth, no ink; as but consisting of a personal piece of folly, nor complicated with uncharitableness. Superfluously we seek a precarious applause abroad; every good man hath his *plaudite* within himself; and though his tongue be silent, is not without loud cymbals in his breast. Conscience will become his panegyrist, and never forget to crown and extol him unto himself.

XXXV. Bless not thyself only that thou wert born in Athens; but, among thy multiplied acknowledgments, lift up one hand unto heaven, that thou wert born of honest parents;

that modesty, humility, patience, and veracity lay in the same egg, and came into the world with thee. From such foundations thou mayest be happy in a virtuous precocity, and make an early and long walk in goodness; so mayest thou more naturally feel the contrariety of vice unto nature, and resist some by the antidote of thy temper. As charity covers, so modesty preventeth, a multitude of sins; withholding from noonday vices, and brazen-browed iniquities, from sinning on the house-top, and painting our follies with the rays of the sun. Where this virtue reigneth, though vice may show its head, it cannot be in its glory. Where shame of sin sets, look not for virtue to arise; for when modesty taketh wing, Astræa* goes soon after.

XXXVI. The heroical vein of mankind runs much in the soldiery and courageous part of the world, and in that form we oftenest find men above men. History is full of the gallantry of that tribe; and when we read their notable acts, we easily find what a difference there is between a life in Plutarch and in Laërtius. Where true fortitude dwells, loyalty, bounty, friendship, and fidelity may be found. A man may confide in persons constituted for noble

* *Astræa*, goddess of Justice, and consequently of all Virtue. Ovid. Met. i. 150. Faerie Queene, v. i. 11.

ends, who dare do and suffer, and who have a hand to burn for their country and their friend. Small and creeping things are the product of petty souls. He is like to be mistaken, who makes choice of a covetous man for a friend, or relieth upon the reed of narrow and poltroon friendship. Pitiful things are only to be found in the cottages of such breasts; but bright thoughts, clear deeds, constancy, fidelity, bounty, and generous honesty, are the gems of noble minds; wherein, to derogate from none, the true heroic English gentleman hath no peer.

Like *Mutius Scævola.* Liv. ii. 12.

PART II.

PUNISH not thyself with pleasure; glut not thy sense with palative delights, nor revenge the contempt of temperance by the penalty of satiety. Were there an age of delight or any pleasure durable, who would not honour Volupia? but the race of delight is short, and pleasures have mutable faces. The pleasures of one age are not pleasures in another, and their lives fall short of our own. Even in our sensual days, the strength of delight is in its seldomness or rarity, and sting in its satiety; mediocrity is its life, and immoderacy its confusion. The luxurious emperors of old inconsiderately satiated themselves with the dainties of sea and land, till, wearied through all varieties, their refections became a study unto them, and they were fain to feed by invention: novices in true epicurism! which by mediocrity, paucity, quick and healthful appetite, makes delights smartly acceptable; whereby Epicurus himself found *Jupiter's brain** in a piece of Cytheridian cheese, and the tongues of nightingales in a dish of onions. Hereby healthful and temperate poverty hath the start of nauseating luxury; unto whose clear and naked appetite every meal is a feast, and in one single dish the first course of Metellus; † who are cheaply hungry, and never lose their hunger or advantage of a craving appetite, because obvious food contents it; while Nero, half famished, could not feed upon a piece of bread, and, lingering after his snowed water, hardly got down an ordinary cup of *calda*.‡ By such circumscriptions of pleasure the contemned philosophers reserved unto themselves the secret of delight, which the *helluo's* of those days lost in their exorbitances. In vain we study delight: it is at the command of every sober mind, and in every sense born with us: but nature, who teacheth us the rule of pleasure, instructeth also in the bounds thereof, and where its line expireth. And therefore, temperate minds, not pressing their

* *Cerebrum Jovis*, for a delicious bit.

† *Metellus* his riotous pontifical supper, the great variety whereat is to be seen in Macrobius. Saturnal. iii. 13.

‡ *Calda*, tepid water with which the ancients tempered their wine. "*Fameque interim et siti interpellante, panem quidem sordidum oblatum adspernatus est, aquæ autem tepidæ aliquantum bibit.*" — Sueton. Nero, 48.

pleasures until the sting appeareth, enjoy their contentations contentedly and without regret; and so escape the folly of excess, to be pleased unto displacency.

II. Bring candid eyes unto the perusal of men's works, and let not Zoilism or detraction blast well-intended labours. He that endureth no faults in men's writings must only read his own, wherein for the most part all appeareth white. Quotation mistakes, inadvertency, expedition, and human lapses, may make, not only moles, but warts, in learned authors; who notwithstanding, being judged by the capital matter, admit not of disparagement. I should unwillingly affirm that Cicero was but slightly versed in Homer, because in his work *De Gloria* he ascribed those verses unto Ajax which were delivered by Hector. What if Plautus in the account of Hercules mistaketh nativity for conception? Who would have mean thoughts of Apollinaris Sidonius, who seems to mistake the river Tigris for Euphrates; and though a good historian and learned bishop of Auvergne had the misfortune to be out in the story of David, making mention of him when the ark was sent
1 Sam. vi. back by the Philistines upon a cart, which was before his time? Though I have no great opinion of Machiavel's learning, yet I shall not presently say that he was but a novice in Ro-

man history, because he was mistaken in placing Commodus after the Emperor Severus. Capital truths are to be narrowly eyed; collateral lapses and circumstantial deliveries not to be too strictly sifted. And if the substantial subject be well forged out, we need not examine the sparks which irregularly fly from it.

III. Let well-weighed considerations, not stiff and peremptory assumptions, guide thy discourses, pen, and actions. To begin or continue our works like Trismegistus of old, *verum certè verum atque verissimum est*, would sound arrogantly unto present ears in this strict inquiring age; wherein, for the most part, *probably* and *perhaps* will hardly serve to mollify the spirit of captious contradictors. If Cardan saith that a parrot is a beautiful bird, Scaliger will set his wits to work to prove it a deformed animal. The compage of all physical truths is not so closely jointed, but opposition may find intrusion; nor always so closely maintained, as not to suffer attrition. Many positions seem quodlibetically constituted, and like a Delphian blade will cut on both sides. Some truths seem almost falsehoods, and some falsehoods almost truths; wherein falsehood and truth seem almost equilibriously stated, and but a few grains of distinction to bear down the balance. Some have digged deep, yet glanced by the royal vein; and a man may come unto the pericardium, but not the heart of truth. Besides, many things are known, as some are seen, that is, by parallaxis, or at some distance from their true and proper beings, the superficial regard of things having a different aspect from their true and central natures. And this moves sober pens unto suspensory and timorous assertions, nor presently to obtrude them as Sibyls' leaves; which after considerations may find to be but folious appearances, and not the central and vital interiors of truth.

IV. Value the judicious, and let not mere acquests in minor parts of learning gain thy pre-existimation. It is an unjust way of compute, to magnify a weak head for some Latin abilities; and to undervalue a solid judgment, because he knows not the genealogy of Hector. When that notable king of France* would have his son to know but one sentence in Latin, had it been a good one, perhaps it had been enough. Natural parts and good judgments rule the world. States are not governed by ergotisms. Many have ruled well, who could not, perhaps, define a Commonwealth; and they who understand not the globe of the earth, command a great part of it. Where natural logic prevails not, artificial too often faileth. Where nature

* Louis XI. "*Qui nescit dissimulare nescit regnare.*"

fills the sails, the vessel goes smoothly on; and when judgment is the pilot, the insurance need not be high. When industry builds upon nature, we may expect pyramids: where that foundation is wanting, the structure must be low. They do most by books, who could do much without them; and he that chiefly owes himself unto himself, is the substantial man.

V. Let thy studies be free as thy thoughts and contemplations: but fly not only upon the wings of imagination; join sense unto reason, and experiment unto speculation, and so give life unto embryon truths and verities yet in their chaos. There is nothing more acceptable unto the ingenious world, than this noble eluctation of truth; wherein, against the tenacity of prejudice and prescription, this century now prevaileth. What libraries of new volumes after-times will behold, and in what a new world of knowledge the eyes of our posterity may be happy, a few ages may joyfully declare; and is but a cold thought unto those, who cannot hope to behold this exantlation of truth, or that obscured virgin half out of the pit: which might make some content with a commutation of the time of their lives, and to commend the fancy of the Pythagorean metempsychosis: whereby they might hope to enjoy this happiness in their third or fourth selves, and behold that in Pythagoras, which they now but foresee in Euphorbus.* The world, which took but six days to make, is like to take six thousand to make out: meanwhile old truths voted down begin to resume their places, and new ones arise upon us; wherein there is no comfort in the happiness of Tully's Elysium,† or any satisfaction from the ghosts of the ancients, who knew so little of what is now well known. Men disparage not antiquity, who prudently exalt new inquiries, and make not them the judges of truth, who were but fellow-inquirers of it. Who can but magnify the endeavours of Aristotle, and the noble start which learning had under him; or less than pity the slender progression made upon such advantages; while many centuries were lost in repetitions and transcriptions sealing up the book of knowledge? And therefore, rather than to swell the leaves of learning by fruitless repetitions, to sing the same song in all ages, nor adventure at essays beyond the attempt of others, many would be content that some would write like Helmont or Paracelsus; and be willing to en-

* Pythagoras, in accordance with his doctrine of metempsychosis, or more correctly metensomatosis, declared that he himself had been present at the siege of Troy as *Euphorbus*. Ovid. Met. xv. 160. Hor. Od. I. xxviii. 11.

† In which Socrates comforted himself that he should converse with the worthies of old. Tusc. Disp. i. xli.

dure the monstrosity of some opinions for divers singular notions requiting such aberrations.

VI. Despise not the obliquities of younger ways, nor despair of better things whereof there is yet no prospect. Who would imagine that Diogenes, who in his younger days was a falsifier of money, should, in the after course of his life, be so great a contemner of metal? Some negroes, who believe the resurrection, think that they shall rise white. Even in this life regeneration may imitate resurrection; our black and vicious tinctures may wear off, and goodness clothe us with candor. Good admonitions knock not always in vain. There will be signal examples of God's mercy, and the angels must not want their charitable rejoices for the conversion of lost sinners. Figures of most angles do nearest approach unto circles, which have no angles at all. Some may be near unto goodness who are conceived far from it; and many things happen, not likely to ensue from any promises of antecedencies. Culpable beginnings have found commendable conclusions, and infamous courses pious retractations. Detestable sinners have proved exemplary converts on earth, and may be glorious in the apartment of Mary Magdalen in heaven. Men are not the same through all divisions of their ages: time, experience, self-reflections, and God's mer-

St. Luke xv. 10.

15

cies, make in some well-tempered minds a kind of translation before death, and men to differ from themselves as well as from other persons. Hereof the old world afforded many examples to the infamy of latter ages, wherein men too often live by the rule of their inclinations; so that, without any astral prediction, the first day gives the last: men are commonly as they were; or rather, as bad dispositions run into worser habits, the evening doth not crown, but sourly conclude, the day.

VII. If the Almighty will not spare us according to his merciful capitulation at Sodom; if his goodness please not to pass over a great deal of bad for a small pittance of good, or to look upon us in the lump; there is slender hope for mercy, or sound presumption of fulfilling half his will, either in persons or nations: they who excel in some virtues being so often defective in others; few men driving at the extent and amplitude of goodness, but computing themselves by their best parts, and others by their worst, are content to rest in those virtues which others commonly want. Which makes this speckled face of honesty in the world; and which was the imperfection of the old philosophers and great pretenders unto virtue; who well declining the gaping vices of intemperance, incontinency, violence, and oppression, were yet blind-

Gen. xviii. 23-33.

ly peccant in iniquities of closer faces; were envious, malicious, contemners, scoffers, censurers, and stuffed with vizard vices, no less depraving the ethereal particle and diviner portion of man. For envy, malice, hatred, are the qualities of Satan, close and dark like himself; and where such brands smoke, the soul cannot be white. Vice may be had at all prices; expensive and costly iniquities which make the noise, cannot be every man's sins; but the soul may be foully inquinated at a very low rate, and a man may be cheaply vicious to the perdition of himself.

VIII. Opinion rides upon the neck of reason; and men are happy, wise, or learned, according as that empress shall set them down in the register of reputation. However, weigh not thyself in the scales of thy own opinion, but let the judgment of the judicious be the standard of thy merit. Self-estimation is a flatterer too readily entitling us unto knowledge and abilities, which others solicitously labour after, and doubtfully think they attain. Surely, such confident tempers do pass their days in best tranquillity; who, resting in the opinion of their own abilities, are happily gulled by such contentation; wherein pride, self-conceit, confidence, and opiniatrity will hardly suffer any to complain of imperfection. To think themselves in the right, or all that right, or only that, which they do or think, is a fallacy of high content; though others laugh in their sleeves, and look upon them as in a deluded state of judgment: wherein, notwithstanding, it were but a civil piece of complacency to suffer them to sleep who would not wake, to let them rest in their securities, nor by dissent or opposition to stagger their contentments.

IX. Since the brow speaks often true, since eyes and noses have tongues, and the countenance proclaims the heart and inclinations, let observation so far instruct thee in physiognomical lines, as to be some rule for thy distinction, and guide for thy affection unto such as look most like men. Mankind, methinks, is comprehended in a few faces, if we exclude all visages which any way participate of symmetries and schemes of look common unto other animals. For as though man were the extract of the world, in whom all were *in coagulato*, which in their forms were *in soluto* and at extension; we often observe that men do most act those creatures, whose constitution, parts, and complexion do most predominate in their mixtures. This is a corner-stone in physiognomy, and holds some truth not only in particular persons, but also in whole nations. There are, therefore, provincial faces, national lips and noses, which testify not only the natures of those countries, but of those which have them elsewhere. Thus we may make England the whole earth, dividing it not only into Europe, Asia, Africa, but the particular regions thereof; and may in some latitude affirm, that there are Egyptians, Scythians, Indians among us, who, though born in England, yet carry the faces and air of those countries, and are also agreeable and correspondent unto their natures. Faces look uniformly unto our eyes: how they appear unto some animals of a more piercing or differing sight, who are able to discover the inequalities, rubs and hairiness of the skin, is not without good doubt; and, therefore, in reference unto man, Cupid is said to be blind. Affection should not be too sharp-eyed, and love is not to be made by magnifying-glasses. If things were seen as they truly are, the beauty of bodies would be much abridged. And, therefore, the Wise Contriver hath drawn the pictures and outsides of things softly and amiably unto the natural edge of our eyes, not leaving them able to discover those uncomely asperities, which make oyster-shells in good faces, and hedgehogs even in Venus's moles.

X. Court not felicity too far, and weary not the favourable hand of fortune. Glorious actions have their times, extent, and *non ultra's.*

All 's Well that ends Well, iv. 3.

To put no end unto attempts were to make prescription of successes, and to bespeak unhappiness at the last; for the line of our lives is drawn with white and black vicissitudes, wherein the extremes hold seldom one complexion. That Pompey should obtain the surname of Great at twenty-five years; that men in their young and active days should be fortunate and perform notable things; is no observation of deep wonder, they having the strength of their fates before them, nor yet acted their parts in the world for which they were brought into it; whereas men of years, matured for counsels and designs, seem to be beyond the vigour of their active fortunes, and high exploits of life, providentially ordained unto ages best agreeable unto them. And, therefore, many brave men, finding their fortune grow faint, and feeling its declination, have timely withdrawn themselves from great attempts, and so escaped the ends of mighty men, disproportionable to their beginnings. But magnanimous thoughts have so dimmed the eyes of many, that forgetting the very essence of fortune, and the vicissitude of good and evil, they apprehend no bottom in felicity, and so have been still tempted on unto mighty actions, reserved for their destructions. For fortune lays the plot of our adversities in the foundation of our felicities, blessing us in

See the story of Polycrates and Amasis, Herod. iii. 40, seq.

the first quadrate, to blast us more sharply in the last. And since in the highest felicities there lieth a capacity of the lowest miseries, she hath this advantage from our happiness to make us truly miserable; for to become acutely miserable we are to be first happy. Affliction smarts most in the most happy state, as having somewhat in it of Belisarius at beggar's bush, or Bajazet in the grate. And this the fallen angels severely understand, who having acted their first part in Heaven, are made sharply miserable by transition, and more afflictively feel the contrary state of Hell.

XI. Carry no careless eye upon the unexpected scenes of things, but ponder the acts of Providence in the public ends of great and notable men, set out unto the view of all for no common memorandums. The tragical exits and unexpected periods of some eminent persons cannot but amuse considerate observators; wherein, notwithstanding, most men seem to see by extramission, without reception or self-reflection, and conceive themselves unconcerned by the fallacy of their own exemption; whereas, the mercy of God hath singled out but few to be the signals of his justice, leaving the generality of mankind to the pædagogy of example. But the inadvertency of our natures not well apprehending this favourable method

and merciful decimation, and that He showeth in some what others also deserve; they entertain no sense of his hand beyond the stroke of themselves. Whereupon the whole becomes necessarily punished, and the contracted hand of God extended unto universal judgments; from whence, nevertheless, the stupidity of our tempers receives but faint impressions, and in the most tragical state of times holds but starts of good motions. So that to continue us in goodness there must be iterated returns of misery, and a circulation in affliction is necessary. And since we cannot be wise by warnings; since plagues are insignificant, except we be personally plagued; since also we cannot be punished unto amendment by proxy or commutation, nor by vicinity, but contaction; there is an unhappy necessity that we must smart in our own skins, and the provoked arm of the Almighty must fall upon ourselves. The capital sufferings of others are rather our monitions than acquitments. There is but One who died salvifically for us, and able to say unto death, Hitherto shalt thou go, and no farther; only one enlivening death, which makes gardens of
1 Cor. xv. 43. graves, and that which was sowed in corruption to arise and flourish in glory: when death itself shall die, and living shall have no period; when the damned shall mourn at the funeral of death;

when life, not death, shall be the wages of sin: Rom. vi.
when the second death shall prove a miserable 23. Rev. vi.
life, and destruction shall be courted. 15-17.

XII. Although their thoughts may seem too severe, who think that few ill-natured men go to heaven; yet it may be acknowledged that good-natured persons are best founded for that place, who enter the world with good dispositions and natural graces, more ready to be advanced by impressions from above, and Christianized unto pieties, who carry about them plain and downright dealing minds, humility, mercy, charity, and virtues acceptable unto God and man. But whatever success they may have as to heaven, they are the acceptable men on earth, and happy is he who hath his quiver full of them for his friends. These are not the dens wherein falsehood lurks, and hypocrisy hides its head, wherein frowardness makes its nest, or where malice, hard-heartedness, and oppression love to dwell; not those by whom the poor get little, and the rich some time lose all; men, not of retracted looks, but who carry their hearts in their faces, and need not to be looked upon with perspectives; not sordidly or mischievously ingrateful; who cannot learn to ride upon the neck of the afflicted, nor load the heavy laden, but who keep the temple of Janus shut by peaceable and quiet tempers; who make not only the best friends, but the best enemies, as easier to forgive than offend, and ready to pass by the second offence before they avenge the first; who make natural Royalists, obedient Subjects, kind and merciful Princes, verified in our own, one of the best-natured Kings of this throne. Of the old Roman Emperors the best were the best-natured, though they made but a small number, and might be writ in a ring. Many of the rest were as bad men as princes; humourists, rather than of good humours; and of good natural parts, rather than of good natures, which did but arm their bad inclinations, and make them wittily wicked.

XIII. With what shift and pains we come into the world we remember not, but 't is commonly found no easy matter to get out of it. Many have studied to exasperate the ways of death, but fewer hours have been spent to soften that necessity. That the smoothest way unto the grave is made by bleeding, as common opinion presumeth, beside the sick and fainting languors which accompany that effusion, the experiment in Lucan and Seneca will make us doubt: under which the noble Stoic so deeply laboured, that, to conceal his affliction, he was fain to retire from the sight of his wife, and not ashamed to implore the merciful hand of his physician to shorten his misery therein.

Tacitus, Annal. xv. 63. 70.

Ovid, the old heroes, and the Stoics, who were so afraid of drowning, as dreading thereby the extinction of their soul, which they conceived to be a fire, stood probably in fear of an easier way of death; wherein the water, entering the possessions of air, makes a temperate suffocation, and kills, as it were, without a fever. Surely many who have had the spirit to destroy themselves, have not been ingenious in the contrivance thereof. 'T was a dull way practised by Themistocles, to overwhelm himself with bull's blood, who being an Athenian, might have held an easier theory of death from the state potion of his country; from which Socrates, in Plato, seemed not to suffer much more than from the fit of an ague. Cato is much to be pitied, who mangled himself with poniards; and Hannibal seems more subtle, who carried his delivery, not in the point, but the pummel of his sword.*

Ovid, Trist i. ii. 51, 52.

Vide Plutarch.

The Egyptians were merciful contrivers, who destroyed their malefactors by asps, charming their senses into an invincible sleep, and killing as it were with Hermes his rod. The Turkish emperor, odious for other cruelty, was herein a remarkable master of mercy, killing his favourite in his sleep, and sending him from the

* Wherein he is said to have carried something, whereby upon a struggle or despair he might deliver himself from all misfortunes. Juvenal says it was carried in a ring. Sat. x. 165.

shade into the house of darkness. He who had been thus destroyed would hardly have bled at the presence of his destroyer: when men are already dead by metaphor, and pass but from one sleep unto another, wanting herein the eminent part of severity to feel themselves to die; and escaping the sharpest attendant of death, the lively apprehension thereof. But to learn to die is better than to study the ways of dying. Death will find some ways to untie or cut the most Gordian knots of life, and make men's miseries as mortal as themselves; whereas evil spirits, as undying substances, are inseparable from their calamities; and, therefore, they everlastingly struggle under their angustias, and, bound up with immortality, can never get out of themselves.

PART III.

IT is hard to find a whole age to imitate, or what century to propose for example. Some have been far more approvable than others; but virtue and vice, panegyrics and satires, scatteringly to be found in all. History sets down not only things laudable, but abominable; things which should never have been, or never have been known; so that noble patterns must be fetched here and there from single persons, rather than whole nations; and from whole nations rather than any one. The world was early bad, and the first sin the most deplorable of any. The younger world afforded the oldest men, and perhaps the best and the worst, when length of days made virtuous habits heroical and immovable; vicious, inveterate and irreclaimable.
And since 't is said that the imaginations of Gen. vi 5
their hearts were evil, only evil, and continu-

ally evil; it may be feared that their sins held pace with their lives, and their longevity swelling their impieties, the longanimity of God would no longer endure such vivacious abominations. Their impieties were surely of a deep dye, which required the whole Element of Water to wash them away, and overwhelmed their memories with themselves; and so shut up the first windows of Time, leaving no histories of those longevous generations, when men might have been properly historians, when Adam might have read long lectures unto Methuselah, and Methuselah unto Noah. For had we been happy in just historical accounts of that unparalleled world, we might have been acquainted with wonders, and have understood not a little of the acts and undertakings of Moses his mighty men, and men of renown of old, which might have enlarged our thoughts, and made the world older unto us. For the unknown part of time shortens the estimation, if not the compute of it. What hath escaped our knowledge, falls not under our consideration; and what is and will be latent, is little better than non-existent.

II. Some things are dictated for our instruction, some acted for our imitation; wherein it is best to ascend unto the highest conformity, and to the honour of the exemplar. He honours

God, who imitates him;* for what we virtuously imitate we approve and admire; and since we delight not to imitate inferiors, we aggrandize and magnify those we imitate; since also we are most apt to imitate those we love, we testify our affection in our imitation of the inimitable. To affect to be like, may be no imitation; to act, and not to be what we pretend to imitate, is but a mimical conformation, and carrieth no virtue in it. Lucifer imitated not God, when he said he would be like the Highest; and he imitated not Jupiter, who counterfeited thunder. Where imitation can go no farther, let admiration step on, whereof there is no end in the wisest form of men. Even angels and spirits have enough to admire in their sublimer natures; admiration being the act of the creature, and not of God, who doth not admire himself. Created natures allow of swelling hyperboles; nothing can be said hyperbolically of God, nor will his attributes admit of expressions above their own exuperances. Trisme-

Salmoneus. Virg. Æn. vi. 585.

* "He prayeth well, who loveth well
Both man and bird and beast.
He prayeth best, who loveth best
All things both great and small;
For the dear God who loveth us,
He made and loveth all."
COLERIDGE.

Cf. St. Matt. vi. 12, 14, 15.

gistus his circle, whose centre is everywhere and circumference nowhere, was no hyperbole. Words cannot exceed, where they cannot express enough. Even the most winged thoughts fall at the setting out, and reach not the portal of Divinity.

III. In bivious theorems, and Janus-faced doctrines, let virtuous considerations state the determination. Look upon opinions as thou dost upon the moon, and choose not the dark hemisphere for thy contemplation. Embrace not the opacous and blind side of opinions, but that which looks most luciferously or influentially unto goodness. It is better to think that there are Guardian Spirits, than that there are no spirits to guard us; that vicious persons are slaves, than that there is any servitude in virtue; that times past have been better than times present, than that times were always bad; and that to be men it sufficeth to be no better than men in all ages, and so promiscuously to swim down the turbid stream, and make up the grand confusion. Sow not thy understanding with opinions, which make nothing of iniquities, and fallaciously extenuate transgressions. Look upon vices and vicious objects with hyperbolical eyes; and rather enlarge their dimensions, that their unseen deformities may not escape thy sense, and their poisonous parts and stings may appear massy and monstrous unto thee: for the undiscerned particles and atoms of evil deceive us, and we are undone by the invisibles of seeming goodness. We are only deceived in what is not discerned, and to err is but to be blind or dim-sighted as to some perceptions.

IV. To be honest in a right line, and virtuous by epitome, be firm unto such principles of goodness as carry in them volumes of instruction and may abridge thy labour. And since instructions are many, hold close unto those, whereon the rest depend; so may we have all in a few, and the law and the prophets in a rule; the Sacred Writ in stenography, and the Scripture in a nut-shell. To pursue the osseous and solid part of goodness, which gives stability and rectitude to all the rest; to settle on fundamental virtues, and bid early defiance unto mother-vices, which carry in their bowels the seminals of other iniquities, makes a short cut in goodness, and strikes not off a head, but the whole neck of Hydra. For we are carried into the dark lake, like the Egyptian river into the sea, by seven principal ostiaries: the mother-sins of that number are the deadly engines of evil spirits that undo us, and even evil spirits themselves; and he who is under the chains thereof is not without a possession. Mary Mag-

Linea recta brevissima.

St. Luke viii. 2. dalene had more than seven devils, if these
with their imps were in her; and he who is
viii. 30. thus possessed, may literally be named Legion. Where such plants grow and prosper, look for no champaign or region void of thorns; but productions like the tree of Goa,* and forests of abomination.

V. Guide not the hand of God, nor order the finger of the Almighty unto thy will and pleasure; but sit quiet in the soft showers of Providence, and favourable distributions in this world, either to thyself or others. And since not only judgments have their errands, but mercies their commissions, snatch not at every favour, nor think thyself passed by if they fall upon thy neighbour. Rake not up envious displacences at things successful unto others, which the Wise Disposer of all things thinks not fit for thyself. Reconcile the events of things unto both beings, that is, of this world and the next; so will there not seem so many riddles in Providence, nor various inequalities in the dispensation of things below. If thou dost not anoint thy face, yet put not on sackcloth at the
Faerie Queene i. iv. 30. felicities of others. Repining at the good draws
on rejoicing at the evils of others, and so falls into

* *Arbor Goa de Ruyz*, or *Ficus Indica*, whose branches send down shoots which root in the ground, from whence there successively rise others, till one tree becomes a wood. Plin. H. N. xii. 5. Milton, P. L. ix. 1101.

that inhuman vice for which so few languages have a name. The blessed spirits above rejoice at our happiness below; but to be glad at the evils of one another is beyond the malignity of hell, and falls not on evil spirits, who, though they rejoice at our unhappiness, take no pleasure at the afflictions of their own society or of their fellow natures. Degenerous heads! who must be fain to learn from such examples, and to be taught from the School of Hell.

VI. Grain not thy vicious stains, nor deepen those swart tinctures which temper, infirmity, or ill habits have set upon thee; and fix not, by iterated depravations, what time might efface, or virtuous washes expunge. He who thus still advanceth in iniquity, deepeneth his deformed hue, turns a shadow into night, and makes himself a negro in the black jaundice; and so becomes one of those lost ones, the disproportionate pores of whose brains afford no entrance unto good motions, but reflect and frustrate all counsels, deaf unto the thunder of the laws, and rocks unto the cries of charitable commiserators. He who hath had the patience of Diogenes, to make orations unto statues, may more sensibly apprehend how all words fall to the ground, spent upon such a surd and earless generation of men, stupid unto all instruction, and rather requiring an exorcist than an orator for their conversion!

VII. Burden not the back of Aries, Leo, or Taurus with thy faults; nor make Saturn, Mars, or Venus guilty of thy follies. Think not to fasten thy imperfections on the stars, and so despairingly conceive thyself under a fatality of being evil. Calculate thyself within; seek not thyself in the moon, but in thine own orb or microcosmical circumference. Let celestial aspects admonish and advertise, not conclude and determine thy ways. For since good and bad stars moralize not our actions, and neither excuse or commend, acquit or condemn our good or bad deeds at the present or last bar; since some are astrologically well disposed who are morally highly vicious; not celestial figures, but virtuous schemes, must denominate and state our
Ps. cxlvii. 4. actions. If we rightly understood the names
Is. xl. 26. whereby God calleth the stars; if we knew his
Cf. Job xxxviii. 31, 32. name for the Dog-star, or by what appellation
Jupiter, Mars, and Saturn obey his will; it might be a welcome accession unto astrology, which speaks great things, and is fain to make use of appellations from Greek and Barbaric systems. Whatever influences, impulsions, or inclinations there be from the lights above, it were a piece of wisdom to make one of those
Sapiens dominabitur astris. wise men who overrule their stars, and with
their own Militia contend with the Host of Heaven. Unto which attempt there want not

auxiliaries from the whole strength of morality, supplies from Christian ethics, influences also and illuminations from above, more powerful than the Lights of Heaven.

VIII. Confound not the distinctions of thy life which nature hath divided; that is, youth, adolescence, manhood, and old age: nor in these divided periods, wherein thou art in a manner four, conceive thyself but one. Let every division be happy in its proper virtues, nor one vice run through all. Let each distinction have its salutary transition, and critically deliver thee from the imperfections of the former; so ordering the whole, that prudence and virtue may have the largest section. Do 1 Cor. xiii.
as a child but when thou art a child, and ride 11. Hor. Sat. ii.
not on a reed at twenty. 3. 248.
He who hath not taken leave of the follies of his youth, and in his maturer state scarce got out of that division, disproportionately divideth his days, crowds up the latter part of his life, and leaves too narrow a corner for the age of wisdom; and so hath room to be a man, scarce longer than he hath been a youth. Rather than to make this confusion, anticipate the virtues of age, and live long without the infirmities of it. So mayest thou count up thy days as some do Adam's, that is, by anticipation; so mayest thou be coetaneous Cf. Rel.
unto thy elders, and a father unto thy contem- Med. xxii. xxxix.
poraries.

IX. While others are curious in the choice of good air, and chiefly solicitous for healthful habitations, study thou conversation, and be critical in thy consortion. The aspects, conjunctions, and configurations of the stars, which mutually diversify, intend, or qualify their influences, are but the varieties of their nearer or farther conversation with one another, and like the consortion of men, whereby they become better or worse, and even exchange their natures. Since men live by examples, and will be imitating something, order thy imitation to thy improvement, not thy ruin. Look not for roses in Attalus his garden,* or wholesome flowers in a venomous plantation. And since there is scarce any one bad, but some others are the worse for him, tempt not contagion by proximity, and hazard not thyself in the shadow of corruption. He who hath not early suffered this shipwreck, and in his younger days escaped this Charybdis, may make a happy voyage, and not come in with black sails into the port. Self-conversation, or to be alone, is better than such consortion. Some schoolmen tell us, that he is properly alone, with whom in the same place there is no other of the same species. Nebuchadnezzar

Vide *Theseus* in Plutarch.

Dan. iv.

* *Omissa deinde regni administratione, hortos fodiebat, gramina seminabat, et noxia innoxiis permiscebat; eaque omnia veneni succo infecta, velut peculiare munus, amicis mittebat.* Justin. Hist. xxxvi. 4.

was alone, though among the beasts of the field; and a wise man may be tolerably said to be alone, though with a rabble of people little better than the beasts about him. Unthinking heads, who have not learned to be alone, are in a prison to themselves, if they be not also with others: whereas, on the contrary, they whose thoughts are in a fair, and hurry within, are sometimes fain to retire into company, to be out of the crowd of themselves. He who must needs have company, must needs have sometimes bad company. Be able to be alone. Lose not the advantage of solitude, and the society of thyself; nor be only content, but delight to be alone and single with Omnipresency. He who is thus prepared, the day is not uneasy, nor the night black unto him. Darkness may bound his eyes, not his imagination. In his bed he may lie, like Pompey and his sons, in all quarters of the earth;* may speculate the universe, and enjoy the whole world in the hermitage of himself. Thus the old ascetic Christians found a paradise in a desert, and with little converse on earth held a conversation in heaven; thus they astronomised in caves, and, though they beheld not the stars, had the glory of heaven before them.

* "*Pompeios Juvenes Asia atque Europa, sed ipsum terra tegit Libyes.*"

X. Let the characters of good things stand indelibly in thy mind, and thy thoughts be active on them. Trust not too much unto suggestions from reminiscential amulets, or artificial memorandums. Let the mortifying Janus of Covarrubias* be in thy daily thoughts, not only on thy hand and signets. Rely not alone upon silent and dumb remembrances. Behold not death's heads till thou dost not see them, nor look upon mortifying objects till thou overlookest them. Forget not how assuefaction unto anything minorates the passion from it; how constant objects lose their hints, and steal an inadvertisement upon us. There is no excuse to forget what everything prompts unto us. To thoughtful observators, the whole world is a phylactery; and everything we see, an item of the wisdom, power, or goodness of God. Happy are they who verify their amulets, and make their phylacteries speak in their lives and actions. To run on in despite of the revulsions and pull-backs of such remoras, aggravates our transgressions. When death's heads on our hands have no influence upon our heads, and

* Don Sebastian de Covarrubias writ three centuries of moral emblems, in Spanish. In the 88th of the second century, he sets down two faces averse, and conjoined, Janus-like; the one a gallant beautiful face, the other a death's-head face, with this motto out of Ovid his Metamorphosis,

"Quid fuerim, quid simque, vide."

fleshless cadavers abate not the exorbitances of the flesh; when crucifixes upon men's hearts suppress not their bad commotions, and His image who was murdered for us withholds not from blood and murder; phylacteries prove but formalities, and their despised hints sharpen our condemnations.

XI. Look not for whales in the Euxine Sea, or expect great matters where they are not to be found. Seek not for profundity in shallowness, or fertility in a wilderness. Place not the expectation of great happiness here below, or think to find heaven on earth; wherein we must be content with embryon felicities, and fruitions of doubtful faces: for the circle of our felicities makes but short arches. In every clime we are in a periscian state;* and, with our light, our shadow and darkness walk about us. Our contentments stand upon the tops of pyramids, ready to fall off, and the insecurity of their enjoyments abrupteth our tranquillities. What we magnify is magnificent, but, like to the Colossus, noble without, stuffed with rubbish and coarse metal within. Even the sun, whose glorious outside we behold, may have dark and smoky entrails. In vain we admire

* The Periscii are those who, living within the polar circle, see the sun move round them, and consequently project their shadows in all directions.

the lustre of anything seen: that which is truly glorious, is invisible. Paradise was but a part of the earth, lost not only to our fruition but our knowledge. And if, according to old dictates, no man can be said to be happy before death; the happiness of this life goes for nothing before it be over, and while we think ourselves happy we do but usurp that name. Certainly, true beatitude groweth not on earth, nor hath this world in it the expectations we have of it. He swims in oil, and can hardly avoid sinking, who hath such light foundations to support him: 't is therefore happy, that we have two worlds to hold on. To enjoy true happiness we must travel into a very far country, and even out of ourselves; for the pearl we seek for is not to be found in the Indian, but in the empyrean ocean.

Eccl. vii. 9. XII. Answer not the spur of fury, and be not prodigal or prodigious in revenge. Make not one in the *Historia horribilis;* flay not thy servant for a broken glass, nor pound him in a mortar who offendeth thee; supererogate not in the worst sense, and overdo not the necessities of evil; humour not the injustice of revenge. Be not stoically mistaken in the equality of sins, nor commutatively iniquous in the valuation of transgressions; but weigh them in the scales of heaven, and by the weights of

See *Vedius Pollio*, Plin. H. N. ix. 23. Calmet on Prov. xxvii. 22.

righteous reason. Think that revenge too high which is but level with the offence. Let thy arrows of revenge fly short; or be aimed like those of Jonathan, to fall beside the mark. Too 1 Sam. xx. 20.
many there be to whom a dead enemy smells well, and who find musk and amber in revenge. The ferity of such minds holds no rule in retaliations; requiring too often a head for a tooth, and the supreme revenge for trespasses which a night's rest should obliterate. But patient meekness takes injuries like pills, not chewing, but swallowing them down, laconically suffering, and silently passing them over; while angered pride makes a noise, like Homerican Juv. Sat. xiii. 112.
Mars, at every scratch of offences. Since women do most delight in revenge, it may seem Sat. xiii. 190.
but feminine manhood to be vindictive. If thou must needs have thy revenge of thine enemy, with a soft tongue break his bones, heap coals Prov. xxv. 15, 21, 22.
of fire on his head, forgive him and enjoy it. To forgive our enemies is a charming way of revenge, and a short Cæsarean conquest, overcoming without a blow; laying our enemies at our feet, under sorrow, shame, and repentance; leaving our foes our friends, and solicitously inclined to grateful retaliations. Thus to return upon our adversaries is a healing way of revenge; and to do good for evil a soft and melting ultion, a method taught from heaven to

keep all smooth on earth.* Common forcible ways make not an end of evil, but leave hatred and malice behind them. An enemy thus reconciled is little to be trusted, as wanting the foundation of love and charity, and but for a time restrained by disadvantage or inability. If thou hast not mercy for others, yet be not cruel unto thyself. To ruminate upon evils, to make critical notes upon injuries, and be too acute in their apprehensions, is to add unto our own tortures, to feather the arrows of our enemies, to lash ourselves with the scorpions of our foes, and to resolve to sleep no more; for injuries long dreamt on, take away at last all rest; and he sleeps but like Regulus who busieth his head about them.†

XIII. Amuse not thyself about the riddles of future things. Study prophecies when they are become histories, and past hovering in their causes. Eye well things past and present, and let conjectural sagacity suffice for things to come. There is a sober latitude for prescience in contingencies of discoverable tempers, whereby discerning heads see sometimes beyond their eyes,

* "Hath any wronged thee? be bravely revenged; sleight it, and the work 's begun; forgive it, 't is finisht: he is below himselfe that is not above an injury." — Quarles's Enchir. ii. 86.

† *Like Regulus.* Dion Cassius relates that, when Regulus fell into the hands of the Carthaginians, he was kept shut up with an Elephant, in order that his sleep might be disturbed.

and wise men become prophetical. Leave cloudy predictions to their periods, and let appointed seasons have the lot of their accomplishments. It is too early to study such prophecies before they have been long made, before some train of their causes have already taken fire, laying open in part what lay obscure and before buried unto us. For the voice of prophecies is like that of whispering-places; they who are near, or at a little distance, hear nothing; those at the farthest extremity will understand all. But a retrograde cognition of times past, and things which have already been, is more satisfactory than a suspended knowledge of what is yet unexistent. And the greatest part of time being already wrapt up in things behind us, it is now somewhat late to bait after things before us; for futurity still shortens, and time present sucks in time to come. What is prophetical in one age, proves historical in another, and so must hold on unto the last of time; when there will be no room for prediction, when Janus shall lose one face, and the long beard of time shall look like those of David's servants, 2 Sam. x. 4.
shorn away upon one side; and when, if the expected Elias should appear, he might say much of what is past, not much of what is to come.

XIV. Live unto the dignity of thy nature,

and leave it not disputable at last, whether thou hast been a man; or, since thou art a composition of man and beast, how thou hast predominantly passed thy days, to state the denomination. Unman not, therefore, thyself by a bestial transformation, nor realize old fables. Expose not thyself by four-footed manners unto monstrous draughts, and caricatura representations. Think not after the old Pythagorean conceit, what beast thou mayest be after death. Be not under any brutal metempsychosis while thou livest, and walkest about erectly under the scheme of man. In thine own circumference, as in that of the earth, let the rational horizon be larger than the sensible, and the circle of reason than of sense; let the divine part be upward, and the region of beast below; otherwise, it is but to live invertedly, and with thy head unto the heels of thy antipodes. Desert not thy title to a divine particle and union with invisibles. Let true knowledge and virtue tell the lower world thou art a part of the higher. Let thy thoughts be of things which have not entered into the hearts of beasts; think of things long passed, and long to come: acquaint thyself with the *choragium* of the stars, and consider the vast expansion beyond them. Let intellectual tubes give thee a glance of things, which visive organs reach not. Have a glimpse of incomprehensibles, and thoughts of things which thoughts but tenderly touch. Lodge immaterials in thy head; ascend unto invisibles; fill thy spirit with spirituals, with the mysteries of faith, the magnalities of religion, and thy life with the honour of God; without which, though giants in wealth and dignity, we are but dwarfs and pigmies in humanity, and may hold a pitiful rank in that triple division of mankind into heroes, men, and beasts. For though human souls are said to be equal, yet is there no small inequality in their operations; some maintain the allowable station of men; many are far below it; and some have been so divine as to approach the *apogeum* of their natures, and to be in the *confinium* of spirits.

XV. Behold thyself by inward optics and the crystalline of thy soul. Strange it is, that in the most perfect sense there should be so many fallacies, that we are fain to make a doctrine, and often to see by art. But the greatest imperfection is in our inward sight, that is, to be ghosts unto our own eyes; and while we are so sharp-sighted as to look through others, to be invisible unto ourselves; for the inward eyes are more fallacious than the outward.*

* "Is it because the mind is like the eye
(Through which it gathers knowledge by degrees),
Whose rays reflect not, but spread outwardly;
Not seeing itself when other things it sees?

The vices we scoff at in others laugh at us within ourselves. Avarice, pride, falsehood lie undiscerned and blindly in us, even to the age of blindness; and, therefore, to see ourselves interiorly, we are fain to borrow other men's eyes; wherein true friends are good informers, and censurers no bad friends. Conscience only, that can see without light, sits in the Areopagy and dark tribunal of our hearts, surveying our thoughts and condemning their obliquities. Happy is that state of vision that can see without light, though all should look as before the creation, when there was not an eye to see, or light to actuate a vision: wherein, notwithstanding, obscurity is only imaginable respectively unto eyes: for unto God there was none; eternal Light was ever; created light was for the creation, not himself; and as he saw before the sun, may still also see without it. In the city
Rev. xxi. 23. of the new Jerusalem there is neither sun nor
xxii. 5. moon; where glorified eyes must see by the archetypal Sun, or the light of God, able to illuminate intellectual eyes, and make unknown visions. Intuitive perceptions in spiritual be-

"No, doubtless; for the mind can backward cast
Upon herself her understanding light;
But she is so corrupt, and so defaced,
As her own image doth herself affright."
Sir John Davies.

Cf. Troilus and Cressida, iii. 3.

ings may, perhaps, hold some analogy unto vision; but yet how they see us, or one another, what eye, what light, or what perception is required unto their intuition, is yet dark unto our apprehension: and even how they see God, or how unto our glorified eyes the beatifical vision will be celebrated, another world must tell us, when perceptions will be new, and we may hope to behold invisibles. Cf. Rel. Med. xlix.

XVI. When all looks fair about, and thou seest not a cloud so big as a hand to threaten thee, forget not the wheel of things: think of sullen vicissitudes, but beat not thy brains to foreknow them. Be armed against such obscurities, rather by submission than foreknowledge. The knowledge of future evils mortifies present felicities, and there is more content in the uncertainty or ignorance of them. This favour our Saviour vouchsafed unto Peter, when he foretold not his death in plain terms, and so by an ambiguous and cloudy delivery damped not the spirit of his disciples. But in the assured foreknowledge of the deluge, Noah lived many years under the affliction of a flood; and Jerusalem was taken unto Jeremiah before it was besieged. And therefore the wisdom of astrologers, who speak of future things, hath wisely softened the severity of their doctrines; and even in their sad predictions, while they

1 Kings xviii. 44.

St. John xxi. 18, 19.

tell us of inclination, not coaction, from the stars, they kill us not with Stygian oaths and merciless necessity, but leave us hope of evasion.

XVII. If thou hast the brow to endure the name of traitor, perjured, or oppressor, yet cover thy face when ingratitude is thrown at thee. If that degenerous vice possess thee, hide thyself in the shadow of thy shame, and pollute not noble society. Grateful ingenuities are content to be obliged within some compass of retribution; and being depressed by the weight of iterated favours, may so labour under their inabilities of requital, as to abate the content from kindnesses. But narrow, self-ended souls make prescription of good offices, and, obliged by often favours, think others still due unto them: whereas, if they but once fail, they prove so perversely ungrateful as to make nothing of former courtesies, and to bury all that is past. Such tempers pervert the generous course of things; for they discourage the inclinations of noble minds, and make beneficency cool unto acts of obligation, whereby the grateful world should subsist, and have their consolation. Common gratitude must be kept alive by the additionary fuel of new courtesies: but generous gratitudes, though but once well obliged, without quickening repetitions or expectation of new favours, have thankful minds forever; for they write not their obligations in sandy, but marble memories, which wear not out but with themselves.

XVIII. Think not silence the wisdom of fools, but, if rightly timed, the honour of wise men who have not the infirmity but the virtue of taciturnity; and speak not out of the abundance, but the well-weighed thoughts of their hearts. Such silence may be eloquence, and speak thy worth above the power of words. Make such a one thy friend, in whom princes may be happy, and great counsels successful. Let him have the key of thy heart, who hath the lock of his own, which no temptation can open;* where thy secrets may lastingly lie, like the lamp in Olybius his urn, alive, and light, but close and invisible.

St. Matt. xii. 34, 36.

XIX. Let thy oaths be sacred, and promises be made upon the altar of thy heart. Call not Jove to witness, with a stone in one hand, and a straw in another; and so make chaff and stubble of thy vows. Worldly spirits, whose interest is their belief, make cobwebs of obligations; and, if they can find ways to elude the urn of the Prætor,† will trust the thunderbolt

Cic. Ep. ad Fam. vii. 12.

* " . . . . keep thy friend
Under thy own life's key."
All 's Well that Ends Well, i. 1. Cf. Ham. iii. 2.

† The vessel into which the ticket of condemnation or acquittal was cast. Dr. Johnson.

of Jupiter; and, therefore, if they should as deeply swear as Osman to Bethlem Gabor, yet whether they would be bound by those chains, and not find ways to cut such Gordian knots, we could have no just assurance. But honest men's words are Stygian oaths, and promises inviolable. These are not the men for whom the fetters of law were first forged; they needed not the solemnness of oaths; by keeping their faith they swear, and evacuate such confirmations.

Knolles's Hist. of the Turks, p. 1383.

Colendo fidem jurant. Curtius.

XX. Though the world be histrionical, and most men live ironically, yet be thou what thou singly art, and personate only thyself. Swim smoothly in the stream of thy nature, and live but one man. To single hearts doubling is discruciating: such tempers must sweat to dissemble, and prove but hypocritical hypocrites. Simulation must be short: men do not easily continue a counterfeiting life, or dissemble unto death. He who counterfeiteth, acts a part; and is, as it were, out of himself: which, if long, proves so irksome, that men are glad to pull off their vizards, and resume themselves again; no practice being able to naturalize such unnaturals, or make a man rest content not to be himself. And therefore, since sincerity is thy temper, let veracity be thy virtue, in words, manners, and actions. To offer at iniquities, which have so little foundations in thee, were to be vicious up-hill, and strain for thy condemnation. Persons viciously inclined want no wheels to make them actively vicious; as having the elater and spring of their own natures to facilitate their iniquities. And therefore so many who are sinistrous unto good actions, are ambidexterous unto bad; and Vulcans in virtuous paths, Achilleses in vicious motions.

XXI. Rest not in the high-strained paradoxes of old philosophy, supported by naked reason and the reward of mortal felicity; but labour in the ethics of faith, built upon heavenly assistance, and the happiness of both beings. Understand the rules, but swear not unto the doctrines of Zeno or Epicurus. Look beyond Antoninus, and terminate not thy morals in Seneca or Epictetus. Let not the twelve, but the two tables be thy Law: let Pythagoras be thy remembrancer, not thy textuary and final instructor; and learn the vanity of the world rather from Solomon than Phocylides. Sleep not in the dogmas of the Peripatus, Academy, or Porticus. Be a moralist of the Mount,* an Epictetus in the faith, and Christianize thy notions.

XXII. In seventy or eighty years a man

* That is, Live according to the rules laid down in our Saviour's Sermon on the Mount. St. Matt. v., vi., vii.

may have a deep gust of the world, know what it is, what it can afford, and what it is to have been a man. Such a latitude of years may hold a considerable corner in the general map of time; and a man may have a curt epitome of the whole course thereof in the days of his own life; may clearly see he hath but acted over his forefathers, what it was to live in ages past, and what living will be in all ages to come.

He is like to be the best judge of time who hath lived to see about the sixtieth part thereof. Persons of short times may know what it is to live, but not the life of man, who, having little behind them, are but Januses of one face, and know not singularities enough to raise axioms of this world: but such a compass of years will show new examples of old things, parallelisms of occurrences through the whole course of time, and nothing be monstrous unto him, who may in that time understand not only the varieties of men, but the variation of himself, and how many men he hath been in that extent of time.

He may have a close apprehension what it is to be forgotten, while he hath lived to find none who could remember his father, or scarce the friends of his youth; and may sensibly see with what a face in no long time oblivion will look upon himself. His progeny may never be his posterity; he may go out of the world less related than he came into it; and, considering the frequent mortality in friends and relations, in such a term of time, he may pass away divers years in sorrow and black habits, and leave none to mourn for himself; orbity may be his inheritance, and riches his repentance.

In such a thread of time, and long observation of men, he may acquire a physiognomical intuitive knowledge; judge the interiors by the outside, and raise conjectures at first sight; and knowing what men have been, what they are, what children probably will be, may in the present age behold a good part and the temper of the next; and since so many live by the rules of constitution, and so few overcome their temperamental inclinations, make no improbable predictions.

Such a portion of time will afford a large prospect backward, and authentic reflection show how far he hath performed the great intention of his being, in the honour of his Maker; whether he hath made good the principles of his nature, and what he was made to be; what characteristic and special mark he hath left, to be observable in his generation; whether he hath lived to purpose or in vain; and what he hath added, acted, or performed, that might considerably speak him a man.

Eccles. xii. In such an age, delights will be undelightful, and pleasures grow stale unto him; antiquated theorems will revive, and Solomon's maxims be demonstrations unto him; hopes or presumptions be over, and despair grow up of any satisfaction below. And having been long tossed in the ocean of this world, he will by that time feel the in-draught of another, unto which this seems but preparatory and without it of no high value. He will experimentally find the emptiness of all things, and the nothing of what is past; and wisely grounding upon true Christian expectations, finding so much past, will wholly fix upon what is to come. He will long for perpetuity, and live as though he made haste to be happy. The last may prove the prime part of his life, and those his best days which he lived nearest heaven.

XXIII. Live happy in the Elysium of a virtuously composed mind, and let intellectual contents exceed the delights wherein mere pleasurists place their paradise. Bear not too slack reins upon pleasure, nor let complexion or contagion betray thee unto the exorbitancy of delight. Make pleasure thy recreation or intermissive relaxation, not thy Diana, life, and profession. Voluptuousness is as insatiable as covetousness. Tranquillity is better than jollity, and to appease pain than to invent pleasure. Our hard entrance into the world, our miserable going out of it, our sicknesses, disturbances, and sad rencounters in it, do clamorously tell us we came not into the world to run a race of delight, but to perform the sober acts and serious purposes of man; which to omit were foully to miscarry in the advantage of humanity, to play away an uniterable life, and to have lived in vain. Forget not the capital end, and frustrate not the opportunity of once living. Dream not of any kind of metempsychosis or transanimation, but into thine own body, and that after a long time; and then also unto wail or bliss, according to thy first and fundamental life. Upon a curricle in this world depends a long course of the next, and upon a narrow scene here an endless expansion hereafter. In vain some think to have an end of their beings with their lives. Things cannot get out of their natures, or be, or not be, in despite of their constitutions. Rational existences in heaven perish not at all, and but partially on earth: that which is thus once, will in some way be always: the first living human soul is still alive, and all Adam hath found no period.

XXIV. Since the stars of heaven do differ 1 Cor. xv. 41.
in glory; since it hath pleased the Almighty hand to honour the north pole with lights above the south; since there are some stars so bright

that they can hardly be looked upon, some so dim that they can scarcely be seen, and vast numbers not to be seen at all even by artificial eyes; read thou the earth in heaven, and things below from above. Look contentedly upon the scattered difference of things, and expect not equality in lustre, dignity, or perfection, in regions or persons below; where numerous numbers must be content to stand like lacteous or nebulous stars, little taken notice of, or dim in their generations. All which may be contentedly allowable in the affairs and ends of this world, and in suspension unto what will be in the order of things hereafter, and the new system of mankind which will be in the world to
St. Matt. xix. 30. come; when the last may be the first, and the first the last; when Lazarus may sit above
St. Matt. xiii. 43. Cæsar, and the just obscure on earth shall shine like the sun in heaven; when personations shall cease, and histrionism of happiness be over; when reality shall rule, and all shall be as they shall be forever.

XXV. When the Stoic said that life would not be accepted if it were offered unto such as knew it,* he spoke too meanly of that state of being which placeth us in the form of men. It more depreciates the value of this life, that men would not live it over again; for although

* *Vitam nemo acciperet, si daretur scientibus.* — Seneca.

they would still live on, yet few or none can endure to think of being twice the same men upon earth, and some had rather never have lived, than to tread over their days once more. Cicero in a prosperous state had not the patience to think of beginning in a cradle again. Job would not only curse the day of his nativity, but also of his renascency, if he were to act over his disasters and the miseries of the dunghill. But the greatest underweening of this life is to undervalue that unto which this is but exordial, or a passage leading unto it. The great advantage of this mean life is thereby to stand in a capacity of a better; for the colonies of heaven must be drawn from earth, and the sons of the first Adam are only heirs unto the second. Thus Adam came into this world with the power also of another; not only to replenish the earth, but the everlasting mansions of heaven. Where we were when the foundations of the earth were laid, when the morning stars sang together, and all the sons of God shouted for joy, He must answer who asked it; who understands entities of preordination, and beings yet unbeing; who hath in his intellect the ideal existences of things, and entities before their extances. Though it looks but like an imaginary kind of existency, to be before we are; yet since we are under the decree or prescience

De Senectute, xxiii.

Job iii.

Job xxxviii. 4-7.

of a sure and omnipotent power, it may be somewhat more than a nonentity to be in that
Cf. Ps. cxxxix. mind, unto which all things are present.

XXVI. If the end of the world shall have the same foregoing signs as the period of empires, states, and dominions in it, that is, corruption of manners, inhuman degenerations, and deluge of iniquities; it may be doubted whether that final time be so far off, of whose day and hour there can be no prescience. But while all men doubt, and none can determine how long the world shall last, some may wonder that it hath spun out so long and unto our days. For if the Almighty had not determined a fixed duration unto it, according to his mighty and merciful designments in it; if he had not said
Job xxxviii. 11. unto it, as he did unto a part of it, hitherto shalt thou go and no further; if we consider the incessant and cutting provocations from the earth; it is not without amazement, how his patience hath permitted so long a continuance unto it; how he, who cursed the earth in the first days of the first man, and drowned it in the tenth generation after, should thus lastingly contend with flesh, and yet defer the last flames. For since he is sharply provoked every moment, yet punisheth to pardon, and forgives to forgive again; what patience could be content to act over such vicissitudes, or accept of repentances

which must have after-penitences, His goodness can only tell us. And surely if the patience of Heaven were not proportionable unto the provocations from earth, there needed an intercessor not only for the sins, but the duration of this world, and to lead it up unto the present computation. Without such a merciful longanimity, the heavens would never be so aged Ps. cii. 25, 26.
as to grow old like a garment. It were in vain to infer from the doctrine of the sphere, that the time might come, when Capella, a noble northern star, would have its motion in the equator; that the northern zodiacal signs would at length be the southern, the southern the northern, and Capricorn become our Cancer. However therefore the wisdom of the Creator hath ordered the duration of the world, yet since the end thereof brings the accomplishment of our happiness, since some would be content that it should have no end, since evil men and spirits do fear it may be too short, since good men hope it may not be too long; the prayer of the saints under the altar will be the sup- Rev. vi. 9, 10.
plication of the righteous world, that his mercy would abridge their languishing expectation, and hasten the accomplishment of their happy state to come.

XXVII. Though good men are often taken Is. lvii. 1.
away from the evil to come; though some in

evil days have been glad that they were old, nor long to behold the iniquities of a wicked world, or judgments threatened by them; yet is it no small satisfaction unto honest minds to leave the world in virtuous well-tempered times, under a prospect of good to come, and continuation of worthy ways acceptable unto God and man. Men who die in deplorable days, which they regretfully behold, have not their eyes closed with the like content; while they cannot avoid the thoughts of proceeding or growing enormities, displeasing unto that Spirit unto whom they are then going, whose honour they desire in all times and throughout all generations. If Lucifer could be freed from his dismal place, he would little care though the rest were left behind. Too many there may be of Nero's mind, who, if their own turn were served, would not regard what became of others; and, when they die themselves, care not if all perish. But good men's wishes extend beyond their lives, for the happiness of times to come, and never to be known unto them. And, therefore, while so many question prayers for the dead, they charitably pray for those who are not yet alive; they are not so enviously ambitious to go to heaven by themselves; they cannot but humbly wish that the little flock might be greater, the narrow gate

Cf. Rel. Med. pt. II. iv.

St. Luke xii. 32.

wider, and that, as many are called, so not a few might be chosen. St. Matt. xxii. 14.

XXVIII. That a greater number of angels remained in heaven than fell from it, the schoolmen will tell us; that the number of blessed souls will not come short of that vast number of fallen spirits, we have the favourable calculation of others. What age or century hath sent most souls unto heaven, He can tell who vouchsafeth that honour unto them. Though the number of the blessed must be complete before the world can pass away; yet since the world itself seems in the wane, and we have no such comfortable prognostics of latter times; since a greater part of time is spun than is to come, and the blessed roll already much replenished; happy are those pieties, which solicitously look about, and hasten to make one of that already much filled and abbreviated list to come.

XXIX. Think not thy time short in this world, since the world itself is not long. The created world is but a small parenthesis in eternity; and a short interposition, for a time, between such a state of duration as was before it and may be after it. And if we should allow of the old tradition, that the world should last six thousand years, it could scarce have the name of old, since the first man lived near a sixth part thereof, and seven Methuselahs would Gen. v. 5, 27.

exceed its whole duration. However, to palliate the shortness of our lives, and somewhat to compensate our brief term in this world, it is good to know as much as we can of it; and also, so far as possibly in us lieth, to hold such a theory of times past, as though we had seen the same. He who hath thus considered the world, as also how therein things long past have been answered by things present; how matters in one age have been acted over in another; and
Eccl. i. 9, 10. how there is nothing new under the sun; may conceive himself in some manner to have lived from the beginning, and to be as old as the world; and if he should still live on, it would be but the same thing.

XXX. Lastly; if length of days be thy portion,
Hor. Ep. i. iv. 13. make it not thy expectation. Reckon not upon long life: think every day the last, and live always beyond thy account. He that so often surviveth his expectation lives many lives, and will scarce complain of the shortness of his days. Time past is gone like a shadow; make time to come present. Approximate thy latter times by present apprehensions of them: be like a neighbour unto the grave, and think there is but little to come. And since there is something of us that will still live on, join both lives together, and live in one but for the other. He who thus ordereth the purposes of

this life, will never be far from the next; and is in some manner already in it, by a happy conformity and close apprehension of it. And if, as we have elsewhere declared, any have been so happy as personally to understand Christian annihilation, ecstasy, exolution, transformation, the kiss of the spouse, and ingression into the divine shadow, according to mystical theology, they have already had a handsome anticipation of heaven, the world is in a manner over, and the earth in ashes unto them.

In his Hydriotaphia, or Urn-Burial.

Hydriotaphia.

Urn-Burial; or, a Discourse of the Sepulchral Urns lately found in Norfolk.

TO MY

WORTHY AND HONOURED FRIEND,

THOMAS LE GROS,

OF CROSTWICK, ESQ.

HEN the funeral pyre was out, and the last valediction over, men took a lasting adieu of their interred friends, little expecting the curiosity of future ages should comment upon their ashes; and having no old experience of the duration of their relics, held no opinion of such after-considerations.

But who knows the fate of his bones, or how often he is to be buried? Who hath the oracle of his ashes, or whither they are to be scattered? The relics of many lie, like the ruins of Pompey's,* in all parts of the earth; and these may seem to have wandered far, when

* "Pompeios juvenes Asia atque Europa, sed ipsum terra tegit Libyæ."

they arrive at your hands, who, in a direct and meridian travel, have but a few miles of known earth between yourself and the pole.*

Brought back by Cimon. Plutarch.

That the bones of Theseus should be seen again in Athens, was not beyond conjecture and hopeful expectation; but that these should arise so opportunely to serve yourself, was a hit of fate and honour beyond prediction.

We cannot but wish these urns might have the effect of theatrical vessels, and great Hippodrome urns in Rome,† to resound the acclamations and honour due unto you. But these are sad and sepulchral pitchers, which have no joyful voices, silently expressing old mortality, the ruins of forgotten times, and can only speak with life, how long in this corruptible frame some parts may be uncorrupted, yet able to outlast bones long unborn, and noblest pile among us.

We present not these as any strange sight or spectacle unknown to your eyes, who have beheld the best of urns and noblest variety of ashes; who are yourself no slender master of antiquities, and can daily command the view of so many imperial faces;‡ which raiseth your

* Little directly but sea between your house and Greenland.

† The great urns in the Hippodrome at Rome, conceived to resound the voices of the people at their shows.

‡ Worthily possessed by that true gentleman, Sir Horatio Townshend, my honoured friend.

thoughts unto old things and consideration of times before you, when even living men were antiquities; when the living might exceed the dead, and to depart this world could not be properly said to go unto the greater number;* and so run up your thoughts upon the ancient of days, the antiquary's truest object, unto whom the eldest parcels are young, and earth itself an infant, and without Egyptian account makes but small noise in thousands.

Which makes the world so many years old.

We were hinted by the occasion, not catched the opportunity to write of old things, or intrude upon the antiquary. We are coldly drawn unto discourses of antiquities, who have scarce time before us to comprehend new things, or make out learned novelties. But seeing they arose as they lay, almost in silence among us, at least in short account suddenly passed over, we were very unwilling they should die again and be buried twice among us.

Besides, to preserve the living, and make the dead to live, to keep men out of their urns, and discourse of human fragments in them, is not impertinent unto our profession, whose study is life and death, who daily behold examples of mortality, and of all men least need artificial mementos or coffins by our bed-side to mind us of our graves.

* *Abiit ad plures.*

'T is time to observe occurrences, and let nothing remarkable escape us. The supinity of elder days hath left so much in silence, or time hath so martyred the records, that the most industrious heads do find no easy work to erect a new Britannia.*

'T is opportune to look back upon old times and contemplate our forefathers. Great examples grow thin, and to be fetched from the passed world. Simplicity flies away, and iniquity comes at long strides upon us. We have enough to do to make up ourselves from present and passed times, and the whole stage of things scarce serveth for our instruction. A complete piece of virtue must be made up from the centos of all ages, as all the beauties of Greece could make but one handsome Venus.

In the time of Henry the Second. Cambden.

When the bones of King Arthur were digged up, the old race might think they beheld therein some originals of themselves. Unto these of our urns none here can pretend relation, and can only behold the relics of those persons, who in their life giving the laws unto their predecessors, after long obscurity, now lie at their mercies. But remembering the early civility they brought upon these countries, and forgetting long-passed mischiefs, we mer-

* Wherein Mr. Dugdale hath excellently well endeavoured.

cifully preserve their bones, and insult not over their ashes.

In the offer of these antiquities, we drive not at ancient families, so long outlasted by them; we are far from erecting your worth upon the pillars of your forefathers, whose merits you illustrate. We honor your old virtues, conformable unto times before you, which are the noblest armoury. And having long experience of your friendly conversation, void of empty formality, full of freedom, constant and generous honesty, I look upon you as a gem of the old rock,* and must profess myself, even to urn and ashes,

Your ever faithful friend,

and servant,

THOMAS BROWNE.

NORWICH, *May* 1, 1658.

* *Adamas de rupe veteri præstantissimus.*

HYDRIOTAPHIA.

CHAPTER I.

IN the deep discovery of the subterranean world, a shallow part would satisfy some inquirers; who, if two or three yards were open about the surface, would not care to rake the bowels of Potosi, and regions towards the centre. Nature hath furnished one part of the earth, and man another. The treasures of time lie high, in urns, coins, and monuments, scarce below the roots of some vegetables. Time hath endless rarities, and shows of all varieties; which reveals old things in heaven, makes new discoveries in earth, and even earth itself a discovery. That great antiquity, America, lay buried for a thousand years; and a large part of the earth is still in the urn unto us.

The rich mountain of Peru.

Though if Adam were made out of an extract of the earth, all parts might challenge a restitution; yet few have returned their bones far lower than they might receive them; not affecting the graves of giants, under hilly and heavy coverings, but, content with less than their own depth, have wished their bones might lie soft, and the earth be light upon them. Even such as hope to rise again would not be content with central interment, or so desperately to place their relics as to lie beyond discovery and in no way to be seen again; which happy contrivance hath made communication with our forefathers, and left unto our view some parts which they never beheld themselves.

Sit tibi terra levis.

Though earth hath engrossed the name, yet water hath proved the smartest grave, which in forty days swallowed almost mankind and the living creation, fishes not wholly escaping, except the salt ocean were handsomely contempered by a mixture of the fresh element.

Many have taken voluminous pains to determine the state of the soul upon disunion; but men have been most fantastical in the singular contrivances of their corporal dissolution; whilst the soberest nations have rested in two ways, of simple inhumation and burning.

That carnal interment or burying was of the elder date, the old examples of Abraham and the patriarchs are sufficient to illustrate, and

Scripture expression . . . tween Satan and the Archangel abo . . . ing the body of Moses. But the pract . . . burning was also of great antiquity, and of n . . . slender extent. For (not to derive the same from Hercules) noble descriptions there are hereof in the Grecian funerals of Homer; in the formal obsequies of Patroclus and Achilles, and somewhat elder in the Theban war, and solemn combustion of Meneceus and Archemorus, contemporary unto Jair, the eighth judge of Israel; confirmable also among the Trojans from the funeral pyre of Hector, burnt before the gates of Troy, and the burning of Penthesilea, the Amazonian queen, and long continuance of that practice in the inward countries of Asia; while as low as the reign of Julian, we find that the king of Chionia burnt the body of his son, and interred the ashes in a silver urn.

Gumbrates, king of Chionia, a country near Persia.

The same practice extended also far west, and, besides Herulians, Getes, and Thracians, was in use with most of the Celtæ, Sarmatians, Germans, Gauls, Danes, Swedes, Norwegians,

of among Cartha-
of greater antiquity
an most opinion, or Pliny
For (besides the old table
g or burying within the city,*
the funeral fire with planed wood,
ching the fire with wine) Manlius, the
, burnt the body of his son. Numa, by
pecial clause of his will, was not burnt, but buried; and Remus was solemnly buried, according to the description of Ovid.†

Cornelius Sylla was not the first whose body was burned in Rome, but of the Cornelian family, which being indifferently, not frequently, used before, from that time spread, and became the prevalent practice; not totally pursued in the highest run of cremation; for when even crows were funerally burnt, Poppæa, the wife of Nero, found a peculiar grave interment. Now as all customs were founded upon some bottom of reason, so there wanted not grounds for this, according to several apprehensions of the most rational dissolution. Some, being of the opinion of Thales, that water was the original of all things, thought it most equal to submit unto the principle of putrefaction, and

* 12 Tab. Pars i. *de jure sacro.* "Hominem mortuum in urbe ne sepelito, neve urito." (Tom. 2.) "Rogum asciâ ne polito." (Tom. 4.)

† "Ultima prolato subdita flamma rogo."

The Scythians, who swore by wind and sword, that is, by life and death, were so far from burning their bodies, that they declined all interment, and made their graves in the air; and the Ichthyophagi, or fish-eating nations about Egypt, affected the sea for their grave, thereby declining visible corruption, and restoring the debt of their bodies. Whereas the old heroes in Homer dreaded nothing more than water or drowning, probably upon the old opinion of the fiery substance of the soul, only extinguishable by that element; and therefore the poet emphatically implieth the total destruction in this kind of death,* which happened to Ajax Oileus.

The old Balearians had a peculiar mode, for they used great urns and much wood, but no fire, in their burials, while they bruised the flesh and bones of the dead, crowded them into urns, and laid heaps of wood upon them. And the Chinese, without cremation or urnal interment of their bodies, make use of trees and much burning, while they plant a pine-tree by their grave, and burn great numbers of printed draughts of slaves and horses over it, civilly content with their companies in effigy, which barbarous nations exact unto reality.

Christians abhorred this way of obsequies,

* Which Magius reads ἐξαπόλωλε.

19

and though they sticked not to give their bodies to be burnt in their lives, detested that mode after death; affecting rather a depositure than absumption, and properly submitting unto the sentence of God, to return not unto ashes, but unto dust again, conformable unto the practice of the patriarchs, the interment of our Saviour, of Peter, Paul, and the ancient martyrs; and so far at last declining promiscuous interment with Pagans, that some have suffered ecclesiastical censures* for making no scruple thereof.

The Mussulman believers will never admit this fiery resolution; for they hold a present trial from their black and white angels in the grave, which they must have made so hollow that they may rise upon their knees.

The Jewish nation, though they entertained the old way of inhumation, yet sometimes admitted this practice. For the men of Jabesh burnt the body of Saul; and, by no prohibited practice, to avoid contagion or pollution in time
Amos vi. 10. of pestilence, burnt the bodies of their friends. And when they burnt not their dead bodies, yet sometimes used great burnings near and about them, deducible from the expressions concerning Jehoram, Zedechiah, and the sumptuous pyre of Asia; and were so little averse

* Martialis, the Bishop. Cyprian.

from Pagan burning, that the Jew, lamenting the death of Cæsar, their friend and revenger on Pompey, frequented the place where his body was burnt, for many nights together. And as they raised noble monuments and mausoleums for their own nation,* so they were not scrupulous in erecting some for others, according to the practice of Daniel, who left that lasting sepulchral pile in Ecbatana for the Median and Persian kings.†

Sueton. in Vita Jul. Cæs.

But even in times of subjection and hottest use they conformed not unto the Roman practice of burning; whereby the prophecy was secured concerning the body of Christ, that it should not see corruption, or a bone should not be broken; which we believe was also providentially prevented, from the soldier's spear and nails that past by the little bones both in his hands and feet; not of ordinary contrivance, that it should not corrupt on the cross, according to the laws of Roman crucifixion, or a hair of his head perish, though observable in Jewish customs to cut the hairs of malefactors.

Nor in their long cohabitation with Egyptians crept into a custom of their exact embalm-

* As that magnificent sepulchral monument erected by Simon. 1 Macc. xiii. 27.

† Κατασκεύασμα θαυμασίως πεποιημένον, whereof a Jewish priest had always the custody unto Josephus's days. Jos. b. 10, Antiq.

ing, wherein deeply slashing the muscles, and taking out the brains and entrails, they had broken the subject of so entire a resurrection, nor fully answered the types of Enoch, Elijah, or Jonah; which yet to prevent or restore was of equal facility unto that rising power, able to break the fasciations and bands of death, to get clear out of the cerecloth and a hundred pounds of ointment, and out of the sepulchre before the stone was rolled from it.

But though they embraced not this practice of burning, yet entertained they many ceremonies agreeable unto Greek and Roman obsequies. And he that observeth their funeral feasts, their lamentations at the grave, their music, and weeping mourners; how they closed the eyes of their friends; how they washed, anointed, and kissed the dead; may easily conclude these were not mere Pagan civilities. But whether that mournful burthen, and treble calling out after Absalom,* had any reference unto the last conclamation and triple valediction used by other nations, we hold but a wavering conjecture.

Civilians make sepulture but of the law of nations; others do naturally found it and discover it also in animals. They that are so thick-skinned as still to credit the story of the

* "O Absalom, Absalom, Absalom!" 2 Sam. xviii. 33.

phœnix, may say something for animal burning. More serious conjectures find some examples of sepulture in elephants, cranes, the sepulchral cells of pismires, and practice of bees; which civil society carrieth out their dead, and hath exequies, if not interments.

CHAPTER II.

THE solemnities, ceremonies, rites of their cremation or interment, so solemnly delivered by authors, we shall not disparage our reader to repeat. Only the last and lasting part in their urns, collected bones and ashes, we cannot wholly omit, or decline that subject, which occasion lately presented in some discovered among us.

In a field of Old Walsingham, not many months past, were digged up between forty and fifty urns, deposited in a dry and sandy soil, not a yard deep, not far from one another; not all strictly of one figure, but most answering these described; some containing two pounds of bones, distinguishable in skulls, ribs, jaws, thigh-bones, and teeth, with fresh impressions of their combustion; besides the extraneous substances, like pieces of small boxes, or combs, handsomely wrought, handles of small brass instruments, brazen nippers, and in one some kind of opal.

Near the same plot of ground, for about six yards' compass, were digged up coals and incinerated substances, which begat conjecture that this was the Ustrina, or place of burning their bodies, or some sacrificing place unto the Manes, which was properly below the surface of the ground, as the aræ and altars unto the gods and heroes above it.

That these were the urns of Romans, from the common custom and place where they were found, is no obscure conjecture; not far from a Roman garrison, and but five miles from Brancaster, set down by ancient record under the name of Brannodunum ; and where the adjoining town, containing seven parishes, in no very different sound, but Saxon termination, still retains the name of Burnham; which, being an early station, it is not improbable the neighbour parts were filled with habitations, either of Romans themselves, or Britons Romanized, which observed the Roman customs.

Nor is it improbable that the Romans early possessed this country; for, though we meet not with such strict particulars of these parts, before the new institution of Constantine, and military charge of the Count of the Saxon shore, and that about the Saxon invasions, the Dalmatian horsemen were in the garrison of Brancaster; yet, in the time of Claudius, Vespasian, and Severus, we find no less than three legions dispersed through the province of Britain; and, as high as the reign of Claudius, a great overthrow was given unto the Iceni, by the Roman lieutenant Ostorius. Not long after, the country was so molested, that, in hope of a better state, Prasutagus bequeathed his kingdom unto Nero and his daughters; and Boadicea, his queen, fought the last decisive battle with Paullinus. After which time and conquest of Agricola, the lieutenant of Vespasian, probable it is they wholly possessed this country, ordering it into garrisons or habitations best suitable with their securities; and so some Roman habitations not improbable in these parts, as high as the time of Vespasian, where the Saxons after seated, in whose thin-filled maps we yet find the name of Walsingham. Now, if the Iceni were but Gammadims, Anconians, or men that lived in an angle, wedge, or elbow of Britain, according to the original etymology, this country will challenge the emphatical appellation, as most properly making the elbow or iken of Icenia.

That Britain was notably populous, is undeniable, from that expression of Cæsar.* That

* "Hominum infinita multitudo est, creberrimaque ædificia fere Gallicis consimilia." — Cæs. de Bello Gal., l. 5.

the Romans themselves were early in no small numbers, seventy thousand, with their associates, slain by Boadicea, affords a sure account. And though not many Roman habitations are now known, yet some by old works, rampires, coins, and urns, do testify their possessions. Some urns have been found at Castor, some also about Southcreek, and, not many years past, no less than ten in a field at Buxton, not near any recorded garrison. Nor is it strange to find Roman coins of copper and silver among us, of Vespasian, Trajan, Adrian, Commodus, Antoninus, Severus, &c.; but the greater number of Diocletian, Constantine, Constans, Valens, with many of Victorinus Posthumius, Tetricus, and the thirty tyrants in the reign of Gallienus; and some as high as Adrianus have been found about Thetford, or Sitomagus, mentioned in the itinerary of Antoninus, as the way from Venta or Castor unto London. But the most frequent discovery is made at the two Casters, by Norwich and Yarmouth, at Burghcastle and Brancaster.

Besides the Norman, Saxon, and Danish pieces of Cuthred, Canutus, William, Matilda, and others, some British coins of gold have been dispersedly found; and no small number of silver pieces near Norwich, with a rude head upon the obverse, and an ill-formed horse on the reverse, with these inscriptions, *Ic. Duro. T.*, whether implying Iceni, Durotriges, Tascia or Trinobantes, we leave to higher conjecture. Vulgar chronology will have Norwich castle as old as Julius Cæsar; but his distance from these parts, and its Gothic form of structure, abridgeth such antiquity. The British coins afford conjecture of early habitation in these parts: though the city of Norwich arose from the ruins of Venta, and, though perhaps not without some habitation before, was enlarged, builded, and nominated by the Saxons. In what bulk or populosity it stood in the old East-Angle monarchy, tradition and history are silent. Considerable it was in the Danish eruptions, when Sueno burnt Thetford and Norwich, and Ulfketel, the governor thereof, was able to make some resistance, and after endeavoured to burn the Danish navy.

How the Romans left so many coins in countries of their conquests seems of hard resolution, except we consider how they buried them under ground, when, upon barbarous invasions, they were fain to desert their habitations in most part of their empire, and the strictness of their laws forbidding to transfer them to any other uses; wherein the Spartans were singular, who, to make their copper money useless, contempered it with vinegar. That the Britons left any, some wonder, since their money was

Plutarch, Vita Lycurgus.

iron and iron rings before Cæsar; and those of after stamp by permission, and but small in bulk and bigness. That so few of the Saxons remain, neither need any wonder, because, overcome by succeeding conquerors upon the place, their coins by degrees passed into other stamps, and the marks of after ages.

Than the time of these urns deposited, or precise antiquity of these relics, nothing is of more uncertainty; for since the lieutenant of Claudius seems to have made the first progress into these parts, since Boadicea was overthrown by the forces of Nero, and Agricola put a full end to these conquests, it is not probable the country was fully garrisoned or planted before; and therefore, however these urns might be of later date, it is not likely they were of higher antiquity.

And the succeeding emperors desisted not from their conquests in these and other parts, as testified by history and medal inscription yet extant; the province of Britain, in so divided a distance from Rome, beholding the faces of many imperial persons, and in large account no fewer than Cæsar, Claudius, Britannicus, Vespasian, Titus, Adrian, Severus, Commodus, Geta, and Caracalla.

A great obscurity herein, because no medal or emperor's coin enclosed, which might denote the date of their interments; — observable in many urns, and found in those of Spittle-fields, by London; which contained the coins of Claudius, Vespasian, Commodus, Antoninus, attended with lacrymatories, lamps, bottles of liquor, and other appurtenances of affectionate superstition, which in these rural interments were wanting.

Stowe's Survey of London.

Some uncertainty there is from the period or term of burning, or the cessation of that practice. Macrobius affirmeth it was disused in his days; but most agree, though without authentic record, that it ceased with the Antonini, — most safely to be understood after the reign of those emperors who assumed the name of Antoninus, extending unto Heliogabalus; — not strictly after Marcus; for about fifty years later we find the magnificent burning and consecration of Severus; and if we so fix this period of cessation, these urns will challenge above thirteen hundred years.

But whether this practice was only then left by emperors and great persons, or generally about Rome, and not in other provinces, we hold no authentic account. For after Tertullian, in the days of Minucius, it was obviously objected upon Christians, that they condemned the practice of burning.* And we find a pas-

* "Execrantur rogos, et damnant ignium sepulturam."

sage in Sidonius, which asserteth that practice in France unto a lower account; and perhaps not fully disused till Christianity was fully established, which gave the final extinction to these sepulchral bonfires.

Whether they were the bones of men, or women, or children, no authentic decision from ancient custom in distinct places of burial; although not improbably conjectured, that the double sepulture, or burying-place of Abraham,* had in it such intention. But from exility of bones, thinness of skulls, smallness of teeth, ribs, and thigh-bones, not improbable that many thereof were persons of minor age, or women; confirmable also from things contained in them. In most were found substances resembling combs, plates like boxes, fastened with iron pins, and handsomely overwrought like the necks or bridges of musical instruments, long brass plates overwrought like the handles of neat implements, brazen nippers to pull away hair, and in one a kind of opal yet maintaining a bluish color.

Now that they accustomed to burn or bury with them things wherein they excelled, delighted, or which were dear unto them, either as farewells unto all pleasure, or vain appre-

* Gen. xxiii. In the cave of a field called Hebron, in the land of Canaan.

hension that they might use them in the other world, is testified by all antiquity;—observable from the gem or beryl ring upon the finger of Cynthia, the mistress of Propertius, when after her funeral pyre her ghost appeared unto him;—and notably illustrated from the contents of that Roman urn preserved by Cardinal Farnese, wherein, besides great number of gems with heads of gods and goddesses, were found an ape of agate, a grasshopper, an elephant of amber, a crystal ball, three glasses, two spoons, and six nuts of crystal. And beyond the content of urns, in the monument of Childeric the First, and fourth king from Pharamond, casually discovered three years past at Tournay, restoring unto the world much gold richly adorning his sword, two hundred rubies, many hundred imperial coins, three hundred golden bees, the bones and horse-shoes of his horse interred with him, according to the barbarous magnificence of those days in their sepulchral obsequies. Although if we steer by the conjecture of many, and Septuagint expression, some trace thereof may be found even with the ancient Hebrews, not only from the sepulchral treasure of David, but the circumcision knives which Joshua also buried.

Some men, considering the contents of these urns, lasting pieces and toys included in them, and the custom of burning with many other nations, might somewhat doubt whether all urns found among us were properly Roman relics, or some not belonging unto our British, Saxon, or Danish forefathers.

Of the form of burial among the ancient Britons, the large discourses of Cæsar, Tacitus, and Strabo are silent. For the discovery whereof, with other particulars, we much deplore the loss of that letter which Cicero expected or received from his brother Quintus, as a resolution of British customs; or the account which might have been made by Scribonius Largus, the physician accompanying the Emperor Claudius, who might have also discovered that frugal bit of the old Britons, which in the bigness of a bean could satisfy their thirst and hunger.

But that the Druids and ruling priests used to burn and bury, is expressed by Pomponius. That Bellinus, the brother of Brennus, and king of the Britons, was burnt, is acknowledged by Polydorus, as also by Amandus Zierexensis in Historia, and Pineda in his Universa Historia (Spanish). That they held that practice in Gallia, Cæsar expressly delivereth. Whether the Britons (probably descended from them, of like religion, language, and manners) did not sometimes make use of burning; or whether at least such as were after civilized unto the Roman life and manners, conformed not unto this practice, we have no historical assertion or denial. But since, from the account of Tacitus, the Romans early wrought so much civility upon the British stock, that they brought them to build temples, to wear the gown, and study the Roman laws and language; that they conformed also unto their religious rites and customs in burials, seems no improbable conjecture.

That burning the dead was used in Sarmatia is affirmed by Gaguinus; that the Sueons and Gothlanders used to burn their princes and great persons is delivered by Saxo and Olaus; that this was the old German practice, is also asserted by Tacitus. And though we are bare in historical particulars of such obsequies in this island, or that the Saxons, Jutes, and Angles burnt their dead, yet came they from parts where it was of ancient practice; the Germans using it, from whom they were descended. And even in Jutland and Sleswick in Anglia Cymbrica, urns with bones were found not many years before us.

But the Danish and Northern nations have raised an era or point of compute from their custom of burning their dead; some deriving it from Unguinus, some from Frotho the Great, who ordained by law that princes and chief commanders should be committed unto the fire, though the common sort had the common grave-interment. So Starkatterus, that old hero, was burnt; and Ringo royally burnt the body of Harold, the king slain by him.

What time this custom generally expired in that nation, we discern no assured period; whether it ceased before Christianity, or upon their conversion by Ausgurius the Gaul, in the time of Ludovicus Pius, the son of Charles the Great, according to good computes; or whether it might not be used by some persons, while for a hundred and eighty years Paganism and Christianity were promiscuously embraced among them, there is no assured conclusion. About which times the Danes were busy in England, and particularly infested this country; where many castles and strong-holds were built by them or against them, and great numbers of names and families still derived from them. But since this custom was probably disused before their invasion or conquest, and the Romans confessedly practised the same since their possession of this island, the most assured account will fall upon the Romans, or Britons Romanized.

However, certain it is that urns, conceived of no Roman original, are often digged up both in Norway and Denmark, handsomely described and graphically represented by the learned physician Wormius; and in some parts of Denmark in no ordinary number, as stands delivered by authors exactly describing those countries. And they contained not only bones, but many other substances in them, as knives, pieces of iron, brass, and wood, and one of Norway a brass gilded jews-harp.

Nor were they confused or careless in disposing the noblest sort, while they placed large stones in circle about the urns or bodies which they interred, somewhat answerable unto the monument of Rollrich stones in England, or sepulchral monument probably erected by Rollo; who after conquered Normandy, where it is not improbable somewhat might be discovered. Meanwhile, to what nation or person belonged that large urn found at Ashbury, containing mighty bones and a buckler; what those large urns found at Little Massingham; or why the Anglesea urns are placed with their mouths downward, remains yet undiscovered.

CHAPTER III.

PLASTERED and whited sepulchres were anciently affected in cadaverous and corruptive burials; and the rigid Jews were wont to garnish the sepulchres of the righteous. Ulysses, in Hecuba, cared not how meanly he lived, so he might find a noble tomb after death. Great princes affected great monuments; and the fair and larger urns contained no vulgar ashes, which makes that disparity in those which time discovereth among us. The present urns were not of one capacity; the largest containing above a gallon; some not much above half that measure. Nor all of one figure, wherein there is no strict conformity in the same or different countries; observable from those represented by Casalius, Bosio, and others, though all found in Italy; while many have handles, ears, and long necks, but most imitate a circular figure, in a spherical and round com-

St. Matt. xxiii.

posure; whether from any mystery, best duration, or capacity, were but a conjecture. But the common form with necks was a proper figure, making our last bed like our first; not much unlike the urns of our nativity, while
Ps. cxxxix. "we lay in the nether part of the earth," and inward vault of our microcosm. Many urns are red, these but of a black color, somewhat smooth, and dully sounding, which begat some doubt whether they were burnt, or only baken in oven or sun, according to the ancient way, in many bricks, tiles, pots, and testaceous works; as the word "testa" is properly to be taken, when occuring without addition, and chiefly intended by Pliny when he commendeth bricks and tiles of two years old, and to make them in the spring. Nor only these concealed pieces, but the open magnificence of antiquity, ran much in the artifice of clay. Hereof the house of Mausolus was built; thus old Jupiter stood in the Capitol; and the statue of Hercules, made in the reign of Tarquinius Priscus, was extant in Pliny's days. And such as declined burning or funeral urns, affected coffins of clay, according to the mode of Pythagoras, a way preferred by Varro. But the spirit of great ones was above these circumscriptions, affecting copper, silver, gold, and porphyry urns, wherein Seve-

rus lay, after a serious view and sentence on that which should contain him. Some of these urns were thought to have been silvered over from sparklings in several pots, with small tinsel parcels, uncertain whether from the earth or the first mixture in them.

Among these urns we could obtain no good account of their coverings; only one seemed arched over with some kind of brick-work. Of those found at Buxton, some were covered with flints; some in other parts with tiles; those at Yarmouth-Caster were closed with Roman bricks; and some have proper earthen covers adapted and fitted to them. But in the Homerical urn of Patroclus, whatever was the solid tegument, we find the immediate covering to be a purple piece of silk. And such as had no covers might have the earth closely pressed into them; after which disposure were probably some of these, wherein we found the bones and ashes half mortared unto the sand and sides of the urn, and some long roots of quich, or dog's-grass, wreathed about the bones.

No lamps, included liquors, lachrymatories, or tear-bottles attended these rural urns, either as sacred unto the Manes, or passionate expressions of their surviving friends; while with rich flames and hired tears they solemnized

Cum lacrymis posuêre.

their obsequies, and in the most lamented monuments made one part of their inscriptions. Some find sepulchral vessels containing liquors which time hath incrassated into jellies. For besides these lachrymatories, notable lamps, with vessels of oils and aromatical liquors, attended noble ossuaries, and some yet retaining a vinosity and spirit in them; which if any have tasted, they have far exceeded the palates of antiquity; liquors not to be computed by years of annual magistrates, but by great conjunctions and the fatal periods of kingdoms.* The draughts of consulary date were but crude unto these, and Opimian † wine but in the must unto them.

In sundry graves and sepulchres we meet with rings, coins, and chalices. Ancient frugality was so severe, that they allowed no gold to attend the corpses, but only that which served to fasten their teeth. ‡ Whether the opaline stone in this urn were burnt upon the finger of the dead, or cast into the fire by some affectionate friend, it will consist with either custom. But other incinerable substances were found so fresh, that they could feel no singe

* About 500 years. Plato.

† "Vinum Opiminianum annorum centum." Petron.

‡ 12 Tabul. l. xi. *de jure sacro.* "Neve aurum addito; ast quo auro dentes vincti erunt, imo cum illo sepelire et urere, ne fraudi esto."

from fire. These upon view were judged to be wood; but sinking in water, and tried by the fire, we found them to be bone or ivory. In their hardness and yellow color, they most resembled box, which, in old expressions, found the epithet * of eternal, and perhaps, in such conservatories, might have passed uncorrupted.

That bay-leaves were found green in the tomb of St. Humbert, after a hundred and fifty years, was looked upon as miraculous. Remarkable it was unto old spectators, that the cypress of the temple of Diana lasted so many hundred years. The wood of the ark and olive rod of Aaron were older at the Captivity. But the cypress of the ark of Noah was the greatest vegetable antiquity, if Josephus were not deceived by some fragments of it in his days;—to omit the moor-logs and fir-trees, found under ground in many parts of England; the undated ruins of winds, floods, and earthquakes; and which, in Flanders, still show from what quarter they fell, as generally lying in a northeast position.

But though we found not these pieces to be wood, according to first apprehension, yet we missed not altogether of some woody substance; for the bones were not so clearly picked, but some coals were found amongst them;—a way

* Plin. lib. xvi. "Inter ξύλα ἀσαπῆ numerat Theophrastus."

to make wood perpetual, and a fit associate for metal, whereon was laid the foundation of the great Ephesian temple, and which were made the lasting tests of old boundaries and landmarks. Whilst we look on these, we admire not observations of coals found fresh after four hundred years. In a long deserted habitation, even egg-shells have been found fresh, not tending to corruption.

In the monument of King Childeric, the iron relics were found all rusty and crumbling into pieces. But our little iron pins, which fastened the ivory works, held well together, and lost not their magnetical quality, though wanting a tenacious moisture for the firmer union of parts. Although it be hardly drawn into fusion, yet that metal soon submitteth unto rust and dissolution. In the brazen pieces we admired not the duration, but the freedom from rust and ill savor upon the hardest attrition: but now exposed unto the piercing atoms of air, in the space of a few months they begin to spot and betray their green entrails. We conceive not these urns to have descended thus naked as they appear, or to have entered their graves without the old habit of flowers. The urn of Philopœmen was so laden with flowers and ribbons, that it afforded no sight of itself. The rigid Lycurgus allowed olive and myrtle.

The Athenians might fairly except against the practice of Democritus, to be buried up in honey; as fearing to embezzle a great commodity of their country, and the best of that kind in Europe. But Plato seemed too frugally politic, who allowed no larger monument than would contain four heroic verses, and designed the most barren ground for sepulture; though we cannot commend the goodness of that sepulchral ground which was set at no higher rate than the mean salary of Judas. Though the earth had confounded the ashes of these ossuaries, yet the bones were so smartly burnt, that some thin plates of brass were found half melted among them; whereby we apprehend, they were not of the meanest carcasses, perfunctorily fired, as sometimes in military, and commonly in pestilence burnings, or after the manner of abject corpses, huddled forth and carelessly burnt, without the Esquiline Port at Rome; which was an affront continued upon Tiberius, while they but half burnt his body, and in the amphitheatre, according to the custom in notable malefactors; whereas Nero seemed not so much to fear his death, as that his head should be cut off, and his body not burnt entire.

Some, finding many fragments of skulls in these urns, suspected a mixture of bones. In none we searched was there cause of such conjecture, though sometimes they declined not that practice. The ashes of Domitian were mingled with those of Julia, of Achilles with those of Patroclus. All urns contained not single ashes. Without confused burnings, they effectually compounded their bones, passionately endeavouring to continue their living unions; and when distance of death denied such conjunctions, unsatisfied affections conceived some satisfaction to be neighbours in the grave, to lie urn by urn, and touch but in their names. And many were so curious to continue their living relations, that they contrived large and family urns, wherein the ashes of their nearest friends and kindred might successively be received, at least some parcels thereof, while their collateral memorials lay in minor vessels about them.

Antiquity held too light thoughts from objects of mortality, while some drew provocatives of mirth from anatomies,* and jugglers showed tricks with skeletons; when fiddlers made not so pleasant mirth as fencers, and men could sit with quiet stomachs while hanging was played before them.† Old considerations made few

* *Sic erimus cuncti, &c. Ergo, dum vivimus, vivamus.*

† *Ἀγχόνην παίζειν.* A barbarous pastime at feasts, when men stood upon a rolling globe, with their necks in a rope, and a knife in their hands, ready to cut it when the stone was rolled away, wherein if they failed, they lost their lives, to the laughter of the spectators. Athenæus.

mementos by skulls and bones upon their monuments. In the Egyptian obelisks and hieroglyphical figures, it is not easy to meet with bones. The sepulchral lamps speak nothing less than sepulture, and in their literal draughts prove often obscene and antic pieces. Where we find D. M. it is obvious to meet with sacrificing "pateras," and vessels of libation, upon old sepulchral monuments. In the Jewish Hypogæum and subterranean cell at Rome was little observable beside the variety of lamps, and frequent draughts of the holy candlestick. In authentic draughts of Antony and Jerome, we meet with thigh-bones, and death's-heads; but the cemeterial cells of ancient Christians and martyrs were filled with draughts of Scripture stories; not declining the flourishes of cypress, palms, and olive, and the mystical figures of peacocks, doves, and cocks; but iterately affecting the portraits of Enoch, Lazarus, Jonas, and the vision of Ezekiel, as hopeful draughts and hinting imagery of the resurrection, —which is the life of the grave and sweetens our habitations in the land of moles and pismires.

Diis Manibus.

Gentile inscriptions precisely delivered the extent of men's lives, seldom the manner of their deaths, which history itself so often leaves obscure in the records of memorable persons. There is scarce any philosopher but dies twice or thrice in Laertius; nor almost any life without two or three deaths in Plutarch; which makes the tragical ends of noble persons more favorably resented by compassionate readers, who find some relief in the election of such differences.

The certainty of death is attended with uncertainties, in time, manner, places. The variety of monuments hath often obscured true graves, and cenotaphs confounded sepulchres. For beside their real tombs, many have found honorary and empty sepulchres. The variety of Homer's monuments made him of various countries. Euripides had his tomb in Africa, but his sepulture in Macedonia. And Severus found his real sepulture in Rome, but his empty grave in Gallia.

Trajanus. Dion.

He that lay in a golden urn eminently above the earth, was not like to find the quiet of these bones. Many of these urns were broke by a vulgar discoverer in hope of enclosed treasure. The ashes of Marcellus were lost above ground upon the like account. Where profit hath prompted, no age hath wanted such miners; for which the most barbarous expilators found the most civil rhetoric. Gold once out of the earth is no more due unto it. What was unreasonably committed to the ground, is reasonably resumed from it. Let monuments and rich fabrics, not riches, adorn men's ashes. The commerce of the living is not to be transferred unto the dead. It is not injustice to take that which none complains to lose, and no man is wronged where no man is possessor.*

What virtue yet sleeps in this "terra damnata" and aged cinders, were petty magic to experiment. These crumbling relics and long-fired particles superannuate such expectations. Bones, hairs, nails, and teeth of the dead, were the treasures of old sorcerers. In vain we revive such practices; present superstition too visibly perpetuates the folly of our forefathers, wherein unto old observation this island was so complete, that it might have instructed Persia.†

Plato's historian of the other world lies twelve days uncorrupted, while his soul was viewing the large stations of the dead. How to keep the corpse seven days from corruption, by anointing and washing, without exenteration, were a hazardable piece of art in our choicest practice. How they made distinct separation of bones and ashes from fiery admixture, hath found no historical solution; though they seemed

* The commission of the Gothic King Theodoric, for finding out sepulchral treasure. Cassiodor. Var. lib. 4.

† "Britannia hodie eam attonite celebrat tantis ceremoniis, ut dedisse Persis videri possit."—Plin. lib. 30.

to make a distinct collection, and overlooked not Pyrrhus's toe.* Some provision they might make by fictile vessels, coverings, tiles, or flat stones upon and about the body, (and in the same field, not far from those urns, many stones were found under ground,) as also by careful separation of extraneous matter, composing and raking up the burnt bones with forks,—observable in that notable lump of Galvanus Martianus, who had the sight of the "vas ustrinum," or vessel wherein they burnt the dead, found in the Esquiline field at Rome, might have afforded clearer solution. But their insatisfaction herein begat that remarkable invention in the funeral pyres of some princes, by incombustible sheets made with a texture of asbestos, incremable flax, or salamander's wool, which preserved their bones and ashes incommixed.

How the bulk of man should sink into so few pounds of bones and ashes, may seem strange unto any who considers not its constitution, and how slender a mass will remain upon an open and urging fire of the carnal composition. Even bones themselves, reduced into ashes, do abate a notable proportion; and consisting much of a volatile salt, when that is fired out, make a light kind of cinders; although their bulk

* Which could not be burnt.

be disproportionable to their weight, when the heavy principle of salt is fired out, and the earth almost only remaineth;—observable in sallow, which makes more ashes than oak, and discovers the common fraud of selling ashes by measure, and not by ponderation.

Old bones, according to Lyserus.

Some bones make best skeletons, some bodies quick and speediest ashes.* Who would expect a quick flame from hydropical Heraclitus? The poisoned soldier, when his belly brake, put out two pyres, in Plutarch. But in the plague of Athens, one private pyre served two or three intruders; and the Saracens, burnt in large heaps by the king of Castile, show how little fuel sufficeth. Though the funeral pyre of Patroclus took up a hundred feet,† a piece of an old boat burnt Pompey; and if the burthen of Isaac were sufficient for a holocaust, a man may carry his own pyre.

From animals are drawn good burning lights, and good medicines against burning. Though the seminal humor seems of a contrary nature to fire, yet the body completed proves a combustible lump, wherein fire finds flame even from bones, and some fuel almost from all parts; though the metropolis of humidity ‡

* Those of young persons not tall nor fat, according to Columbus.

† Ἑκατόμπεδον ἔνθα καὶ ἔνθα.

‡ The brain. Hippocrates.

seems least disposed unto it, which might render the skulls of these urns less burned than other bones. But all flies or sinks before fire almost in all bodies. When the common ligament is dissolved, the attenuable parts ascend; the rest subside in coal, calx, or ashes.

To burn the bones of the king of Edom for lime (Amos ii. 1) seems no irrational ferity; but to drink of the ashes of dead relations,* a passionate prodigality. He that hath the ashes of his friend, hath an everlasting treasure. Where fire taketh leave, corruption slowly enters. In bones well burnt, fire makes a wall against itself, experimented in copels and tests of metals, which consist of such ingredients. What the sun compoundeth, fire analyzeth, not transmuteth. That devouring agent leaves almost always a morsel for the earth, whereof all things are but a colony, and which, if time permits, the mother element will have in their primitive mass again.

He that looks for urns and old sepulchral relics, must not seek them in the ruins of temples, where no religion anciently placed them. These were found in a field, according to ancient custom, in noble or private burial; the old practice of the Canaanites, the family of Abraham, and the burying-place of Joshua, in the borders of

* As Artemisia of her husband, Mausolus.

his possessions; and also agreeable unto Roman practice to bury by highways, whereby their monuments were under eye, memorials of themselves and mementos of mortality unto living passengers; whom the epitaphs of great ones were fain to beg to stay and look upon them, — *Siste, viator.* a language, though sometimes used, not so proper in church inscriptions. The sensible rhetoric of the dead, to exemplarity of good life, first admitted the bones of pious men and martyrs within church walls, which, in succeeding ages, crept into promiscuous practice. While Constantine was peculiarly favored to be admitted unto the church porch; and the first thus buried in England was in the days of Cuthred.

Christians dispute how their bodies should lie in the grave. In urnal interment they clearly escaped this controversy. Though we decline the religious consideration, yet in cemeterial and narrower burying-places, to avoid confusion and cross position, a certain posture were to be admitted; which even Pagan civility observed. The Persians lay north and south; the Megarians and Phœnicians placed their heads to the east; the Athenians, some think, towards the west, which Christians still retain; and Beda will have it to be the posture of our Saviour. That he was crucified with his face towards the west, we will not contend with tradition and probable account; but we applaud not the hand of the painter in exalting his cross so high above those on either side, since hereof we find no authentic account in history, and even the crosses found by Helena pretend no such distinction from longitude or dimension.

To be knaved out of our graves, to have our skulls made drinking-bowls, and our bones turned into pipes, to delight and sport our enemies, are tragical abominations escaped in burning burials.

Urnal interments and burnt relics lie not in fear of worms, or to be a heritage for serpents. In carnal sepulture corruptions seem peculiar unto parts, and some speak of snakes out of the spinal marrow. But while we suppose common worms in graves, 't is not easy to find any there; few in churchyards above a foot deep; fewer, or none, in churches, though in fresh decayed bodies. Teeth, bones, and hair, give the most lasting defiance to corruption.

In a hydropical body, ten years buried in a church-yard, we met with a fat concretion, where the nitre of the earth, and the salt and lixivious liquor of the body, had coagulated large lumps of fat into the consistence of the hardest Castile soap; whereof part remaineth with us.

After a battle with the Persians, the Roman corpses decayed in a few days, while the Persian bodies remained dry and uncorrupted.

Bodies in the same ground do not uniformly dissolve, nor bones equally moulder; whereof, in the opprobrious disease, we expect no long duration.

The body of the Marquis of Dorset seemed sound and handsomely cereclothed, that after seventy-eight years was found uncorrupted.* Common tombs preserve not beyond powder. A firmer consistence and compage of parts might be expected from arefaction, deep burial, or charcoal. The greatest antiquities of mortal bodies may remain in petrified bones, whereof, though we take not in the pillar of Lot's wife, or metamorphosis of Ortelius,† some may be older than pyramids, in the petrified relics of the general inundation. When Alexander opened the tomb of Cyrus, the remaining bones discovered his proportion, whereof urnal fragments afford but a bad conjucture, and have this disadvantage of grave-interments, that they leave us ignorant of most personal discoveries.

* Of Thomas, Marquis of Dorset, whose body being buried, 1530, was, 1608, upon the cutting open of the cerecloth, found perfect, and nothing corrupted, the flesh not hardened, but in color, proportion, and softness like an ordinary corpse, newly to be interred. See Burton's Description of Leicestershire.

† In his Map of Russia.

For since bones afford not only rectitude and stability, but figure unto the body, it is no impossible physiognomy to conjecture at fleshy appendencies, and after what shape the muscles and carnous parts might hang in their full consistencies. A full spread cariola * shows a well-shaped horse behind; handsome-formed skulls give some analogy of fleshly resemblance. A critical view of bones makes a good distinction of sexes. Even color is not beyond conjecture; since it is hard to be deceived in the distinction of negroes' skulls.† Dante's characters are to be found in skulls as well as faces. ‡ Hercules is not only known by his foot; other parts make out their comproportions and inferences upon whole or parts. And since the dimensions of the head measure the whole body, and the figure thereof gives conjecture of the principal faculties, physiognomy outlives ourselves, and ends not in our graves.

* That part next the haunch-bones.

† For their extraordinary thickness.

‡ The poet Dante, in his view of Purgatory, found gluttons so meagre and extenuated, that he conceited them to have been in the siege of Jerusalem, and that it was easy to have discovered Homo or Omo in their faces; M being made by the two lines of their cheeks, arching over the eyebrows to the nose, and their sunk eyes making O O, which makes up Omo.

"Parean l' occhiaje anella senza gemme:
Chi nel viso degli uomini legge O M O,
Ben avria quivi conosciuto l' emme."

Purg. xxiii. 31.

Severe contemplators observing these lasting relics, may think them good monuments of persons past, little advantage to future beings; and, considering that power which subdueth all things unto itself, that can resume the scattered atoms, or identify out of anything, conceive it superfluous to expect a resurrection out of relics. But the soul subsisting, other matter, clothed with due accidents, may salve the individuality. Yet the saints, we observe, arose from graves and monuments about the holy city. Some think the ancient patriarchs so earnestly desired to lay their bones in Canaan, as hoping to make a part of that resurrection, and, though thirty miles from Mount Calvary, at least to lie in that region which should produce the first-fruits of the dead. And if, according to learned conjecture, the bodies of men shall rise where their greatest relics remain, many are not like to err in the topography of their resurrection, though their bones or bodies be after translated by angels into the field of Ezekiel's vision, or, as some will order it, into the Valley of Judgment, or Jehosaphat.

CHAPTER IV.

CHRISTIANS have handsomely glossed the deformity of death, by careful consideration of the body, and civil rites, which take off brutal terminations; and, though they conceived all reparable by a resurrection, cast not off all care of interment. And since the ashes of sacrifices burnt upon the altar of God were carefully carried out by the priest, and deposed in a clean field; since they acknowledged their bodies to be the lodging of Christ and temples of the Holy Ghost, they devolved not all upon the sufficiency of soul existence; and therefore with long services and full solemnities concluded their last exequies, wherein, to all distinctions, the Greek devotion seems most pathetically ceremonious.

Christian invention hath chiefly driven at rites which speak hopes of another life, and hints of a resurrection. And if the ancient

Gentiles held not the immortality of their better part, and some subsistence after death, in several rites, customs, actions, and expressions, they contradicted their own opinions; wherein Democritus went high, even to the thought of a resurrection, as scoffingly recorded by Pliny.* What can be more express than the expression of Phocyllides? † or who could expect from Lucretius ‡ a sentence of Ecclesiastes? Before Plato could speak, the soul had wings in Homer, which fell not, but flew out of the body into the mansions of the dead; who also observed that handsome distinction of Demas and Soma, for the body conjoined to the soul, and body separated from it. Lucian spoke much truth in jest, when he said, that part of Hercules which proceeded from Alcmena perished, that from Jupiter remained immortal. Thus Socrates was content that his friends should bury his body, so they would not think they buried Socrates, and, regarding only his immortal part, was indifferent to be burnt or buried. From such considerations Diogenes might con-

* "Similis reviviscendi promissa Democrito vanitas, qui non revixit ipse. Quæ, malum, ista dementia est, iterari vitam morte!" — Plin. lib. 7, c. 56.

† Καὶ τάχα δ' ἐκ γαίης ἐλπίζομεν ἐς φάος ἐλθεῖν
Λείψαν' ἀποιχομένων, κ. τ. λ.

‡ "Cedit enim retro de terrâ quod fuit ante
In terram," &c.

demn sepulture, and, being satisfied that his soul could not perish, grow careless of corporal interment. The Stoics, who thought the souls of wise men had their habitation about the moon, might make slight account of subterraneous deposition; whereas the Pythagoreans and transcorporating philosophers, who were to be often buried, held great care of their interment. And the Platonics rejected not a due care of the grave, though they put their ashes to unreasonable expectations, in their tedious term of return and long-set revolution.

Men have lost their reason in nothing so much as their religion, wherein stones and clouts make martyrs; and since the religion of one seems madness unto another, to afford an account or rational of old rites, requires no rigid reader. That they kindled the pyre aversely, or turning their face from it, was a handsome symbol of unwilling ministration. That they washed their bones with wine and milk; that the mother wrapped them in linen, and dried them in her bosom, the first fostering part and place of their nourishment; that they opened their eyes towards heaven before they kindled the fire, as the place of their hopes or original, were no improper ceremonies. Their last valediction, thrice uttered by the attendants,* was

* "Vale, vale, vale; nos te ordine, quo natura permittet, sequemur."

also very solemn, and somewhat answered by Christians, who thought it too little, if they threw not the earth thrice upon the interred body. That in strewing their tombs, the Romans affected the rose, the Greeks amaranthus and myrtle; that the funeral pyre consisted of sweet fuel, cypress, fir, larix, yew, and trees perpetually verdant, lay silent expressions of their surviving hopes. Wherein Christians, who deck their coffins with bays, have found a more elegant emblem; for that tree seeming dead, will restore itself from the root, and its dry and exsuccous leaves resume their verdure again; which, if we mistake not, we have also observed in furze. Whether the planting of yew in churchyards holds not its original from ancient funeral rites, or as an emblem of resurrection from its perpetual verdure, may also admit conjecture.

They made use of music to excite or quiet the affections of their friends, according to different harmonies. But the secret and symbolical hint was the harmonical nature of the soul, which, delivered from the body, went again to enjoy the primitive harmony of heaven, from whence it first descended; which, according to its progress traced by antiquity, came down by Cancer, and ascended by Capricornus.

They burnt not children before their teeth

appeared, as apprehending their bodies too tender a morsel for fire, and that their gristly bones would scarce leave separable relics after the pyral combustion. That they kindled not fire in their houses for some days after, was a strict memorial of the late afflicting fire. And mourning without hope, they had a happy fraud against excessive lamentation, by a common opinion that deep sorrows disturbed their ghosts.*

That they buried their dead on their backs, or in a supine position, seems agreeable unto profound sleep and common posture of dying, contrary to the most natural way of birth, nor unlike our pendulous posture in the doubtful state of the womb. Diogenes was singular, who preferred a prone situation in the grave; and some Christians like neither, who decline the figure of rest, and make choice of an erect posture.

Russians, &c.

That they carried them out of the world with their feet forward, not inconsonant unto reason, as contrary unto the native posture of man, and his production first into it, and also agreeable unto their opinions, while they bid adieu unto the world, not to look again upon it; whereas Mahometans, who think to return to a delightful life again, are carried forth with

* *Tu manes ne lœde meos.*

their heads forward, and looking toward their houses.

They closed their eyes, as parts which first die, or first discover the sad effects of death. But their iterated clamations to excitate their dying or dead friends, or revoke them unto life again, was a vanity of affection, as not presumably ignorant of the critical tests of death, by apposition of feathers, glasses, and reflection of figures, which dead eyes represent not; which, however not strictly verifiable in fresh and warm cadavers, could hardly elude the test in corpses of four or five days.

That they sucked in the last breath of their expiring friends, was surely a practice of no medical institution, but a loose opinion that the soul passed out that way, and a fondness of affection from some Pythagorical foundation, that the spirit of one body passed into another, which they wished might be their own.

That they poured oil upon the pyre, was a tolerable practice, while the intention rested in facilitating the ascension. But to place good omens in the quick and speedy burning, to sacrifice unto the winds for a despatch in this office, was a low form of superstition.

The Archimime, or jester, attending the funeral train, and imitating the speeches, gesture, and manners of the deceased, was too light for such solemnities, contradicting their funeral orations and doleful rites of the grave.

That they buried a piece of money with them as a fee of the Elysian ferryman, was a practice full of folly. But the ancient custom of placing coins in considerable urns, and the present practice of burying medals in the noble foundations of Europe, are laudable ways of historical discoveries, in actions, persons, chronologies; and posterity will applaud them.

We examine not the old laws of sepulture, exempting certain persons from burial or burning. But hereby we apprehend that these were not the bones of persons planet-struck or burnt with fire from heaven; no relics of traitors to their country, self-killers, or sacrilegious malefactors, persons in old apprehension unworthy of the earth, condemned unto the Tartarus of hell and bottomless pit of Pluto, from whence there was no redemption.

Nor were only many customs questionable in order to their obsequies, but also sundry practices, fictions, and conceptions, discordant or obscure, of their state and future beings. Whether unto eight or ten bodies of men to add one of a woman, as being more inflammable, and unctuously constituted for the better pyral combustion, were any rational practice; or whether the complaint of Periander's wife be tolerable, that, wanting her funeral burning, she suffered intolerable cold in hell, according to the constitution of the infernal house of Pluto, wherein cold makes a great part of their tortures; it cannot pass without some question.

Why the female ghosts appear unto Ulysses before the heroes and masculine spirits; why the Psyche, or soul, of Tiresias is of the masculine gender,* who, being blind on earth, sees more than all the rest in hell; why the funeral suppers consisted of eggs, beans, smallage, and lettuce, since the dead are made to eat asphodels † about the Elysian meadows; why, since there is no sacrifice acceptable, nor any propitiation for the covenant of the grave, men set up the deity of Morta, and fruitlessly adored divinities without ears; it cannot escape some doubt.

The dead seem all alive in the human "hades" of Homer, yet cannot well speak, prophesy, or know the living, except they drink blood, wherein is the life of man. And therefore the souls of Penelope's paramours, conducted by Mercury, chirped like bats, and those which followed Hercules made a noise, but like a flock of birds.

The departed spirits know things past and to

* Ψυχὴ Θηβαίου Τειρεσίαο σκῆπτρον ἔχων. Homer.

† Lucian.

come, yet are ignorant of things present. Agamemnon foretells what should happen unto Ulysses, yet ignorantly inquires what is become of his own son. The ghosts are afraid of swords in Homer; yet Sibylla tells Æneas in Virgil, the thin habit of spirits was beyond the force of weapons. The spirits put off their malice with their bodies, and Cæsar and Pompey accord in Latin hell; yet Ajax, in Homer, endures not a conference with Ulysses; and Deiphobus appears all mangled in Virgil's ghosts; yet we meet with perfect shadows among the wounded ghosts of Homer.

Since Charon, in Lucian, applauds his condition among the dead, whether it be handsomely said of Achilles, that living contemner of death, that he had rather be a ploughman's servant than emperor of the dead; how Hercules's soul is in hell and yet in heaven, and Julius's soul in a star, yet seen by Æneas in hell; (except the ghosts were but images and shadows of the soul, received in higher mansions, according to the ancient division of body, soul, and image, or simulacrum of them both,) we leave our readers to judge. The particulars of future beings must needs be dark unto ancient theories, which Christian philosophy yet determines but in a cloud of opinions. A dialogue between two infants in the womb, concerning the state of this world, might handsomely illustrate our ignorance of the next, whereof methinks we yet discourse in Plato's den, and are but embryon philosophers.

Pythagoras escapes, in the fabulous hell of Dante, among that swarm of philosophers, wherein, whilst we meet with Plato and Socrates, Cato is to be found in no lower place than Purgatory. Among all the set, Epicurus is most considerable, whom men make honest without an Elysium, who contemned life without encouragement of immortality, and, making nothing after death, yet made nothing of the king of terrors.

Were the happiness of the next world as closely apprehended as the felicities of this, it were a martyrdom to live; and unto such as consider none hereafter, it must be more than death to die, which makes us amazed at those audacities that durst be nothing and return into their chaos again. Certainly such spirits as could contemn death, when they expected no better being after, would have scorned to live had they known any. And therefore we applaud not the judgments of Machiavel, that Christianity makes men cowards; or that with the confidence of but half dying, the despised virtues of patience and humility have abased the spirits of men, which Pagan principles exalted; but rather regulated the wildness of audacities, in the attempts, grounds, and eternal sequels of death, wherein men of the boldest spirits are often prodigiously temerarious. Nor can we extenuate the valor of ancient martyrs, who contemned death in the uncomfortable scene of their lives, and in their decrepit martyrdoms did probably lose not many months of their days, or parted with life when it was scarce worth the living; for (beside that long time past holds no consideration unto a slender time to come) they had no small disadvantage from the constitution of old age, which naturally makes men fearful, and complexionally superannuated from the bold and courageous thoughts of youth and fervent years. But the contempt of death from corporal animosity promoteth not our felicity. They may sit in the orchestra and noblest seats of heaven who have held up shaking hands in the fire, and humanly contended for glory.

Meanwhile Epicurus lies deep in Dante's hell, wherein we meet with tombs enclosing souls which denied their immortalities. But whether the virtuous heathen, who lived better than he spake, or, erring in the principles of himself, yet lived above philosophers of more specious maxims, lie so deep as he is placed; at least so low as not to rise against Christians, who, believing or knowing that truth, have lastingly denied it in their practice and conversation, — were a query too sad to insist on.

But all or most apprehensions rested in opinions of some future being, which, ignorantly or coldly believed, begat those perverted conceptions, ceremonies, sayings, which Christians pity or laugh at. Happy are they which live not in that disadvantage of time, when men could say little for futurity but from reason; whereby the noblest minds fell often upon doubtful deaths and melancholy dissolutions. With those hopes Socrates warmed his doubtful spirits against that cold potion; and Cato, before he durst give the fatal stroke, spent part of the night in reading the immortality of Plato, thereby confirming his wavering hand unto the animosity of that attempt.

It is the heaviest stone that melancholy can throw at a man, to tell him he is at the end of his nature; or that there is no farther state to come, unto which this seems progressional, and otherwise made in vain. Without this accomplishment, the natural expectation and desire of such a state were but a fallacy in nature. Unsatisfied considerators would quarrel at the justice of their constitutions, and rest content that Adam had fallen lower; whereby, by knowing no other original, and deeper ignorance of themselves, they might have enjoyed the happiness of inferior creatures, who in tranquillity possess their constitutions, as having not the apprehension to deplore their own natures; and being framed below the circumference of these hopes, or cognition of better being, the wisdom of God hath necessitated their contentment. But the superior ingredient and obscured part of ourselves, whereto all present felicities afford no resting contentment, will be able at last to tell us we are more than our present selves, and evacuate such hopes in the fruition of their own accomplishments.

CHAPTER V.

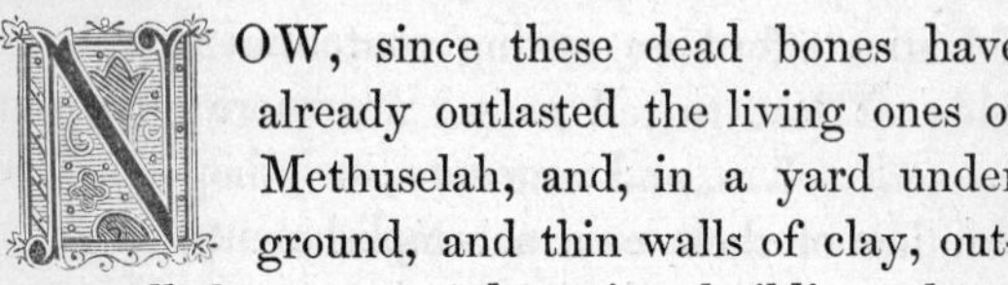

OW, since these dead bones have already outlasted the living ones of Methuselah, and, in a yard under ground, and thin walls of clay, outworn all the strong and specious buildings above it, and quietly rested under the drums and tramplings of three conquests; what prince can promise such diuturnity unto his relics, or might not gladly say,

"Sic ego componi versus in ossa velim."

Time, which antiquates antiquities, and hath an art to make dust of all things, hath yet spared these minor monuments. In vain we hope to be known by open and visible conservatories, when to be unknown was the means of their continuation, and obscurity their protection.

If they died by violent hands, and were thrust into their urns, these bones become considerable, and some old philosophers would honor them, whose souls they conceived most pure, which were thus snatched from their bodies,* and to retain a stronger propension unto them; whereas, they weariedly left a languishing corpse, and with faint desires of reunion. If they fell by long and aged decay, yet wrapped up in the bundle of time, they fall into indistinction, and make but one blot with infants. If we begin to die when we live, and long life be but a prolongation of death, our life is a sad composition; we live with death, and die not in a moment. How many pulses made up the life of Methuselah, were work for Archimedes. Common counters sum up the life of Moses's man.† Our days become considerable, like petty sums by minute accumulations, where numerous fractions make up but small round numbers, and our days of a span long make not one little finger.‡

If the nearness of our last necessity brought a nearer conformity unto it, there were a happiness in hoary hairs, and no calamity in half senses. But the long habit of living indisposeth us for dying; when avarice makes us the sport

* Βίῃ λιπόντων σῶμα ψυχαὶ καθαρώταται. "Vi corpus relinquentium animæ purissimæ." — Oracula Chaldaica cum scholiis Pselli et Phethonis.

† In the psalm of Moses.

‡ According to the ancient arithmetic of the hand, wherein the little finger of the right hand, contracted, signified a hundred.

of death; when even David grew politically cruel; and Solomon could hardly be said to be the wisest of men. But many are too early old, and before the date of age. Adversity stretcheth our days, misery makes Alcmena's nights, and time hath no wings unto it. But the most tedious being is that which can unwish itself, content to be nothing, or never to have been; which was beyond the malecontent of Job, who cursed not the day of his life, but his nativity, content to have so far been as to have a title to future being, although he had lived here but in a hidden state of life, and as it were an abortion.

One night as long as three.

What song the Sirens sang, or what name Achilles assumed when he hid himself among women, though puzzling questions,* are not beyond all conjecture. What time the persons of these ossuaries entered the famous nations of the dead,† and slept with princes and counsellors, might admit a wide solution. But who were the proprietaries of these bones, or what bodies these ashes made up, were a question above antiquarianism; not to be resolved by man, nor easily perhaps by spirits, except we consult the provincial guardians or tutelary observators. Had they made as good provision for their

* The puzzling questions of Tiberius unto grammarians. Marcel. Donatus in Suet.

† Κλυτὰ ἔθνεα νεκρῶν. Hom. Job.

names as they have done for their relics, they had not so grossly erred in the art of perpetuation. But to subsist in bones, and be but pyramidally extant, is a fallacy in duration. Vain ashes, which in the oblivion of names, persons, times, and sexes, have found unto themselves a fruitless continuation, and only arise unto late posterity, as emblems of mortal vanities, antidotes against pride, vainglory, and madding vices. Pagan vainglories, which thought the world might last forever, had encouragement for ambition; and finding no Atropos unto the immortality of their names, were never damped with the necessity of oblivion. Even old ambitions had the advantage of ours, in the attempts of their vainglories, who, acting early, and before the probable meridian of time, have by this time found great accomplishment of their designs, whereby the ancient heroes have already outlasted their monuments and mechanical preservations. But in this latter scene of time we cannot expect such mummies unto our memories, when ambition may fear the prophecy of Elias, and Charles the Fifth can never expect to live within two Methuselahs of Hector.*

That the world may last but six thousand years.

And therefore restless inquietude for the diuturnity of our memories unto present considera-

* Hector's fame lasting above two lives of Methuselah, before that famous prince, Charles, was extant.

tions, seems a vanity almost out of date, and superannuated piece of folly. We cannot hope to live so long in our names as some have done in their persons. One face of Janus holds no proportion unto the other. 'T is too late to be ambitious. The great mutations of the world are acted, or time may be too short for our designs. To extend our memories by monuments, whose death we daily pray for, and whose duration we cannot hope, without injury to our expectations, in the advent of the last day, were a contradiction to our beliefs. We, whose generations are ordained in this setting part of time, are providentially taken off from such imaginations; and being necessitated to eye the remaining particle of futurity, are naturally constituted unto thoughts of the next world, and cannot excusably decline the consideration of that duration, which maketh pyramids pillars of snow, and all that 's past a moment.

Circles and right lines limit and close all bodies, and the mortal right-lined circle must conclude and shut up all. There is no antidote against the opium of time, which temporally considereth all things. Our fathers find their graves in our short memories, and sadly tell us how we may be buried in our survivors. Gravestones tell truth scarce forty years.*

Θ, the character of death.

* Old ones being taken up, and other bodies laid under them.

Generations pass while some trees stand, and old families last not three oaks. To be read by bare inscriptions, like many in Gruter;* to hope for eternity by enigmatical epithets, or first letters of our names; to be studied by antiquaries, who we were, and have new names given us, like many of the mummies,† are cold consolations unto the students of perpetuity, even by everlasting languages.

To be content that times to come should only know there was such a man, not caring whether they knew more of him, was a frigid ambition in Cardan,‡ disparaging his horoscopal inclination and judgment of himself. Who cares to subsist like Hippocrates's patients, or Achilles's horses in Homer, under naked nominations, without deserts and noble acts, which are the balsam of our memories, the "entelechia" and soul of our subsistences? Yet to be nameless in worthy deeds exceeds an infamous history. The Canaanitish woman lives more happily without a name, than Herodias with one. And who had not rather have been the good thief than Pilate?

* Gruteri Inscriptiones Antiquæ.

† Which men show in several countries, giving them what names they please, and unto some the names of the old Egyptian kings out of Herodotus.

‡ "Cuperem notum esse quod sim, non opto ut sciatur qualis sim." — Card. in Vitâ propriâ.

But the iniquity of oblivion blindly scattereth her poppy, and deals with the memory of men without distinction to merit of perpetuity. Who can but pity the founder of the pyramids? Erostratus lives that burnt the Temple of Diana; he is almost lost that built it. Time hath spared the epitaph of Adrian's horse, confounded that of himself. In vain we compute our felicities by the advantage of our good names, since bad have equal durations; and Thersites is like to live as long as Agamemnon. Who knows whether the best of men be known, or whether there be not more remarkable persons forgot than any that stand remembered in the known account of time? Without the favor of the everlasting register, the first man had been as unknown as the last, and Methuselah's long life had been his only chronicle.

Oblivion is not to be hired. The greater part must be content to be as though they had not been, to be found in the register of God, not in the record of man. Twenty-seven names make up the first story, and the recorded names ever since contain not one living century. The number of the dead long exceedeth all that shall live. The night of time far surpasseth the day; and who knows when was the equinox? Every hour adds unto that current arithmetic, which scarce stands one moment.

Before the flood.

And since death must be the Lucina of life, and even Pagans could doubt whether thus to live were to die; since our longest sun sets at right declensions, and makes but winter arches, and therefore it cannot be long before we lie down in darkness, and have our light in ashes;* since the brother of death daily haunts us with dying mementos, and time, that grows old itself, bids us hope no long duration, diuturnity is a dream and folly of expectation.

Darkness and light divide the course of time, and oblivion shares with memory a great part even of our living beings. We slightly remember our felicities, and the smartest strokes of affliction leave but short smart upon us. Sense endureth no extremities, and sorrows destroy us or themselves. To weep into stones are fables. Afflictions induce callosities; miseries are slippery, or fall like snow upon us, which, notwithstanding, is no unhappy stupidity. To be ignorant of evils to come, and forgetful of evils past, is a merciful provision in nature, whereby we digest the mixture of our few and evil days, and our delivered senses not relapsing into cutting remembrances, our sorrows are not kept raw by the edge of repetitions. A great part of antiquity contented their hopes of subsistency

* According to the custom of the Jews, who placed a lighted wax-candle in a pot of ashes by the corpse.

with a transmigration of their souls; a good way to continue their memories, while, having the advantage of plural successions, they could not but act something remarkable in such variety of beings, and enjoying the fame of their passed selves, make accumulation of glory unto their last durations. Others, rather than be lost in the uncomfortable night of nothing, were content to recede into the common being, and make one particle of the public soul of all things, which was no more than to return into their unknown and divine original again. Egyptian ingenuity was more unsatisfied, contriving their bodies in sweet consistencies to attend the return of their souls. But all was vanity, feeding the wind and folly.* The Egyptian mummies, which Cambyses or time hath spared, avarice now consumeth. Mummy is become merchandise, Mizraim cures wounds, and Pharaoh is sold for balsams.

In vain do individuals hope for immortality, or any patent from oblivion, in preservations below the moon. Men have been deceived even in their flatteries above the sun, and studied conceits to perpetuate their names in heaven. The various cosmography of that part hath already varied the names of contrived constella-

* Omnia vanitas et pastio venti, νομὴ ἀνέμου καὶ βόσκησις, ut olim Aquila et Symmachus.

tions. Nimrod is lost in Orion, and Osiris in the Dog-star. While we look for incorruption in the heavens, we find they are but like the earth, durable in their main bodies, alterable in their parts; whereof, beside comets and new stars, perspectives begin to tell tales, and the spots that wander about the sun, with Phaethon's favor, would make clear conviction.

There is nothing strictly immortal but immortality. Whatever hath no beginning, may be confident of no end; which is the peculiar of that necessary essence that cannot destroy itself, and the highest strain of omnipotency to be so powerfully constituted, as not to suffer even from the power of itself. All others have a dependent being, and within the reach of destruction. But the sufficiency of Christian immortality frustrates all earthly glory, and the quality of either state after death makes a folly of posthumous memory. God, who can only destroy our souls, and hath assured our resurrection, either of our bodies or names hath directly promised no duration. Wherein there is so much of chance, that the boldest expectants have found unhappy frustration; and to hold long subsistence seems but a scape in oblivion. But man is a noble animal, splendid in ashes, and pompous in the grave, solemnizing nativities and deaths with equal lustre, nor omitting ceremonies of bravery in the infamy of his nature.

Life is a pure flame, and we live by an invisible sun within us. A small fire sufficeth for life; great flames seemed too little after death, while men vainly affected precious pyres, and to burn like Sardanapalus. But the wisdom of funeral laws found the folly of prodigal blazes, and reduced undoing fires unto the rule of sober obsequies, wherein few could be so mean as not to provide wood, pitch, a mourner, and an urn.*

Five languages † secured not the epitaph of Gordianus. The man of God lives longer without a tomb than any by one, invisibly interred by angels, and adjudged to obscurity, though not without some marks directing human discovery. Enoch and Elias, without either tomb or burial, in an anomalous state of being, are the great examples of perpetuity, in their long and living memory, in strict account being still on this side death, and having a late part yet to act

* According to the epitaph of Rufus and Beronica in Gruterus:

"Nec ex
Eorum bonis plus inventum est, quam
Quod sufficeret ad emendam pyram
Et picem quibus corpora cremarentur,
Et præfica conducta et olla empta."

† Hebrew, Greek, Latin, Egyptian, and Arabic, defaced by Licinius the Emperor.

upon this stage of earth. If in the decretory term of the world we shall not all die, but be changed, according to received translation, the last day will make but few graves; at least, quick resurrections will anticipate lasting sepultures. Some graves will be opened before they be quite closed, and Lazarus be no wonder; when many that feared to die shall groan that they can die but once. The dismal state is the second and living death, when life puts despair on the damned, when men shall wish the coverings of mountains, not of monuments, and annihilation shall be courted.

While some have studied monuments, others have studiously declined them; and some have been so vainly boisterous, that they durst not acknowledge their graves; wherein Alaricus seems more subtle, who had a river turned to hide his bones at the bottom. Even Sylla, who thought himself safe in his urn, could not prevent revenging tongues, and stones thrown at his monument. Happy are they whom privacy makes innocent, who deal so with men in this world, that they are not afraid to meet them in the next; who, when they die, make no commotion among the dead, and are not touched with that poetical taunt of Isaiah.

Isaiah xiv. 9 *et seq.*

Pyramids, arches, obelisks, were but the irregularities of vainglory and wild enormities of ancient magnanimity. But the most magnanimous resolution rests in the Christian religion, which trampleth upon pride, and sits on the neck of ambition, humbly pursuing that infallible perpetuity, unto which all others must diminish their diameters, and be poorly seen in angles of contingency.

Angulus contingentiæ, the least of angles.

Pious spirits, who passed their days in raptures of futurity, made little more of this world than the world that was before it, while they lay obscure in the chaos of preordination and night of their forebeings. And if any have been so happy as truly to understand Christian annihilation, ecstasis, exolution, liquefaction, transformation, the kiss of the spouse, gustation of God, and ingression into the divine shadow, they have already had a handsome anticipation of heaven; the glory of the world is surely over, and the earth in ashes unto them.

To subsist in lasting monuments, to live in their productions, to exist in their names and predicament of chimeras, was large satisfaction unto old expectations, and made one part of their Elysium. But all this is nothing in the metaphysics of true belief. To live indeed, is to be again ourselves, which being not only a hope but an evidence in noble believers, 't is all one to lie in St. Innocent's churchyard,*

* In Paris, where bodies soon consume.

as in the sands of Egypt,* ready to be anything, in the ecstasy of being ever, and as content with six feet as the "moles" of Adrianus.†

> "Tabesne cadavera solvat
> An rogus, haud refert."
>
> LUCAN.

* Beneath the pyramids.

† A stately mausoleum, or sepulchral pile, built by Adrianus in Rome, where now standeth the castle of St. Angelo.

FROM

THE GARDEN OF CYRUS.

FROM

The Garden of Cyrus,

or the Quincuncial* Lozenge.

AND therefore Providence hath arched and paved the great house of the world, with colours of mediocrity, that is, blue and green, above and below the sight, moderately terminating the *acies* of the eye. For most plants, though green above ground, maintain their original white below it, according to the candour of their seminal pulp: and the rudimental leaves do first appear in that colour, observable in seeds sprouting in water upon their first foliation. Green seeming to be the first supervenient, or above-ground complexion of vegetables, separable in many upon ligature or inhumation, as succory, endive, artichokes, and which is also lost upon fading in the autumn.

* *Quincunx.* An arrangement or disposition of things by *fives* in a square, one being placed in the middle of the square.

And this is also agreeable unto water itself, the alimental vehicle of plants, which first altereth into this colour. And, containing many vegetable seminalities, revealeth their seeds by greenness; and therefore soonest expected in rain or standing water, not easily found in distilled or water strongly boiled; wherein the seeds are extinguished by fire and decoction, and therefore last long and pure without such alteration, affording neither uliginous coats, gnat-worms, *acari*, hair-worms, like crude and common water; and therefore most fit for wholesome beverage, and with malt makes ale and beer without boiling. What large water-drinkers some plants are, the canary-tree and birches in some northern countries, drenching the fields about them, do sufficiently demonstrate. How water itself is able to maintain the growth of vegetables, and without extinction of their generative or medical virtues,—besides the experiment of Helmont's tree, we have found in some which have lived six years in glasses. The seeds of scurvy-grass growing in water-pots, have been fruitful in the land; and *assarum* after a year's space, and once casting its leaves in water, in the second leaves hath handsomely performed its vomiting operation.

Nor are only dark and green colours, but shades and shadows, contrived through the great volume of nature, and trees ordained not only to protect and shadow others, but by their shades and shadowing parts to preserve and cherish themselves: the whole radiation or branchings shadowing the stock and the root; —the leaves, the branches and fruit, too much exposed to the winds and scorching sun. The calicular leaves enclose the tender flowers, and the flowers themselves lie wrapped about the seeds, in their rudiment and first formations, which being advanced, the flowers fall away; and are therefore contrived in variety of figures, best satisfying the intention; handsomely observable in hooded and gaping flowers, and the butterfly blooms of leguminous plants, the lower leaf closely involving the rudimental cod, and the alary or wingy divisions embracing or hanging over it.

But seeds themselves do lie in perpetual shades, either under the leaf, or shut up in coverings; and such as lie barest have their husks, skins, and pulps about them, wherein the nib and generative particle lieth moist and secured from the injury of air and sun. Darkness and light hold interchangeable dominions, and alternately rule the seminal state of things. Light unto Pluto* is darkness unto Jupiter.

* "Lux orco, tenebræ Jovi; tenebræ orco, lux Jovi."—Hippocr. de Diæta. S. Hevelii Selenographia.

Legions of seminal ideas lie in their second chaos and Orcus of Hippocrates; till, putting on the habits of their forms, they show themselves upon the stage of the world, and open dominion of Jove. They that held the stars of heaven were but rays and flashing glimpses of the empyreal light, through holes and perforations of the upper heaven, took off the natural shadows of stars; while according to better discovery the poor inhabitants of the moon have but a polary life, and must pass half their days in the shadow of that luminary.

Light that makes things seen, makes some things invisible: were it not for darkness and the shadow of the earth, the noblest part of the creation had remained unseen, and the stars in heaven as invisible as on the fourth day, when they were created above the horizon with the sun, or there was not an eye to behold them. The greatest mystery of religion is expressed by adumbration, and in the noblest part of Jewish types we find the cherubims shadowing the mercy-seat. Life itself is but the shadow of death, and souls departed but the shadows of the living. All things fall under this name. The sun itself is but the dark *simulachrum*, and light but the shadow of God.

Lastly, it is no wonder that this quincuncial order was first and is still affected as grateful unto the eye. For all things are seen quincuncially; for at the eye the pyramidal rays from the object receive a decussation, and so strike a second base upon the *retina* or hinder coat, the proper organ of vision; wherein the pictures from objects are represented, answerable to the paper, or wall in the dark chamber; after the decussation of the rays at the hole of the horny-coat, and their refraction upon the crystalline humour, answering the *foramen* of the window, and the convex or burning-glasses, which refract the rays that enter it. And if ancient anatomy would hold, a like disposure there was of the optic or visual nerves in the brain, wherein antiquity conceived a concurrence by decussation. And this not only observable in the laws of direct vision, but in some part also verified in the reflected rays of sight. For making the angle of incidence equal to that of reflection, the visual ray returneth quincuncially, and after the form of a V; and the line of reflection being continued unto the place of vision, there ariseth a semi-decussation which makes the object seen in a perpendicular unto itself, and as far below the reflectent, as it is from it above; observable in the sun and moon beheld in water.

And this is also the law of reflection in moved bodies and sounds, which, though not made by decussation, observe the rule of equality between incidence and reflection: whereby whispering places are framed by elliptical arches laid sidewise; where the voice being delivered at the focus of one extremity, observing an equality unto the angle of incidence, it will reflect unto the focus of the other end, and so escape the ears of the standers in the middle.

A like rule is observed in the reflection of the vocal and sonorous line in echoes, which cannot therefore be heard in all stations. But happening in woody plantations, by waters, and able to return some words, if reached by a pleasant and well dividing voice, there may be heard the softest notes in nature.

And this not only verified in the way of sense, but in animal and intellectual receptions: things entering upon the intellect by a pyramid from without, and thence into the memory by another from within, the common decussation being in the understanding as is delivered by Bovillus. Whether the intellectual and fantastical lines be not thus rightly disposed, but magnified, diminished, distorted, and ill-placed, in the mathematics of some brains, whereby they have irregular apprehensions of things, perverted notions, conceptions, and incurable hallucinations, were no unpleasant speculation.

Car. Bovillus de Intellectu.

And if Egyptian philosophy may obtain, the

scale of influences was thus disposed, and the genial spirits of both worlds do trace their way in ascending and descending pyramids, mystically apprehended in the letter X, and the open bill and straddling legs of a stork, which was imitated by that character.

Of this figure Plato made choice to illustrate the motion of the soul, both of the world and man: while he delivereth that God divided the whole conjunction lengthwise, according to the figure of a Greek X, and then turning it about reflected it into a circle; by the circle implying the uniform motion of the first orb, and by the right lines, the planetical and various motions within it. And this also with application unto the soul of man, which hath a double aspect, one right, whereby it beholdeth the body, and objects without; another circular and reciprocal, whereby it beholdeth itself. The circle declaring the motion of the indivisible soul, simple, according to the divinity of its nature, and returning into itself; the right lines respecting the motion pertaining unto sense and vegetation; and the central decussation, the wondrous connection of the several faculties conjointly in one substance. And so conjoined the unity and duality of the soul, and made out the three substances so much considered by him; that is, the indivisible or divine, the divisible or corporeal, and that third, which was the *systasis* or harmony of those two, in the mystical decussation.

And if that were clearly made out which Justin Martyr took for granted, this figure hath had the honour to characterize and notify our blessed Saviour, as he delivereth in that borrowed expression from Plato, "Decussavit eum in universo," the hint whereof he would have Plato derive from the figure of the brazen serpent, and to have mistaken the letter X for T. Whereas it is not improbable he learned these and other mystical expressions in his learned observations of Egypt, where he might obviously behold the mercurial characters, the handed crosses, and other mysteries not thoroughly understood in the sacred letter X; which, being derivative from the stork, one of the ten sacred animals, might be originally Egyptian, and brought into Greece by Cadmus of that country.

To enlarge this contemplation unto all the mysteries and secrets accommodable unto this number, were inexcusable Pythagorism, yet cannot omit the ancient conceit of five surnamed the number of justice;* as justly dividing between the digits, and hanging in the centre of nine, described by square numeration, which

* δίκη.

angularly divided will make the decussated number; and so agreeable unto the quincuncial ordination, and rows divided by equality, and just decorum, in the whole com-plantation; and might be the original of that common game among us, wherein the fifth place is sovereign, and carrieth the chief intention; — the ancients wisely instructing youth, even in their recreations, unto virtue, that is, early to drive at the middle point and central seat of justice.

Nor can we omit how agreeable unto this number an handsome division is made in trees and plants, since Plutarch, and the ancients have named it the divisive number; justly dividing the entities of the world, many remarkable things in it, and also comprehending the general division of vegetables.* And he that considers how most blossoms of trees, and greatest number of flowers, consist of five leaves, and therein doth rest the settled rule of nature, — so that in those which exceed there is often found, or easily made, a variety, — may readily discover how nature rests in this number, which is indeed the first rest and pause of numeration in the fingers, the natural organs thereof. Nor in

* Δένδρον, Θάμνος, Φρύγανον, Πόα, *arbor*, *frutex*, *suffrutex*, *herba*, and that fifth which comprehendeth the *fungi* and *tubera*, whether to be named Ἄσχιον or γύμνον, comprehending also *conferva marina salsa*, and sea-cords, of so many yards length.

the division of the feet of perfect animals doth nature exceed this account. And even in the joints of feet, which in birds are most multiplied, surpasseth not this number; so progressionally making them out in many,* that from five in the fore-claw she descendeth unto two in the hindmost; and so in four feet makes up the number of joints in the five fingers or toes of man.

Not to omit the quintuple section of a cone,† of handsome practice in ornamental garden-plots, and in same way discoverable in so many works of nature, in the leaves, fruits, and seeds of vegetables, and scales of some fishes; so much considerable in glasses, and the optic doctrine; wherein the learned may consider the crystalline humour of the eye in the cuttle-fish and loligo.

He that forgets not how antiquity named this the conjugal or wedding number, and made it the emblem of the most remarkable conjunction, will conceive it duly appliable unto this handsome economy and vegetable combination: and may hence apprehend the allegorical sense of that obscure expression of Hesiod,‡ and afford no improbable reason why Plato admitted his nuptial guests by fives, in the kindred of the married couple.

Plato de Leg. 6.

* As herons, bitterns, and long-clawed fowls.

† *Elleipsis, parabola, hyperbole, circulus, triangulum.*

‡ *πέμπτας, id est, nuptias multas.* Rhodig.

And though a sharper mystery might be implied in the number of the five wise and foolish virgins, which were to meet the bridegroom, yet was the same agreeable unto the conjugal number, which ancient numerists made out by two and three, the first parity and imparity, the active and passive digits, the material and formal principles in generative societies. And not discordant even from the customs of the Romans, who admitted but five torches in their nuptial solemnities. Whether there were any mystery, or not, implied, the most generative animals were created on this day, and had accordingly the largest benediction. And under a quintuple consideration, wanton antiquity considered the circumstances of generation, while by this number of five they naturally divided the nectar of the fifth planet.*

Plutarch. Problem. Rom. i.

The same number in the Hebrew mysteries and cabalistical accounts was the character of generation,† declared by the letter E, the fifth in their alphabet, according to that cabalistical dogma; if Abram had not had this letter added unto his name, he had remained fruitless, and without the power of generation: not only because hereby the number of his name attained

* ". . . . . oscula quæ Venus
Quinta parte sui nectaris imbuit."
Hor. lib. i. od. 13.

† Archang. Dog. Cabal.

two hundred forty-eight, the number of the affirmative precepts, but because, as in created natures there is a male and female, so in divine and intelligent productions, the mother of life and fountain of souls in cabalistical technology is called *Binah*, whose seal and character was E. So that, being sterile before, he received the power of generation from that measure and mansion in the archetype: and was made conformable unto Binah. And upon such involved considerations, the ten of Sarai was exchanged into five.* If any shall look upon this as a stable number, and fitly appropriable unto trees, as bodies of rest and station, he hath herein a great foundation in nature, who observing much variety in legs and motive organs of animals, as two, four, six, eight, twelve, fourteen, and more, hath passed over five and ten, and assigned them unto none, or very few, as the *Phalangium monstrosum Brasilianum* (*Clusii et Jac. de Laet. Cur. Poster. Americæ Descript.*), if perfectly described. And for the stability of this number, he shall not want the sphericity of its nature, which multiplied in itself will return into its own denomination, and bring up the rear of the account. Which is also one of the numbers that makes up the mystical name of God, which consisting of letters de-

* *Jod* into *He*.

noting all the spherical numbers, ten, five, and six, emphatically sets forth the notion of Trismegistus, and that intelligible sphere, which is the nature of God.

Many expressions by this number occur in Holy Scripture, perhaps unjustly laden with mystical expositions, and little concerning our order. That the Israelites were forbidden to eat the fruit of their new-planted trees before the fifth year, was very agreeable unto the natural rules of husbandry; fruits being unwholesome and lash,* before the fourth or fifth year. In the second day or feminine part of five, there was added no approbation. For in the third or masculine day, the same is twice repeated; and a double benediction enclosed both creations, whereof the one, in some part, was but an accomplishment of the other. That the trespasser was to pay a fifth part above the head or principal, makes no secret in this number, and implied no more than one part above the principal; which being considered in four parts, the additional forfeit must bear the name of a fifth. The five golden mice had plainly their determination from the number of the princes. That five should put to flight an hundred might have nothing mystically implied; considering a rank

Lev. vi.

* "*lash.*] Soft and watery, but without flavour." — Forby's Vocabulary of East Anglia.

of soldiers could scarce consist of a lesser number. Saint Paul had rather speak five words in a known, than ten thousand in an unknown tongue; that is, as little as could well be spoken; a simple proposition consisting of three words, and a complexed one not ordinarily short of five.

More considerables there are in this mystical account, which we must not insist on. And therefore, why the radical letters in the Pentateuch should equal the number of the soldiery of the tribes? Why our Saviour in the wilderness fed five thousand persons with five barley loaves; and again, but four thousand with no less than seven of wheat? Why Joseph designed five changes of raiment unto Benjamin; and David took just five pebbles* out of the brook against the Pagan champion; — we leave it unto arithmetical divinity, and theological explanation.

Yet if any delight in new problems, or think it worth the enquiry, whether the critical physician hath rightly hit the nominal notation of *quinque?* Why the ancients mixed five or three, but not four parts of water unto their wine; and Hippocrates observed a fifth proportion in the mixture of water with milk, as in dysenteries and bloody fluxes? Under what

* τέσσαρα ἕνκε, four and one, or five. Scalig.

abstruse foundation astrologers do figure the good or bad fate from our children, in good fortune;* or the fifth house of their celestial schemes? Whether the Egyptians described a star by a figure of five points, with reference unto the five capital aspects,† whereby they transmit their influences, or abstruser considerations? Why the cabalistical doctors, who conceive the whole sephiroth, or divine emanations to have guided the ten-stringed harp of David, whereby he pacified the evil spirit of Saul, in strict numeration do begin with the *perihypate meson*, or *si fa ut*, and so place the *tiphereth* answering *c sol fa ut*, upon the fifth string? or whether this number be oftener applied unto bad things and ends, than good in Holy Scripture, and why? he may meet with abstrusities of no ready resolution.

If any shall question the rationality of that magic, in the cure of the blind man by Serapis, commanded to place five fingers on his altar, and then his hand on his eyes? Why, since the whole comedy is primarily and naturally comprised in four parts,‡ and antiquity permitted not so many persons to speak in one scene, yet would not comprehend the same in

* Ἀγαθὴ τυχή, *bona fortuna*, the name of the fifth house.

† Conjunct, opposite, sextile, trigonal, tetragonal.

‡ Πρότασις, ἐπίτασις, κατάστασις, καταστροφή.

more or less than five acts? Why amongst sea-stars nature chiefly delighteth in five points? And since there are found some of no fewer than twelve, and some of seven, and nine, there are few or none discovered of six or eight?* If any shall enquire why the flowers of rue properly consist of four leaves, the first and third flower have five? Why, since many flowers have one leaf or none, as Scaliger will have it, divers three, and the greatest number consist of five divided from their bottoms, there are yet so few of two? or why nature, generally beginning or setting out with two opposite leaves at the root, doth so seldom conclude with that order and number at the flower? He shall not pass his hours in vulgar speculations.

Unifolium nullifolium.

If any shall further query why magnetical philosophy excludeth decussations, and needles transversely placed do naturally distract their verticities? Why geomancers do imitate the quintuple figure, in their mother characters of acquisition and amission, &c., somewhat answering the figures in the lady or speckled beetle?

* *Why amongst sea-stars, &c.*] The far greater number of this group of *Radiata* is pentagonal, or five-rayed. But there occur in many species individuals which vary from the rule. In the British Museum there are specimens of *Ophiura elegans* and *Asterias reticulata* with but four rays; of some unnamed species with 4, 5, 6, and 7; of *A. variolata* with 4, 5, 6, 7, and 8 rays; of *A. endica* with 8 and 9; and *A. papposa* with from 12 to 15 rays.

With what equity chiromantical conjecturers decry these decussations in the lines and mounts of the hand? What that decussated figure intendeth in the medal of Alexander the Great? Why the goddesses sit commonly cross-legged in ancient draughts, since Juno is described in the same as a veneficial posture to hinder the birth of Hercules? If any shall doubt why at the amphidromical feasts, on the fifth day after the child was born, presents were sent from friends, of polypuses and cuttle-fishes? Why five must be only left in that symbolical mutiny among the men of Cadmus? Why Proteus in Homer, the symbol of the first matter, before he settled himself in the midst of his sea-monsters, doth place them out by fives? Why the fifth year's ox was acceptable sacrifice unto Jupiter? Or why the noble Antoninus in some sense doth call the soul itself a rhombus? He shall not fall on trite or trivial disquisitions. And these we invent and propose unto acuter inquirers, nauseating crambe verities and questions over-queried. Flat and flexible truths are beat out by every hammer; but Vulcan and his whole forge sweat to work out Achilles his armour. A large field is yet left unto sharper discerners to enlarge upon this order, to search out the *quaternios* and figured draughts of this nature, and (moderating the study of names, and mere nomenclature of plants), to erect generalities, disclose unobserved proprieties, not only in the vegetable shop, but the whole volume of nature; affording delightful truths, confirmable by sense and ocular observation, which seems to me the surest path to trace the labyrinth of truth.* For though discursive inquiry and rational conjecture may leave handsome gashes and flesh-wounds; yet without conjunction of this, expect no mortal or dispatching blows unto error.

But the quincunx † of heaven runs low, and 't is time to close the five ports of knowledge. We are unwilling to spin out our awaking thoughts into the phantasms of sleep, which often continueth precogitations; making cables of cobwebs, and wildernesses of handsome groves. Beside, Hippocrates hath spoke so little, and the oneirocritical masters have left such frigid interpretations from plants, that there is little encouragement to dream of Paradise itself. Nor will the sweetest delight of gardens afford much comfort in sleep; wherein the dulness of that sense shakes hands with de-

De Insomniis. Artemidorus et Apomazar.

* *and (moderating the study of names, and mere nomenclature of plants), to erect generalities, &c.*] In these observations the importance and necessity of endeavouring to approximate to the true natural system of plants, is very curiously and sagaciously anticipated by our author.

† *Hyades*, near the horizon about midnight, at that time.

lectable odours; and though in the bed of Cleopatra,* can hardly with any delight raise up the ghost of a rose.

Night, which Pagan theology could make the daughter of Chaos, affords no advantage to the description of order; although no lower than that mass can we derive its genealogy. All things began in order, so shall they end, and so shall they begin again; according to the ordainer of order and mystical mathematics of the city of heaven.

Though Somnus in Homer be sent to rouse up Agamemnon, I find no such effects in these drowsy approaches of sleep. To keep our eyes open longer, were but to act our Antipodes. The huntsmen are up in America, and they are already past their first sleep in Persia. But who can be drowsy at that hour which freed us from everlasting sleep? or have slumbering thoughts at that time, when sleep itself must end, and as some conjecture all shall awake again.

* Strewed with roses.

FROM

VULGAR ERRORS.

[THE following passages are selected as specimens from different parts of the "Enquiries into Vulgar and Common Errors."]

Vulgar Errors.

Adam's error.

ADAM, upon the expostulation of God, replied, "I heard thy voice in the garden, and because I was naked I hid myself." In which reply there was included a very gross mistake, and if with pertinacity maintained, a high and capital error. For thinking by this retirement to obscure himself from God, he infringed the omnisciency and essential ubiquity of his Maker; who, as he created all things, so is he beyond and in them all, not only in power, as under his subjection, or in his presence, as being in his cognition, but in his very essence, as being the soul of their causalities and the essential cause of their existences. Certainly his posterity, at this distance and after so perpetuated an impairment, cannot but condemn the poverty of his conception, that thought to obscure himself from his Creator in the shade of the garden, who had beheld him before in the darkness of his chaos and the great obscurity of nothing; that thought to fly from God which could not fly himself; or imagined that one tree should conceal his nakedness from God's eye, as another had revealed it unto his own. Those tormented spirits, that wish the mountains to cover them, have fallen upon desires of minor absurdity, and chosen ways of less improbable concealment. Though this be also as ridiculous unto reason as fruitless unto their desires; for he that laid the foundations of the earth cannot be excluded the secrecy of the mountains; nor can there anything escape the perspicacity of those eyes which were before light, and in whose optics there is no opacity. This is the consolation of all good men, unto whom his ubiquity affordeth continual comfort and security; and this is the affliction of hell, unto whom it affordeth despair and remediless calamity. For those restless spirits that fly the face of the Almighty, being deprived of the fruition of his eye, would also avoid the extent of his hand; which being impossible, their sufferings are desperate and their afflictions without evasion, until they can get out of Trismegistus's circle, that is, to extend their wings above the universe and pitch beyond ubiquity.

Of adherence unto antiquity.

BUT the mortalest enemy unto knowledge, and that which hath done the greatest execution upon truth, hath been a peremptory adhesion unto authority, and more especially the establishing of our belief upon the dictates of antiquity. For (as every capacity may observe) most men of ages present so superstitiously do look on ages past, that the authorities of the one exceed the reasons of the other; whose persons indeed, being far removed from our times, their works, which seldom with us pass uncontrolled either by contemporaries or immediate successors, are now become out of the distance of envies; and the further removed from present times, are conceived to approach the nearer unto truth itself. Now hereby methinks we manifestly delude ourselves, and widely walk out of the track of truth.

For, first, men hereby impose a thraldom on their times, which the ingenuity of no age should endure, or indeed the presumption of any did ever yet enjoin. Thus Hippocrates, about two thousand years ago, conceived it no injustice either to examine or refute the doctrines of his predecessors; Galen the like, and Aristotle most of any. Yet did not any of these conceive themselves infallible, or set down their dictates as verities irrefragable; but when they either deliver their own inventions or reject other men's opinions, they proceed with judgment and ingenuity, establishing their assertions, not only with great solidity, but submitting them also unto the correction of future discovery.

Secondly, men that adore times past, consider not that those times were once present; that is, as our own are at this instant, and we ourselves unto those to come as they unto us at present. As we rely on them, even so will those on us, and magnify us hereafter, who at present condemn ourselves; which very absurdity is daily committed amongst us even in the esteem and censure of our own times. And, to speak impartially, old men, from whom we should expect the greatest example of wisdom, do most exceed in this point of folly; commending the days of their youth they scarce remember, at least well understood not; extolling those times their younger years have heard their fathers condemn, and condemning those times the gray heads of their posterity shall commend. And thus is it the humor of many heads to extol the days of their forefathers and declaim against the wickedness of times present; which notwithstanding they cannot handsomely do, without the borrowed help and satires of times past, condemning the vices of their times by the expressions of vices in times which they commend, which cannot but argue the community of vice in both. Horace, therefore, Juvenal, and Persius were no prophets, although their lines did seem to indigitate and point at our times. There is a certain list of vices committed in all ages and declaimed against by all authors, which will last as long as human nature; or digested into commonplaces may serve for any theme, and never be out of date until doomsday.

The erroneous disposition of the people.

AS for popular errors, they are more nearly founded upon an erroneous inclination of the people, as being the most deceptible part of mankind, and ready with open arms to receive the encroachments of error; which condition of theirs, although deducible from many grounds, yet shall we evidence it but from a few, and such as most nearly and undeniably declare their natures.

How unequal discerners of truth they are, and openly exposed unto error, will first appear from their unqualified intellectuals, unable to umpire the difficulty of its dissensions. For error, to speak largely, is a false judgment of things, or an assent unto falsity. Now whether the object whereunto they deliver up their assent be true or false, they are incompetent judges.

For the assured truth of things is derived from the principles of knowledge, and causes which determine their verities; whereof their uncultivated understandings scarce holding any theory, they are but bad discerners of verity, and in the numerous track of error but casually do hit the point and unity of truth.

Their understanding is so feeble in the discernment of falsities and averting the errors of reason, that it submitteth unto the fallacies of sense, and is unable to rectify the error of its sensations. Thus the greater part of mankind, having but one eye of sense and reason, conceive the earth far bigger than the sun, the fixed stars lesser than the moon, their figures plain, and their spaces from earth equidistant. For thus their sense informeth them, and herein their reason cannot rectify them; and therefore hopelessly continuing in mistakes, they live and die in their absurdities, passing their days in perverted apprehensions and conceptions of the world, derogatory unto God and the wisdom of the creation.

Again, being so illiterate in the point of intellect and their sense so incorrected, they are further indisposed ever to attain unto truth, as commonly proceeding in those ways which have most reference unto sense, and wherein there lieth most notable and popular delusion. For being unable to wield the intellectual arms of reason, they are fain to betake themselves unto wasters and the blunter weapons of truth, affecting the gross and sensible ways of doctrine, and such as will not consist with strict and subtile reason. Thus unto them a piece of rhetoric is a sufficient argument of logic, an apologue of Æsop beyond a syllogism in Barbara; parables than propositions, and proverbs more powerful than demonstrations. And therefore are they led rather by example than precept, receiving persuasions from visible inducements before intellectual instructions. And therefore also they judge of human actions by the event; for being uncapable of operable circumstances or rightly to judge the prudentiality of affairs, they only gaze upon the visible success, and thereafter condemn or cry up the whole progression. And so from this ground in the lecture of Holy Scripture, their apprehensions are commonly confined unto the literal sense of the text; from whence have ensued the gross and duller sort of heresies. For not attaining the deuteroscopy and second intention of the words, they are fain to omit their superconsequences, coherencies, figures, or tropologies, and are not sometimes persuaded by fire beyond their literalities. And therefore all things invisible but unto intellectual discernments, to humour the grossness of their comprehensions, have been degraded from their proper forms, and God himself dishonoured into manual expressions. And so likewise, being unprovided or unsufficient for higher speculations, they will always betake themselves unto sensible representations, and can hardly be restrained the dulness of idolatry; a sin or folly not only derogatory unto God, but men; overthrowing their reason as well as his divinity; in brief, a reciprocation, or rather an inversion of the creation, making God one way, as he made us another; that is, after our image, as he made us after his own.

Moreover, their understanding, thus weak in itself, and perverted by sensible delusions, is yet further impaired by the dominion of their appetite, that is, the irrational and brutal part of the soul; which, lording it over the sovereign faculty, interrupts the actions of that noble part, and chokes those tender sparks which Adam hath left them of reason; and therefore they do not only swarm with errors, but vices depending thereon. Thus they commonly affect no man any further than he deserts his reason or complies with their aberrancies. Hence they embrace not virtue for itself, but its reward; and the argument from pleasure or utility is far more powerful than that from virtuous honesty;

which Mahomet and his contrivers well understood, when he set out the felicity of his heaven by the contentments of flesh and the delights of sense, slightly passing over the accomplishment of the soul and the beatitude of that part which earth and visibilities too weakly affect. But the wisdom of our Saviour and the simplicity of his truth proceeded another way, defying the popular provisions of happiness from sensible expectations, placing his felicity in things removed from sense, and the intellectual enjoyment of God. And therefore the doctrine of the one was never afraid of universities, or endeavoured the banishment of learning like the other. And though Galen doth sometimes nibble at Moses, and beside the Apostate Christian, some heathens have questioned his philosophical part or treatise of the creation; yet is there surely no reasonable Pagan that will not admire the rational and well-grounded precepts of Christ, whose life, as it was conformable unto his doctrine, so was that unto the highest rules of reason, and must therefore flourish in the advancement of learning, and the perfection of parts best able to comprehend it.

Again, their individual imperfections being great, they are moreover enlarged by their aggregation; and being erroneous in their single numbers, once huddled together they will be error itself. For being a confusion of knaves and fools, and a farraginous concurrence of all conditions, tempers, sexes, and ages, it is but natural if their determinations be monstrous and many ways inconsistent with truth. And therefore wise men have always applauded their own judgment in the contradiction of that of the people; and their soberest adversaries have ever afforded them the style of fools and madmen; and to speak impartially, their actions have often made good these epithets. Had Orestes been judge, he would not have acquitted that Lystrian rabble of madness, who, upon a visible miracle, falling into so high a conceit of Paul and Barnabas, that they termed the one Jupiter, the other Mercurius; that they brought oxen and garlands, and were hardly restrained from sacrificing unto them; did notwithstanding suddenly after fall upon Paul, and, having stoned him, drew him for dead out of the city. It might have hazarded the sides of Democritus had he been present at that tumult of Demetrius, when, the people flocking together in great numbers, some cried one thing and some another, and the assembly was confused, and the most part knew not wherefore they were come together; notwithstanding, all with one voice for the space of two hours cried out, "Great is Diana of the Ephesians." It had overcome the patience of Job, as it did the meekness of Moses, and would surely have mastered any but the longanimity and lasting sufferance of God, had they beheld the mutiny in the wilderness, when, after ten great miracles in Egypt and some in the same place, they melted down their stolen ear-rings into a calf, and monstrously cried out, "These be thy gods, O Israel, which brought thee up out of the land of Egypt." It much accuseth the impatience of Peter, who could not endure the staves of the multitude, and is the greatest example of lenity in our Saviour, when he desired of God forgiveness unto those, who, having one day brought him into the city in triumph, did presently after act all dishonour upon him, and nothing could be heard but "Crucifige" in their courts. Certainly he that considereth these things in God's peculiar people will easily discern how little of truth there is in the ways of the multitude; and though sometimes they are flattered with that aphorism, will hardly believe the voice of the people to be the voice of God.

Lastly, being thus divided from truth in themselves, they are yet farther removed by advenient deception. For true it is, (and I hope I shall not offend their vulgarities if I say,) they are daily mocked into error by subtler devisors, and have been expressly deluded by all professions and ages. Thus the priests of elder time have put upon them many incredible conceits, not only deluding their apprehensions with ariolation, soothsaying, and such oblique idolatries, but winning their credulities unto the literal and downright adorement of cats, lizards, and beetles. And thus also in some Christian churches, wherein is presumed an irreprovable truth, if all be true that is suspected, or half what is related, there have not wanted many strange deceptions, and some thereof are still confessed by the name of pious frauds. Thus Theudas, an impostor, was able to lead away four thousand into the wilderness, and the delusions of Mahomet almost the fourth part of mankind. Thus all heresies, how gross soever, have found a welcome with the people. For thus many of the Jews were wrought into the belief that Herod was the Messias; and David George of Leyden, and Arden, were not without a party amongst the people, who maintained the same opinion of themselves almost in our days.

Saltinbancoes, quacksalvers, and charlatans deceive them in lower degrees. Were Æsop alive, the Piazza and Pont-Neuf could not but speak their fallacies; meanwhile there are too many, whose cries cannot conceal their mischief. For their impostures are full of cruelty and worse than any other, deluding not only unto pecuniary defraudations, but the irreparable deceit of death.

Astrologers, which pretend to be of Cabala with the stars, (such I mean as abuse that worthy inquiry,) have not been wanting in their deceptions; who, having won their belief unto principles whereof they make great doubt themselves, have made them believe that arbitrary events below have necessary causes above; whereupon their credulities assent unto any prognostics, and daily swallow the predictions of men, which, considering the independency of their causes and contingency in their events, are only in the prescience of God.

Fortune-tellers, jugglers, geomancers, and the like incantatory impostors, though commonly men of inferior rank, and from whom without illumination they can expect no more than from themselves, do daily and professedly delude them; unto whom (what is deplorable in men and Christians) too many applying themselves, betwixt jest and earnest, betray the cause of truth, and insensibly make up the legionary body of error.

Statists and politicians, unto whom "ragione di stato" is the first considerable, as though it were their business to deceive the people, as a maxim do hold that truth is to be concealed from them; unto whom although they reveal the visible design, yet do they commonly conceal the capital intention. And therefore have they ever been the instruments of great designs, yet seldom understood the true intention of any; accomplishing the drifts of wiser heads, as inanimate and ignorant agents the general design of the world; who though in some latitude of sense and in a natural cognition perform their proper actions, yet do they unknowingly concur unto higher ends, and blindly advance the great intention of nature. Now how far they may be kept in ignorance, a great example there is in the people of Rome, who never knew the true and proper name of their own city. For beside that common appellation received by the citizens, it had a proper and secret name concealed from them. "Cujus alterum nomen dicere secretis ceremoniarum nefas habetur," says Pliny; lest the name thereof being discovered unto their enemies, their penates and patronal gods might be called forth by charms and incantations. For according unto the tradition of magicians, the tutelary spirits will not remove at common appellations, but at the proper names of things whereunto they are protectors.

Thus having been deceived by themselves, and continually deluded by others, they must needs be stuffed with errors, and even overrun with these inferior falsities; whereunto whosoever shall resign their reasons, either from the root of deceit in themselves, or inability to resist such trivial ingannations from others, although their condition and fortunes may place them many spheres above the multitude, yet are they still within the line of vulgarity, and democratical enemies of truth.

THE falling of salt is an authentic presagement of ill luck, nor can every temper contemn it; from whence notwithstanding nothing can be naturally feared; nor was the same a general prognostic of future evil among the ancients, but a particular omination concerning the breach of friendship. For salt, as incorruptible, was the symbol of friendship, and, before the other service, was offered unto their guests; which, if it casually fell, was accounted ominous, and their amity of no duration. But whether salt were not only a symbol of friendship with man, but also a figure of amity and reconciliation with God, and was therefore observed in sacrifices, is a higher speculation.

Of the falling of salt.

TO break the egg-shell after the meat is out, we are taught in our childhood, and practise it all our lives; which nevertheless is

Of breaking the egg-shell.

but a superstitious relic, according to the judgment of Pliny, "Huc pertinet ovorum, ut exsorbuerit quisque, calices protinus frangi, aut eosdem cochlearibus perforari"; and the intent hereof was to prevent witchcraft; for lest witches should draw or prick their names therein, and veneficiously mischief their persons, they broke the shell, as Dalecampius hath observed.

Of the true-lover's knot.

THE true lover's knot is very much magnified, and still retained in presents of love among us; which, though in all points it doth not make out, had perhaps its original from "Nodus Herculanus," or that which was called Hercules's knot, resembling the snaky complication in the caduceus or rod of Hermes; and in which form the zone or woollen girdle of the bride was fastened, as Turnebus observeth in his "Adversaria."

Of the cheek burning or ear tingling.

WHEN our cheek burneth or ear tingleth, we usually say that somebody is talking of us, which is an ancient conceit, and ranked among superstitious opinions by Pliny. "Absentes tinnitu aurium præsentire sermones de se receptum est," according to that distich noted by Dalecampius.

"Garrula, quid totis resonas mihi noctibus, auris?
Nescio quem dicis nunc meminisse mei."

Which is a conceit hardly to be made out without the concession of a signifying Genius, or universal Mercury, conducting sounds unto their distant subjects, and teaching us to hear by touch.

WHEN we desire to confine our words, we commonly say they are spoken under the rose; which expression is commendable, if the rose, from any natural property, may be the symbol of silence, as Nazianzen seems to imply in these translated verses: —

Of speaking under the rose.

"Utque latet rosa verna suo putamine clausa,
Sic os vincla ferat, validisque arctetur habenis,
Indicatque suis prolixa silentia labris."

And is also tolerable, if by desiring a secrecy to words spoke under the rose, we only mean in society and compotation, from the ancient custom in symposiac meetings to wear chaplets of roses about their heads; and so we condemn not the German custom, which over the table describeth a rose in the ceiling. But more considerable it is, if the original were such as Lemnius and others have recorded, that the rose was the flower of Venus, which Cupid consecrated unto Harpocrates, the god of silence, and was therefore an emblem thereof, to conceal the pranks of venery; as is declared in this tetrastich:—

> "Est rosa flos Veneris, cujus quo facta laterent,
> Harpocrati matris, dona dicavit Amor;
> Inde rosam mensis hospes suspendit amicis,
> Convivæ ut sub eâ dicta tacenda sciant."

Of smoke following the fair.

THAT smoke doth follow the fairest, is a usual saying with us and in many parts of Europe; whereof although there seem no natural ground, yet is it the continuation of a very ancient opinion, as Petrus Victorius and Casaubon have observed from a passage in Athenæus; wherein a parasite thus describeth himself:—

> "To every table first I come,
> Whence Porridge I am called by some;
> A Capaneus at stairs I am,
> To enter any room a ram;
> Like whips and thongs to all I ply,
> Like smoke unto the fair I fly."

Of sitting cross-legged.

TO sit cross-legged, or with our fingers pectinated or shut together, is accounted bad, and friends will persuade us from it. The same conceit religiously possessed the ancients, as is observable from Pliny,—"Poplites alternis genibus imponere nefas olim"; and also from

Athenæus, that it was an old veneficious practice, and Juno is made in this posture to hinder the delivery of Alcmæna. And therefore, as Pierius observeth, in the medal of Julia Pia, the right hand of Venus was made extended, with the inscription of Venus Genetrix; for the complication or pectination of the fingers was a hieroglyphic of impediment, as in that place he declareth.

THE set and statary time of paring of nails and cutting of hair is thought by many a point of consideration; which is perhaps but the continuation of an ancient superstition. For piaculous it was unto the Romans to pare their nails upon the Nundinæ, observed every ninth day; and was also feared by others in certain days of the week, according to that of Ausonius, "Ungues Mercurio, barbam Jove, Cypride crines," and was one part of the wickedness that filled up the measure of Manasses, when 't is delivered that "he observed times." * Of the paring of nails.

A COMMON fashion it is to nourish hair upon the moles of the face; which is the perpetuation of a very ancient custom, and, Of hair upon moles.

* 2 Chronicles xxxiii. 6.

though innocently practised among us, may have a superstitious original, according to that of Pliny, "Nævos in facie tondere religiosum habent nunc multi." From the like might proceed the fears of polling elvelocks, or complicated hairs of the head, and also of locks longer than the other hair; they being votary at first, and dedicated upon occasion, preserved with great care, and accordingly esteemed by others, as appears by that of Apuleius, "Adjuro per dulcem capilli tui nodulum."

Of lions' heads upon spouts.

A CUSTOM there is in most parts of Europe to adorn aqueducts, spouts, and cisterns with lions' heads; which, though no illaudable ornament, is of an Egyptian genealogy, who practised the same under a symbolical illation. For because, the sun being in Leo, the flood of Nilus was at the full, and water became conveyed into every part, they made the spouts of their aqueducts through the head of a lion. And upon some celestial respects it is not improbable the great Mogul or Indian king doth bear for his arms a lion and the sun.

Of the picture of God.

THE picture of the Creator, or God the Father, in the shape of an old man, is a dangerous piece, and in this fecundity of sects may revive the Anthropomorphites; which, although maintained from the expression of Daniel, "I beheld where the Ancient of days did sit, whose hair of his head was like the pure wool," yet may it be also derivative from the hieroglyphical description of the Egyptians, who, to express their Eneph, or Creator of the world, described an old man in a blue mantle, with an egg in his mouth, which was the emblem of the world. Surely those heathens, that, notwithstanding the exemplary advantage in heaven, would endure no pictures of sun or moon, as being visible unto all the world, and needing no representation, do evidently accuse the practice of those pencils that will describe invisibles. And he that challenged the boldest hand unto the picture of an echo, must laugh at this attempt, not only in the description of invisibility, but circumscription of ubiquity, and fetching under lines incomprehensible circularity.

The pictures of the Egyptians were more tolerable, and in their sacred letters more veniably expressed the apprehension of Divinity. For though they implied the same by an eye upon a sceptre, by an eagle's head, a crocodile, and the like, yet did these manual descriptions pretend no corporal representations; nor could the people misconceive the same unto real correspondencies. So though the Cherub carried some apprehension of Divinity, yet was it not conceived to be the shape thereof; and so perhaps, because it is metaphorically predicated of God that he is a consuming fire, he may be harmlessly described by a flaming representation. Yet if, as some will have it, all mediocrity of folly is foolish, and, because an unrequitable evil may ensue, an indifferent convenience must be omitted, we shall not urge such representments; we could spare the holy lamb for the picture of our Saviour, and the dove or fiery tongues to represent the Holy Ghost.

Of the sun, moon, and winds.

THE sun and moon are usually described with human faces. Whether herein there be not a Pagan imitation, and those visages at first implied Apollo and Diana, we may make some doubt; and we find the statue of the sun was framed with rays about the head, which were the indeciduous and unshaven locks of Apollo. We should be too iconomachal * to question the pictures of the winds as commonly drawn in human heads, and with their cheeks distended; which notwithstanding we find condemned by Minucius, as answering poetical

* Quarrelsome with pictures.

fancies, and the gentile description of Æolus, Boreas, and the feigned deities of the winds.

Of the sun dancing.

WE shall not, I hope, disparage the resurrection of our Redeemer, if we say the sun doth not dance on Easter day. And though we would willingly assent unto any sympathetical exultation, yet cannot conceive therein any more than a tropical expression. Whether any such motion there were in that day wherein Christ arose, Scripture hath not revealed, which hath been punctual in other records concerning solary miracles; and the Areopagite that was amazed at the eclipse took no notice of this. And if metaphorical expressions go so far, we may be bold to affirm, not only that one sun danced, but two arose that day; that light appeared at his nativity, and darkness at his death, and yet a light at both; for even that darkness was a light unto the Gentiles, illuminated by that obscurity; that 't was the first time the sun set above the horizon; that although there were darkness above the earth, there was light beneath it; nor dare we say that hell was dark if he were in it.

Of the devil.

A CONCEIT there is, that the devil commonly appeareth with a cloven hoof; wherein, although it seem excessively ridiculous, there may be somewhat of truth; and the ground thereof at first might be his frequent appearing in the shape of a goat, which answers that description. This was the opinion of ancient Christians concerning the apparition of Panites, Fauns, and Satyrs; and in this form we read of one that appeared unto Antony in the wilderness. The same is also confirmed from expositions of Holy Scripture, for whereas it is said, "Thou shalt not offer unto devils," the original word is "seghnirim," that is, rough and hairy goats, because in that shape the devil most often appeared; as is expounded by the rabbins, as Tremellius hath also explained, and as the word Ascimah, the god of Emath, is by some conceived. Nor did he only assume this shape in elder times, but commonly in later days, especially in the place of his worship, if there be any truth in the confession of witches, and as in many stories it stands confirmed by Bodinus. And therefore a goat is not improperly made the hieroglyphic of the devil, as Pierius hath expressed it. So might it be the emblem of sin, as it was in the sin-offering; and so likewise of wicked and sinful men, according to the expression of Scripture in the method of the last distribution, when our Saviour shall separate the sheep from the goats, that is, the sons of the Lamb from the children of the devil.

Of spots on the nails.

THAT temperamental dignotions and conjecture of prevalent humours may be collected from spots in our nails, we are not averse to concede, but yet not ready to admit sundry divinations vulgarly raised upon them. Nor do we observe it verified in others, what Cardan discovered as a property in himself, to have found therein some signs of most events that ever happened unto him; or that there is much considerable in that doctrine of chiromancy, that spots in the top of the nails do signify things past, in the middle things present, and at the bottom events to come; that white specks presage our felicity, blue ones our misfortunes; that those in the nail of the thumb have significations of honor, those in the forefinger of riches, and so respectively in other fingers, (according to planetical relations, from whence they receive their names,) as Tricassus hath taken up, and Picciolus well rejecteth.

We shall not proceed to query what truth there is in palmistry, or divination from those lines in our hands of high denomination. Although, if anything be therein, it seems not confinable unto man; but other creatures are also considerable; as is the forefoot of the mole, and especially of the monkey; wherein we have observed the table line, that of life, and of the liver.

Of lights burning blue.

THAT candles and lights burn dim and blue at the apparition of spirits, may be true, if the ambient air be full of sulphurous spirits, as it happeneth ofttimes in mines, where damps and acid exhalations are able to extinguish them; and may be also verified, when spirits do make themselves visible by bodies of such effluviums. But of lower consideration is the common foretelling of strangers, from the fungus parcels about the wicks of candles; which only signifieth a moist and pluvious air about them, hindering the avolation of the light and favillous particles; whereupon they are forced to settle upon the snast.

Of the wearing of coral.

THOUGH coral doth properly preserve and fasten the teeth in men, yet is it used in children to make an easier passage for them, and for that intent is worn about their necks. But whether this custom were not superstitiously founded, as presumed an amulet or defensative against fascination, is not beyond all doubt. For the same is delivered by Pliny. "Aruspices religiosum coralli gestamen amoliendis periculis arbitrantur; et surculi infantiæ adalligati, tutelam habere creduntur."

A STRANGE kind of exploration and peculiar way of rhabdomancy is that which is used in mineral discoveries, that is, with a forked hazel, commonly called Moses's rod, which, freely held forth, will stir and play if any mine be under it. And though many there are who have attempted to make it good, yet, until better information, we are of opinion with Agricola, that in itself it is a fruitless exploration, strongly scenting of Pagan derivation and the "virgula divina," proverbially magnified of old. The ground whereof were the magical rods in poets, that of Pallas in Homer, that of Mercury that charmed Argus, and that of Circe which transformed the followers of Ulysses; too boldly usurping the name of Moses's rod, from which notwithstanding, and that of Aaron, were probably occasioned the fables of all the rest. For that of Moses must needs be famous unto the Egyptians, and that of Aaron unto many other nations, as being preserved in the ark

Of the divining-rod.

until the destruction of the temple built by Solomon.

Of discovering matters by book or staff.

A PRACTICE there is among us to determine doubtful matters by the opening of a book, and letting fall a staff; which notwithstanding are ancient fragments of Pagan divinations. The first an imitation of "Sortes Homericæ" or "Virgilianæ," drawing determinations from verses casually occurring. The same was practised by Severus, who entertained ominous hopes of the empire, from that verse in Virgil, "Tu regere imperio populos, Romane, memento"; and Gordianus, who reigned but few days, was discouraged by another, that is, "Ostendent terris hunc tantum fata, nec ultra Esse sinunt." Nor was this only performed in heathen authors, but upon the sacred texts of Scripture, as Gregorius Turonensis hath left some account, and as the practice of the Emperor Heraclius, before his expedition into Asia Minor, is delivered by Cedrenus.

As for the divination or decision from the staff, it is an augurial relic, and the practice thereof is accused by God himself. "My people ask counsel at their stocks, and their staff declareth unto them."* Of this kind of rhab-

* Hosea iv. 12.

domancy was that practised by Nabuchadonosor in that Chaldean miscellany delivered by Ezekiel, — "The king of Babylon stood at the parting of the way, at the head of two ways, to use divination; he made his arrows bright, he consulted with images, he looked in the liver; at his right hand was the divination for Jerusalem." * That is, as Estius expounded it, the left way leading unto Rabbah, the chief city of the Ammonites, and the right unto Jerusalem, he consulted idols and entrails, he threw up a bundle of arrows to see which way they would light; and falling on the right hand, he marched towards Jerusalem. A like way of belomancy, or divination by arrows, hath been in request with Scythians, Alanes, Germans, with the Africans and Turks of Algiers. But of another nature was that which was practised by Elisha, when, by an arrow shot from an eastern window, he presignified the destruction of Syria; or when, according unto the three strokes of Joash with an arrow upon the ground, he foretold the number of his victories. For thereby the spirit of God particulared the same, and determined the strokes of the king unto three, which the hopes of the prophet expected in twice that number.

We are unwilling to enlarge concerning many

* Ezekiel xxi. 21.

other; only referring unto sober examination, what natural effects can reasonably be expected, when to prevent the ephialtes or nightmare we hang up a hollow stone in our stables; when for amulets against agues we use the chips of gallows and places of execution; when for warts we rub our hands before the moon; or commit any maculated part unto the touch of the dead. Swarms hereof our learned Selden and critical philologers might illustrate, whose abler performances our adventures do but solicit. Meanwhile I hope they will plausibly receive our attempts, or candidly correct our misconjectures.

Miscellaneous Papers.

FRAGMENT ON MUMMIES.

WISE Egypt, prodigal of her embalmments, wrapped up her princes and great commanders in aromatical folds, and, studiously extracting from corruptible bodies their corruption, ambitiously looked forward to immortality; from which vainglory we have become acquainted with many remnants of the old world, who could discourse unto us of the great things of yore, and tell us strange tales of the sons of Misraim, and ancient braveries of Egypt. Wonderful indeed are the preserves of time, which openeth unto us mummies from crypts and pyramids, and mammoth bones from caverns and excavations; whereof man hath found the best preservation, appearing unto us in some sort fleshly, while beasts must be fain of an osseous continuance.

In what original this practice of the Egyptians had root, divers authors dispute; while some place the origin hereof in the desire to prevent the separation of the soul, by keeping the body untabified, and alluring the spiritual part to remain by sweet and precious odours. But all this was but fond inconsideration. The soul, having broken its * * * *, is not stayed by bands and cerecloths, nor to be recalled by Sabæan odours, but fleeth to the place of invisibles, the *ubi* of spirits, and needeth a surer than Hermes's seal to imprison it to its medicated trunk, which yet subsists anomalously in its indestructible case, and, like a widow looking for her husband, anxiously awaits its return.

* * * * *

Of Joseph it is said, that they embalmed him; and he was put in a coffin in Egypt. When the Scripture saith that the Egyptians mourned for him three score and ten days, some doubt may be made, from the practices as delivered by Herodotus, who saith that the time allowed for preserving the body and mourning was seventy days. Amongst the Rabbins, there is an old tradition, that Joseph's body was dried by smoke, and preserved in the river Nile, till the final departure of the children of Israel from Egypt, according to the Targum of Uzziel. Sckichardus delivereth it as the opinion of R. Abraham Seba, that this was done in contempt of Egypt, as unworthy of the depositure of that great patriarch; also as a type of the infants who were drowned in that river, whereto Sckichardus subjoineth that it was physically proper to prevent corruption. The Rabbins likewise idly dream that these bones were carried away by Moses about a century after, when they departed into Egypt, though how a coffin could be preserved in that large river, so as to be found again, they are not agreed; and some fly after their manner to Schem-hamphorasch, which most will regard as vain babblings.

That mummy is medicinal, the Arabian Doctor Haly delivereth, and divers confirm; but of the particular uses thereof, there is much discrepancy of opinion. While Hofmannus prescribes the same to epileptics, Johan de Muralto commends the use thereof to gouty persons; Bacon likewise extols it as a stiptic: and Junkenius considers it of efficacy to resolve coagulated blood. Meanwhile, we hardly applaud Francis the First of France, who always carried mummies with him as a panacea against all disorders; and were the efficacy thereof more clearly made out, scarce conceive the use thereof allowable in physic, exceeding the barbarities of Cambyses, and turning old heroes unto unworthy potions. Shall Egypt lend out her ancients unto chirurgeons and apothecaries, and Cheops and Psammitticus be weighed unto us for drugs? Shall we eat of Chamnes and Amosis in electuaries and pills, and be cured by cannibal mixtures? Surely such diet is dismal vampirism; and exceeds in horror the black banquet of Domitian, not to be paralleled except in those Arabian feasts, wherein Ghoules feed horribly.

But the common opinion of the virtues of mummy bred great consumption thereof, and princes and great men contended for this strange panacea, wherein Jews dealt largely, manufacturing mummies from dead carcasses, and giving them the names of kings, while specifics were compounded from crosses and gibbet leavings. There wanted not a set of Arabians who counterfeited mummies so accurately, that it needed great skill to distinguish the false from the true. Queasy stomachs would hardly fancy the doubtful potion, wherein one might so easily swallow a cloud for his Juno, and defraud the fowls of the air while in conceit enjoying the conserves of Canopus.

* * * * *

Radzivil hath a strange story of some mummies which he had stowed in seven chests, and was carrying on shipboard from Egypt, when a priest on the mission, while at his prayers, was tormented by two ethnic spectres or devils, a man and a woman, both black and horrible; and at the same time a great storm at sea, which threatened shipwreck, till at last they were enforced to pacify the enraged sea, and put those demons to flight by throwing their mummy freight overboard, and so with difficulty escaped. What credit the relation of the worthy person deserves, we leave unto others. Surely, if true, these demons were Satan's emissaries, appearing in forms answerable unto Horus and Mompta, the old deities of Egypt, to delude unhappy men. For those dark caves and mummy repositories are Satan's abodes, wherein he speculates and rejoices on human vainglory, and keeps those kings and conquerors, whom alive he bewitched, whole for that great day, when he will claim his own, and marshal the kings of Nilus and Thebes in sad procession unto the pit.

Death, that fatal necessity which so many would overlook, or blinkingly survey, the old Egyptians held continually before their eyes. Their embalmed ancestors they carried about at their banquets, as holding them still a part of their families, and not thrusting them from their places at feasts. They wanted not likewise a sad preacher at their tables to admonish them daily of death, surely an unnecessary discourse while they banqueted in sepulchres. Whether this were not making too much of death, as tending to assuefaction, some reason there is to doubt; but certain it is that such practices would hardly be embraced by our modern gourmands, who like not to look on faces of *morta*, or be elbowed by mummies.

Yet in those huge structures and pyramidal immensities, of the builders whereof so little is known, they seemed not so much to raise sepulchres or temples to death, as to contemn and disdain it, astonishing heaven with their audacities, and looking forward with delight to their interment in those eternal piles. Of their living habitations they made little account, conceiving of them but as *hospitia*, or inns, while they adorned the sepulchres of the dead, and, planting thereon lasting bases, defied the crumbling touches of time and the misty vaporousness of oblivion. Yet all were but Babel vanities. Time sadly overcometh all things, and is now dominant, and sitteth upon a sphinx, and looketh unto Memphis and old Thebes, while his sister Oblivion reclineth semisomnous on a pyramid, gloriously triumphing, making puzzles of Titanian erections, and turning old glories into dreams. History sinketh beneath her cloud. The traveller, as he paceth amazedly through those deserts, asketh of her, who builded them? and she mumbleth something, but what it is he heareth not.

Egypt itself is now become the land of obliviousness, and doteth. Her ancient civility is gone, and her glory hath vanished as a phantasma. Her youthful days are over, and her face hath become wrinkled and tetric. She poreth not upon the heavens, astronomy is dead unto her, and knowledge maketh other cycles. Canopus is afar off, Memnon resoundeth not to the sun, and Nilus heareth strange voices. Her monuments are but hieroglyphically sempiternal. Osiris and Anubis, her averruncous deities, have departed, while Orus yet remains dimly shadowing the principle of vicissitude and the effluxion of things, but receiveth little oblation.

* * * * *

On Dreams.

HALF our days we pass in the shadow of the earth; and the brother of death exacteth a third part of our lives. A good part of our sleep is peered out with visions and fantastical objects, wherein we are confessedly deceived. The day supplieth us with truths; the night with fictions and falsehoods, which uncomfortably divide the natural account of our beings. And, therefore, having passed the day in sober labours and rational enquiries of truth, we are fain to betake ourselves unto such a state of being, wherein the soberest heads have acted all the monstrosities of melancholy, and which unto open eyes are no better than folly and madness.

Happy are they that go to bed with grand music, like Pythagoras, or have ways to compose the fantastical spirit, whose unruly wanderings take off inward sleep, filling our heads with St. Anthony's visions, and the dreams of Lipara in the sober chambers of rest.

Virtuous thoughts of the day lay up good treasures for the night; whereby the impressions of imaginary forms arise into sober similitudes, acceptable unto our slumbering selves and preparatory unto divine impressions.* Hereby Solomon's sleep was happy. Thus prepared, Jacob might well dream of angels upon a pillow of stone. And the best sleep of Adam might be the best of any after.†

That there should be divine dreams seems unreasonably doubted by Aristotle. That there are demoniacal dreams we have little reason to doubt. Why may there not be angelical? If there be guardian spirits, they may not be inactively about us in sleep; but may sometimes order our dreams: and many strange hints, instigations, or discourses, which are so amazing unto us, may arise from such foundations.

But the phantasms of sleep do commonly walk in the great road of natural and animal

* *Virtuous thoughts, &c.*] See an exquisite passage on Dreams in *Religio Medici* (*ante*, pp. 145-147).

† *the best sleep of Adam, &c.*] The only sleep of Adam recorded is that which God caused to fall upon him, and which resulted in the creation of woman. It does not very clearly appear whether Sir Thomas calls it the ***best*** sleep of Adam in allusion to its origin or its result.

dreams, wherein the thoughts or actions of the day are acted over and echoed in the night. Who can therefore wonder that Chrysostom should dream of St. Paul, who daily read his epistles; or that Cardan, whose head was so taken up about the stars, should dream that his soul was in the moon! Pious persons, whose thoughts are daily busied about heaven, and the blessed state thereof, can hardly escape the nightly phantasms of it, which though sometimes taken for illuminations, or divine dreams, yet rightly perpended may prove but animal visions, and natural night-scenes of their awaking contemplations.

Many dreams are made out by sagacious exposition, and from the signature of their subjects; carrying their interpretation in their fundamental sense and mystery of similitude, whereby, he that understands upon what natural fundamental every notion dependeth may, by symbolical adaptation, hold a ready way to read the characters of Morpheus. In dreams of such a nature, Artemidorus, Achmet, and Astrampsichus, from Greek, Egyptian, and Arabian oneiro-criticism, may hint some interpretation: who, while we read of a ladder in Jacob's dream, will tell us that ladders and scalary ascents signify preferment; and while we consider the dream of Pharaoh, do teach us that rivers overflowing speak plenty, lean oxen, famine and scarcity; and therefore it was but reasonable in Pharaoh to demand the interpretation from his magicians, who, being Egyptians, should have been well versed in symbols and the hieroglyphical notions of things. The greatest tyrant in such divinations was Nabuchodonosor, while, besides the interpretation, he demanded the dream itself; which being probably determined by divine immission, might escape the common road of phantasms, that might have been traced by Satan.

When Alexander, going to besiege Tyre, dreamt of a Satyr, it was no hard exposition for a Grecian to say, "Tyre will be thine." He that dreamed that he saw his father washed by Jupiter and anointed by the sun, had cause to fear that he might be crucified, whereby his body would be washed by the rain, and drop by the heat of the sun. The dream of Vespasian was of harder exposition; as also that of the Emperor Mauritius, concerning his successor Phocas. And a man might have been hard put to it to interpret the language of Æsculapius, when to a consumptive person he held forth his fingers; implying thereby that his cure lay in dates, from the homonomy of the Greek, which signifies dates and fingers.

We owe unto dreams that Galen was a physician, Dion an historian, and that the world hath seen some notable pieces of Cardan; yet, he that should order his affairs by dreams, or make the night a rule unto the day, might be ridiculously deluded; wherein Cicero is much to be pitied, who having excellently discoursed of the vanity of dreams, was yet undone by the flattery of his own, which urged him to apply himself unto Augustus.

However dreams may be fallacious concerning outward events, yet may they be truly significant at home; and whereby we may more sensibly understand ourselves. Men act in sleep with some conformity unto their awaked senses; and consolations or discouragements may be drawn from dreams which intimately tell us ourselves. Luther was not like to fear a spirit in the night, when such an apparition would not terrify him in the day. Alexander would hardly have run away in the sharpest combats of sleep, nor Demosthenes have stood stoutly to it, who was scarce able to do it in his prepared senses.

Persons of radical integrity will not easily be perverted in their dreams, nor noble minds do pitiful things in sleep. Crassus would have hardly been bountiful in a dream, whose fist was so close awake. But a man might have lived all his life upon the sleeping hand of Antonius.*

There is an art to make dreams, as well as their interpretations; and physicians will tell us that some food makes turbulent, some gives quiet dreams. Cato, who doated upon cabbage, might find the crude effects thereof in his sleep; wherein the Egyptians might find some advantage by their superstitious abstinence from onions. Pythagoras might have [had] calmer sleeps, if he [had] totally abstained from beans. Even Daniel, the great interpreter of dreams, in his leguminous diet seems to have chosen no advantageous food for quiet sleeps, according to Grecian physic.

To add unto the delusion of dreams, the fantastical objects seem greater than they are; and being beheld in the vaporous state of sleep, enlarge their diameters unto us; whereby it may prove more easy to dream of giants than pigmies. Democritus might seldom dream of atoms, who so often thought of them. He almost might dream himself a bubble extending unto the eighth sphere. A little water makes a sea; a small puff of wind a tempest. A grain of sulphur kindled in the blood may make a

* *sleeping hand of Antonius.*] Who awake was *open-handed* and liberal, in contrast with the *close-fistedness* of Crassus, and therefore would have been munificent in his dreams.

flame like Ætna; and a small spark in the bowels of Olympias a lightning over all the chamber.

But, beside these innocent delusions, there is a sinful state of dreams. Death alone, not sleep, is able to put an end unto sin; and there may be a night-book of our iniquities; for beside the transgressions of the day, casuists will tell us of mortal sins in dreams, arising from evil precogitations; meanwhile human law regards not noctambulos; and if a night-walker should break his neck, or kill a man, takes no notice of it.

Dionysius was absurdly tyrannical to kill a man for dreaming that he had killed him; and really to take away his life, who had but fantastically taken away his. Lamia was ridiculously unjust to sue a young man for a reward, who had confessed that pleasure from her in a dream which she had denied unto his awaking senses: conceiving that she had merited somewhat from his fantastical fruition and shadow of herself. If there be such debts, we owe deeply unto sympathies; but the common spirit of the world must be ready in such arrearages.

If some have swooned, they may have also died in dreams, since death is but a confirmed swooning. Whether Plato died in a dream, as some deliver, he must rise again to inform us. That some have never dreamed is as improbable as that some have never laughed. That children dream not the first half-year; that men dream not in some countries, with many more, are unto me sick men's dreams; dreams out of the ivory gate,* and visions before midnight.

* *the ivory gate.*] The poets suppose two gates of sleep, the one of horn, from which true dreams proceed; the other of ivory, which sends forth false dreams.

Letters.

To his Son, a Lieutenant of his Majesty's ship the Marie Rose, at Portsmouth.

[May or June, 1667.]

DEAR SONNE, — I am very glad you are returned from the strayghts mouth once more in health and safetie. God continue his mercifull providence over you. I hope you maintaine a thankful heart and daylie bless him for your great deliverances in so many fights and dangers of the sea, whereto you have been exposed upon several seas, and in all seasons of the yeare. When you first under tooke this service, you cannot butt remember that I caused you to read the description of all the sea fights of note, in Plutark, the Turkish history, and others; and withall gave you the description of fortitude left by Aristotle, "Fortitudinis est inconcussum δύσπληκτον a mortis metu et constantem in malis et intrepidum ad pericula esse, et malle honestè mori quam turpiter servari et victoriæ causam præstare. Præterea autem fortitudinis est laborare et tolerare. Accedit autem fortitudini audacia et animi præstantia et fiducia, et confidentia, ad hæc industria et tolerantia." That which I then proposed for your example, I now send you for your commendation. For, to give you your due, in the whole cours of this warre, both in fights and other sea affairs, hazards and perills, you have very well fullfilled this character in yourself. And allthough you bee not forward in commending yourself, yett others have not been backward to do it for you, and have so earnestly expressed your courage, valour, and resolution; your sober, studious, and observing cours of life; your generous and obliging disposition, and the notable knowledge you have obtayned in military and all kind of sea affayres, that it affoordeth no small comfort unto mee. And I would by no meanes omitt to declare the same unto yourself, that you may not want that encouragement which you so well deserve. They that do well need not commend themselves; others will be readie enough to do it for them. And because you may understand how well I have heard of you, I would not omitt to communicate this unto you. Mr. Scudamore, your sober and learned chaplaine, in your voyage with Sir Jeremie Smith, gives you no small commendations for a sober, studious, courageous, and diligent person; that he had not met with any of the fleet like you, so civill, observing, and diligent to your charge, with the reputation and love of all the shippe; and that without doubt you would make a famous man, and a reputation to your country. Captain Fenne, a meere rough seaman, sayd that if hee were to choose, hee would have your company before any he knewe. Mr. W. B. of Lynn, a stout volunteer in the Dreadnought, sayd, in my hearing, that you were a deserving person, and of as good a reputation as any young man in the fleet. Another, who was with you at Schellinck's, highly commended your sobrietie, carefullnesse, undaunted and lasting courage through all the cours of the warre; that you had acquired no small knowledge in navigation, as well as the military part. That you understood every thing that belonged unto a shippe; and had been so strict and criticall an observer of the shipps in the fleet, that you could name any shippe sayling at some distance; and by some private mark and observation which you had made, would hardly mistake one, if seventie shippes should sayle at a reasonable distance by you. You are much obliged to Sir Thomas Allen, who upon all occasions speakes highly of you;* and is to be held to the fleet by encouragement and preferment: for I would not have him leave the sea, which otherwise probably he might, having parts to make himself considerable by divers other wayes. Mr. I. told mee you were compleately constituted to do your country service, honour, and reputation, as being exceeding faythfull, valiant, diligent, generous, vigilant, observing, very knowing, and a scholar. How you behaved yourself in the Foresight, at the hard service at Bergen, in Norway, captain Brookes, the commander, expressed unto many before his death, not long after, in Suffolk; and particularly unto my lord of Sandwich, then admiral, which thoughe you would not tell me yourself, yet was I informed from a person of no ordinary qualitie, C. Harland, who when you came aboard the admiral after the taking of the East India shippes, heard my lord of Sandwich, to speak thus unto you. "Sir, you are a person whom I am glad to see, and must be better acquainted with you, upon the account which captain Brooke gave mee of you. I must encourage such persons and give them their due, which will stand so

* There is evidently some omission here, either in the original or the copy; the following sentence appears to be Sir Thomas Allen's remark, the beginning of which is apparently wanting.

firmely and courageously unto it upon extremities, wherein true valour is best discovered. Hee told mee you were the only man that stuck closely and boldly to him unto the last, and that after so many of his men and his lieutenant was slayne, hee could not have well knowne what to have done without you." Butt beside these I must not fayle to tell you how well I like it, that you are not only Marti but Mercurio, and very much pleased to find how good a student you have been at sea, and particularly with what success you have read divers bookes there, especially Homer and Juvenal with Lubines notes. Being much surprised to find you so perfect therein that you had them in a manner without booke, and could proceed in any verse I named unto you. I am glad you can overcome Lucan. The other bookes which I sent, are, I perceive, not hard unto you, and having such industrie adjoined unto your apprehension and memorie, you are like to proceed [not only] a noble navigator, butt a great schollar, which will be much to your honour and my satisfaction and content. I am much pleased to find that you take the draughts of remarkable things where ere you go; for that may bee very usefull, and will fasten themselves the better in your memorie. . . . . .

To his Daughter, Mrs. Lyttleton.

Sept. 15, [1681.]

DEARE BETTY, — Tho it were noe wonder this very tempestious and stormy winter, yet I am sorry you had such an uncomfortable sight as to behold a ship cast away so neer you; this is noe strange tho unwelcom sight at Yarmouth, Cromer, Winterton, and sea towns: tho you could not saue them, I hope they were the better for your prayers, both those that perishd and those that scapd. Some wear away in calmes, some are caried away in storms: we come into the world one way, there are many gates to goe out of it. God giue us grace to fit and prepare our selues for that necessity, and to be ready to leaue all when and how so ever he shall call. The prayers of health are most like to be acceptable; sickness may choak our devotions, and we are accepted rather by our life then our death: we have a rule how to lead the one, the other is uncertain, and may come in a moment. God, I hope, will spare you to serve him long, who didst begin early to serve him. . . . . Your self is not impatient, you will haue noe cause to be sad: giue no way unto melancholy, which is purely sadnes without a reasonable cause. . . . .

Resolves.

[Found in one of Sir Thomas Browne's Commonplace-Books.]

TO be sure that no day pass, without calling upon God in a solemn formed prayer, seven times within the compass thereof; that is, in the morning, and at night, and five times between; taken up long ago from the example of David and Daniel, and a compunction and shame that I had omitted it so long, when I heedfully read of the custom of the Mahometans to pray five times in the day.

To pray and magnify God in the night, and my dark bed, when I could not sleep: to have short ejaculations whenever I awaked; and when the four-o'clock bell * awoke me, or my first dis-

* A bell which tolls (or ought to toll, if the old sexton does not oversleep himself) in pursuance of the will of a person who, after wandering about for a considerable time on Mousehold

covery of the light, to say the collect of our liturgy, Eternal God, who hath safely brought me to the beginning of this day, &c.

To pray in all places where privacy inviteth; in any house, highway, or street; and to know no street or passage in this city which may not witness that I have not forgot God and my Saviour in it: and that no parish or town where I have been may not say the like.

To take occasion of praying upon the sight of any church, which I see or pass by, as I ride about.

Since the necessities of the sick, and unavoidable diversions of my profession, keep me often from church, yet to take all possible care that I might never miss sacraments upon their accustomed days.

To pray daily and particularly for sick patients, and in general for others, wheresoever, howsoever, and under whose care soever; and at the entrance into the house of the sick, to say, The peace and mercy of God be in this place.

Heath, having lost his way in a winter-night's storm, at length was directed to the city by the tolling of a bell in the Church of St. Peter, Mancroft, the residence of Sir Thomas Browne.

After a sermon, to make a thanksgiving, and desire a blessing, and to pray for the minister.

In tempestuous weather, lightning, and thunder, either night or day, to pray for God's merciful protection upon all men, and His mercy upon their souls, bodies, and goods.

Upon sight of beautiful persons, to bless God in his creatures, to pray for the beauty of their souls, and to enrich them with inward graces to be answerable unto the outward. Upon sight of deformed persons, to send them inward graces, and enrich their souls, and give them the beauty of the resurrection.

Cambridge: Electrotyped and Printed by Welch, Bigelow, & Co.